JESUS

A Revolutionary Biography

John Dominic Crossan

HarperSanFrancisco
A Division of HarperCollins*Publishers*

*To Robert W. Funk and my fellow members of
the Westar Institute's Jesus Seminar for their courage,
collegiality, and consistency*

Quotations from the Bible are taken from the New Revised Standard Version, copyright © 1989 by the Division of Christian Education of the National Council of the Churches of Christ in the United States of America.
Quotations from the *Q Gospel* are taken from Burton L. Mack, *The Lost Gospel: The Book of Q and Christian Origins.* Copyright © 1993, HarperSanFrancisco.
Quotations from the *Gospel of Thomas* are taken from Marvin Meyer, *The Gospel of Thomas: The Hidden Sayings of Jesus.* Copyright © 1992, HarperSanFrancisco.
Quotations from Josephus are taken from *Josephus.* 10 vols. Loeb Classical Library. Copyright © 1926–1965, Harvard Univ. Press.

Text design by Margery Cantor

FIRST EDITION

Library of Congress Cataloging-in-Publication Data:
Crossan, John Dominic.
    Jesus : a revolutionary biography / John Dominic Crossan. — 1st ed.
      p. cm.
    ISBN 0-06-061661-X. — ISBN 0-061662-8 (pbk.)
    ISBN 0-06-061669-5 (international edition)
    1. Jesus Christ—Biography. 2. Jesus Christ—Historicity.
    I. Title.
    BT301.2.C77   1994
    232.9'01—dc20
    [B]   93-24685
                                             CIP

94 95 96 97 98 RRD(H) 10 9 8 7 6 5 4 3 2 1

This edition is printed on acid-free paper that meets the American National Standards Institute Z39.48 Standard.

Rome, Museo Nazionale delle Terme. (Alinari/Art Resource, NY.)

The picture on the cover of this book and the above relief, from which it is taken, are not so much decoration as summary of this book. The relief is one of two twin-registered polychrome marble plaques containing biblical scenes and dating to the first years of the fourth century C.E.

Twin scenes of free healing frame a central image of open eating, which are, as this book maintains, the heart of Jesus' original vision and program. At left Jesus heals the paralytic who carries off his bed, as in Mark 2:1–12. And at right the widow's son at Nain arises from his bier, as in Luke 7:11–16. Jesus faces inward at the plaque's half-broken left side; he presumably looked inward at the right, which is totally broken. In the lower center are four figures in typical pose for a pagan meal with the dead. The middle two are "reclining" behind a barely visible curved bolster while the outer pair seem to be serving them. They have six baskets—that is, lots of food—and are both eating and drinking (note goblet in right hand of third from left). That classical scene in the lower center is subsumed into a multiplication of the loaves (but no sign of fishes), as in Mark 6:35–44 or John 6:5–13, by its conjunction with the upper center scene where three disciples, at left, lead toward Jesus, at right. Finally, Jesus himself is designated as a teacher or philosopher by the scroll in his hand. In both cases he wears the pallium of Greek wisdom rather than the toga of Roman power. But, while in the scene to the left he wears both outer pallium and inner tunic, in the center he wears the pallium without the tunic, leaving his right shoulder and body bare. He is portrayed as not just any type of philosopher but, precisely, a Cynic philosopher.

We find Jesus healing, eating, teaching, and more like a Cynic philosopher than anything else—in other words, this book in iconographic miniature.

Contents

PROLOGUE

From Christ to Jesus

TRYING to find the actual Jesus is like trying, in atomic physics, to locate a submicroscopic particle and determine its charge. The particle cannot be seen directly, but on a photographic plate we see the lines left by the trajectories of larger particles it put in motion. By tracing these trajectories back to their common origin, and by calculating the force necessary to make the particles move as they did, we can locate and describe the invisible cause. Admittedly, history is more complex than physics; the lines connecting the original figure to the developed legends cannot be traced with mathematical accuracy; the intervention of unknown factors has to be allowed for. Consequently, results can never claim more than probability; but "probability," as Bishop Butler said, "is the very guide of life."

Morton Smith, *Jesus the Magician*
(San Francisco: Harper & Row, 1982)

This book gives my own reconstruction of the historical Jesus derived from twenty-five years of scholarly research on what actually happened in Galilee and Jerusalem during the early first century of the common era. But why should any such research be necessary at all? Have we not, for Jesus, this first-century Mediterranean Jewish peasant, four biographies, by Matthew, Mark, Luke, and John—individuals all directly or indirectly connected with him, and all writing within, say, seventy-five years of his death? Is that not equal to or even better than the research on the contemporary Roman emperor, Tiberius, for whom we have biographies by Velleius Paterculus, Tacitus, Suetonius, and Dio Cassius, only the first of whom was directly connected with him, the others writing from seventy-five to two hundred years after his death? Why, then, with such abundant documentation, is there a need for any scholarly search for the historical Jesus?

It is precisely that *fourfold* record that constitutes the core problem. If you read the four gospels vertically and consecutively, from start to finish and one after another, you get a generally persuasive impression of unity, harmony, and agreement. But if you read them horizontally and comparatively, focusing on this or that unit and comparing it across two, three, or four versions, it is disagreement rather than agreement that strikes you most forcibly. And those divergences stem not from the random vagaries of memory and recall but from the coherent and consistent theologies of the individual texts. The gospels are, in other words, interpretations. Hence, of course, despite there being only one Jesus, there can be more than one gospel, more than one interpretation.

That core problem is compounded by another one. Those four gospels do not represent all the early gospels available or even a random sample within them but are instead a calculated collection known as the canonical gospels. This becomes clear in studying other gospels either discerned as sources inside the official four or else discovered as documents outside them.

An example of a source hidden inside the four canonical gospels is the reconstructed document known as *Q*, from the German word *Quelle*, meaning "source," which is now imbedded within both Luke and Matthew. Those two authors also use Mark as a regular source, so *Q* is discernible wherever they agree with one another but lack a Markan parallel. Since, like Mark, that document has its own generic integrity and theological consistency apart from its use as a *Quelle* or source for others, I refer to it in this book as the *Q Gospel.*

An example of a document discovered outside the four canonical gospels is the *Gospel of Thomas,* which was found at Nag Hammadi, in Upper Egypt, in the winter of 1945 and is, in the view of many scholars, completely independent of the canonical gospels—Matthew, Mark, Luke, and John. It is also most strikingly different from them, especially in its format, and is, in fact, much closer to that of the *Q Gospel* than to any of the canonical foursome. It identifies itself, at the end, as a gospel, but it is in fact a collection of the sayings of Jesus given without any compositional order and lacking descriptions of deeds or miracles, crucifixion or resurrection stories, and especially any overall narratival or biographical framework. The existence of such *other* gospels means that the canonical foursome is a spectrum of approved interpretation forming a strong central vision that was later able to render apocryphal, hidden, or censored any other gospels too far off its right or left wing.

Suppose that in such a situation you wanted to know not just what early believers wrote about Jesus but what you would have seen and heard if you had been a more or less neutral observer in the early decades of the first century. Clearly, some people ignored him, some worshiped him, and others crucified him. But what if you wanted to move behind the screen of credal interpretation and, without in any way denying or negating the validity of faith, give an accurate but impartial account of the historical Jesus as distinct from the confessional Christ? That is what the academic or scholarly study of the historical Jesus is about, at least when it is not a disguise for doing theology and calling it history, doing autobiography and calling it biography, doing Christian apologetics and calling it academic scholarship. Put another way, no matter how fascinating result and conclusion may be, they are only as good as the theory and method on which they are based.

My method locates the historical Jesus where three independent vectors cross. That triangulation serves as internal discipline and mutual corrective, since all must intersect at the same point for any of them to be correct. It is like three giant searchlights coming together on a single object in the night sky.

The first vector is *cross-cultural anthropology*, based not just on this or that society but on what is common across history to all those of the same ecological and technological type. What do the scholars in this field tell us about ancient Mediterranean—as distinct from, say, contemporary American—culture? About an agrarian as distinct from an industrial society? What do they tell us about trance and possession, curing and healing, magic and exorcism? About imperial and colonial situations, elites and peasants, politics and family, taxes and debts, class and gender? This information is crucial since it has no direct connection to Jesus and is therefore not likely to be skewed for or against him. If, for example, we are tempted to describe Jesus as a literate middle-class carpenter, cross-cultural anthropology reminds us that there was no middle class in ancient societies and that peasants are usually illiterate; so how could Jesus become what never existed at his time?

The second vector is *Greco-Roman and especially Jewish history* in the first quarter of Jesus' century. What is primary here is the situation of the Jewish homeland as a colony of the Roman Empire, as the land bridge between Syria to the north and Egypt to the south, and as a political unit ruled either directly by Roman governors or indirectly by Herodian rulers. I focus here especially on the works of the aristocratic Jewish historian Josephus, who has two separate and parallel accounts for that period. Normally, elite authors tell us very little about the lower classes or the peasants except when these groups rebel or revolt. But throughout the century leading up to the First Roman-Jewish War in 66 C.E. there was consistent peasant unrest, so I pay very great attention to what Josephus tells us about protesters and prophets, bandits and messiahs, but I also try to imagine those levels of peasant unrest that smolder below the surface and never get recorded until they burst forth openly and overtly.

The third and most difficult vector is *the literary or textual* one. Let me give you some background, some general conclusions accepted by most critical scholars today. First, gospels are found not only inside but also outside the New Testament itself. Second, therefore, the four New Testament gospels are neither a total collection of all those available nor a random sampling from among them. They are, rather, a deliberate arrangement in which some gospels were accepted and included while others were rejected and excluded. Third, three successive levels—involving *retention* of original Jesus materials, *development* of those retained materials, and *creation* of totally new materials—are found alike in gospels both inside and outside the New Testament. Fourth, differences and discrepancies among accounts and versions are not due primarily to vagaries of memory or divergences in emphasis but to quite deliberate theological interpretations of Jesus. Finally, and in summary, what those first Christians experienced as the continuing presence of the risen Jesus or the abiding empowerment of the Spirit gave the transmitters of the Jesus tradition a creative freedom we would never have dared postulate had such a conclusion not been forced upon us by the evidence. Even when, for example, Matthew and Luke are using Mark as a source for what Jesus said or did or what others said or did in relation to Jesus, they are unnervingly free about omission and addition, about change, correction, or creation in their own individual accounts—but always, of course, subject to their own particular interpretation of Jesus. The gospels are neither histories nor biographies, even within the ancient tolerances for those genres. Each is what it was eventually called—a *Gospel* or a *Good News*—and thereby comes a double warning. *Good* is always such within some individual or community's opinion or interpretation. And *News*, since it is already a plural, is not a word we usually pluralize a second time.

Faced with all those laminated layers of development and interpretation, I follow two basic strategies to base my reconstruction on the most plausibly original materials. I focus especially on the earliest stratum of the tradition, on materials I date to the period between 30 and 60 C.E. And I never build on anything that has only a single independent attestation. All professional journalists operate by that standard, and critical historians should follow their good example. A single attestation may of course be quite accurate, but I try to build my picture upward from the most multiple toward that single one. Multiple or at least plural independent attestations in the primary stratum point to the earliest available material. That is a methodological discipline, a process that may not guarantee truth but at least makes dishonesty more difficult.

Those who wish to explore this subject in more detail and complexity may go to the much longer book on which this one is based. Fuller citation, argumentation, and documentation are available in my 1991 book *The Historical Jesus: The Life of a Mediterranean Jewish Peasant*, published, like this one, by Harper San Francisco. This present book is a more popular version of that one, but it is also something more. Every chapter contains something beyond the parent volume. And the cumulative impact of this historical biography is, I trust, more compelling and dramatic precisely because of its compact, direct presentation. It has benefited from debates and discussions, from questions and objections, and from rethinking and reconsidering that earlier book in the years since its first publication.

One detail has not changed, however, from one book to the other: my endeavor was to reconstruct the historical Jesus as accurately and honestly as possible. It was not my purpose to find a Jesus whom I liked or disliked, a Jesus with whom I agreed or disagreed. So I conclude by reproducing here an imaginary dialogue taken from an article of mine that appeared in the Christmas 1991 issue of the *Christian Century*. The historical Jesus is speaking to me:

> "I've read your book, Dominic, and it's quite good. So now you're ready to live by my vision and join me in my program?"
>
> "I don't think I have the courage, Jesus, but I did describe it quite well, didn't I, and the method was especially good, wasn't it?"
>
> "Thank you, Dominic, for not falsifying the message to suit your own incapacity. That at least is something."
>
> "Is it enough, Jesus?"
>
> "No, Dominic, it is not."

ONE

A Tale of Two Gods

WHEREAS Providence . . . has . . . adorned our lives with the highest good: *Augustus* . . . and has in her beneficence granted us and those who will come after us [a Savior] who has made war to cease and who shall put everything [in peaceful] order . . . with the result that the birthday of our God signalled the beginning of Good News for the world because of him . . . therefore . . . the Greeks in Asia *Decreed* that the New Year begin for all the cities on September 23 . . . and the first month shall . . . be observed as the Month of Caesar, beginning with 23 September, the birthday of Caesar.

Decree of calendrical change on marble stelae
in the Asian temples dedicated to the Roman
Empire and Augustus, its first emperor

And the angel said to her, "Do not be afraid, Mary, for you have found favor with God. And behold, you will conceive in your womb and bear a son, and you shall call his name Jesus. He will be great, and will be called the Son of the

1

Most High; and the Lord God will give to him the throne of his father David, and he will reign over the house of Jacob for ever; and of his kingdom there will be no end. . . . The Holy Spirit will come upon you, and the power of the Most High will overshadow you; therefore the child to be born will be called holy, the Son of God.". . .

And the angel said to them, "Be not afraid; for behold I bring you good news of a great joy which will come to all the people; for to you is born this day in the city of David a Savior, who is Christ the Lord."

> Message of the angels to the Virgin Mary at
> Nazareth and to the shepherds at Bethlehem
> (Luke 1:31–35 and 2:10–11)

∞   The Trojan Caesar Comes

Twice within a hundred years, on different shores of that cruel and beautiful Mediterranean Sea, a man was acclaimed *son of god* when alive and, more simply, *god* when dead. Octavius, however, stood at the height of the Roman aristocracy, Jesus near the bottom of the Jewish peasantry. No surprise, then, that for the former's life story we have exact dates and precise places, and for the latter's, neither.

Gaius Octavius was born on 23 September 63 B.C.E. and became the adopted son and legal heir of Julius Caesar, who was assassinated on 15 March 44 B.C.E. After Caesar's deification by the Roman Senate on 1 January 42 B.C.E., Octavius became immediately *divi filius,* son of a divine one. But even where those secure dates were easily available, it took mythology over history, faith over fact, and poetry over chronicle to tell the tale of Octavius becoming Augustus.

As early as 40 B.C.E., after a decade of civil war, the poet Virgil wrote rhapsodically in his *Fourth Eclogue* of an imagined child newly born into a world newly peaceful as Octavius and Anthony were sealing future friendship at Brundisium, on the heel of Italy. This was to be that child's future in a world of ecstatic peace:

> *But when maturing years make you a man,*
> *Even the merchant will give up the sea,*
> *The pine will not become a trading ship,*
> *For every land will furnish everything.*
> *The soil will not endure the hoe, nor vines*
> *The pruning hook; the vigorous plowman will*
> *Release his oxen from their yokes; no dyes*
> *Will teach bright-colored falsehood to pure wool:*
> *The ram, in the meadow by himself, will blush*
> *Sweet crimson murex-color, then will change*
> *His fleece to saffron, while, spontaneously,*
> *Vermilion clothes the young lambs as they graze.*

But apart completely from such an ideal vision, even ordinary, everyday, normal peace would not arrive for another decade, when, off Actium, on Greece's western coast, Cleopatra's battle flotilla would pick up the defeated Anthony and head home to Alexandria and the asp.

Virgil, combining magnificently musical poetry with consummately political propaganda, moved immediately to give Octavius and his Julian heritage a mythological genealogy worthy of the new Roman order. He went back for inspiration to the only possible source, to Homer—the "bible," if ever there was one, of Greco-Roman paganism. He fused together Homer's two Greek epics—the *Iliad*, about waging war abroad, and the *Odyssey*, about coming home again—into his own Latin *Aeneid*. Julius Caesar and Gaius Octavius were celebrated as heirs to an ancient and even divine ancestry. For Aeneas—son of a human father, Anchises, and a divine mother, Aphrodite—had saved both his father and his own son from the embers of Troy's destruction and brought that son, Julus, to Italy as sire of the Julian family. In the words of the *Aeneid*'s first book:

> *The Trojan Caesar comes, to circumscribe*
> *Empire with Ocean, fame with heaven's stars.*
> *Julius his name, from Julus handed down:*
> *All tranquil shall you take him heavenward*
> *In time, laden with plunder of the East,*
> *And he with you shall be invoked in prayer . . .*

And grim with iron frames, the gates of War
Will then be shut.

Even where all the dates and places were exactly known, mythology alone was adequate for a radically new vision of Roman society. But whether we term it mythology, ideology, theology, or propaganda, at its root was the historical fact that Octavius had ended twenty years of civil strife by emerging as the one and only victor. He was now Augustus, a title poised with marvelous ambiguity between humanity and divinity. He was also Princeps, a title poised with equal ambiguity between kingship and citizenship. Call him first among equals, with all the equals dead. And, lest we sneer too readily at this mixture of history and mythology, remember that we are always better at separating such mixtures in other lives, in different societies, and in alien cultures. Our own mixture we too seldom see at all. In any case, the Roman Senate deified Augustus on 17 September 14 C.E., a scant month after his death on 19 August. He was now divine not only by ancestry or adoption but in his own right as well because of all he had done to unify Roman power internally and to consolidate Roman power externally. Which returns the discussion to Jesus.

∞ The Future of the Past

Of the four gospels inside the New Testament only Matthew and Luke give any account of Jesus' birth or early years. And thereafter they, like Mark and John, proceed immediately to his adult life, the point where Mark and John begin their own narratives. It is, however, the presence rather than the absence of an infancy story that requires explanation. Before his death, for example, Augustus had left for safekeeping with the Vestal Virgins a list of his accomplishments, which were to be inscribed on bronze tablets before his mausoleum in Rome. He begins that account, in a copy from the Temple of Rome and Augustus at Ankara, in central Turkey, with these words:

> At the age of nineteen on my own responsibility and at my
> own expense I raised an army, with which I successfully

championed the liberty of the republic when it was oppressed by the tyranny of a faction.

So the *Res Gestae Divi Augusti* or *Achievements of the Divine Augustus* begins not with his birth or infancy, but with the events of 44 B.C.E. Augustus is already an adult, and Anthony is dismissed to anonymity as merely a faction.

The key question, then, is not just what Matthew and Luke tell us about the mode, place, and time of Jesus' birth but, more pointedly, why they tell us anything at all. What are those infancy stories supposed to do? They are not so much the first chapters of Jesus' life, from which other chapters about the rest of his infancy and youth have been, as it were, hidden or lost, as they are overtures, condensed intertwinings of the dominant themes in the respective gospels to which they serve as introduction and summary. And, of course, since those gospels have separate and distinct visions of Jesus' adult life, so must they also have separate and distinct visions of his infancy-as-overture. That explains, at least in general, what strikes the careful reader immediately—namely, the differences between those twin accounts and the difficulties in integrating them into a single coherent and consecutive version. Luke alone, for example, has the shepherds and the angels, the inn and the manger, the earlier presentation and the later finding in the Temple, while Matthew alone has Herod and the Magi, the slaughter of the innocents, and the flight into Egypt. But now for some specific details.

John and Jesus

The opening chapters of Luke tell the story of two births, and they face in two directions simultaneously: into the past, assimilating the birth of John the Baptist into that of the ancient patriarchs, prophets, and heroes of the Hebrew Scriptures (which Christians had adopted in its enlarged Greek translation as their Old Testament); and into the future, asserting the primacy of Jesus' birth over that of the Baptist and thus over all those preceding figures with which the latter had been associated.

In the Old Testament there are several stories of birth despite marital infertility—infertility that often continues into an advanced age, when all hope would normally have been abandoned. The archetypal instance is the barren couple Sarah and Abraham in Genesis 18:10–11, to whom God promised a son even though "Abraham and Sarah were old, advanced in age." There is here a double miracle, not only over infertility but over age as well. Another example, but only over infertility, is that of the prophet Samuel's parents in 1 Samuel 1–2, where God hears the prayer and promise of Hannah and grants her and Elkanah a son. In both cases, of course, the son born of such divine intervention is thereby destined for greatness. It was through Isaac that the Jews would become the children of Abraham, and it was through Samuel that they would receive the monarchy in which David would be the ideal king. Greatness later on, when everybody was paying attention, is retrojected onto earlier origins, when nobody was interested. A marvelous life and death demands and gets, in retrospect, a marvelous conception and birth. Thus the situation of Sarah and Abraham or of Elkanah and Hannah serves as a model for that of Elizabeth and Zechariah, who, according to Luke 1:7, "had no child, because Elizabeth was barren, and both were advanced in years." The conception of John the Baptist continues and even consummates that Old Testament model in which the predestined child is born to an infertile and/or aged couple so that its very conception announces that predestination to greatness. That is one half of Luke's program; the other is even more significant.

The twin infancies of John and Jesus are told in such detailed parallelism with one another that even a casual reading discerns this fact, and scholarly probings serve only to increase its specifics. Imagine it as a drama with five parallel acts.

The first act is the *angelic announcements* to Zechariah about John's conception in Luke 1:5–25 and to Mary about Jesus' conception in 1:26–38. This first parallelism is very pronounced, presumably to draw attention to the entire structure of the composition. Compare, for example, the angel's "Do not be afraid" to Zechariah in 1:13 and to Mary in 1:30; or the questioning of the angel by Zechariah in 1:18 ("How will I know that this is so? For I am an old man, and my wife is getting on in years") and by Mary in 1:34 ("How can this be, since I am a virgin?"). But, especially within such parallelism in form, notice the difference in content already evident in that last comparison. The angel Gabriel says of John in 1:15 that "he will be great before the Lord" but of Jesus in 1:32 that "he will be great, and will be called the Son of the Most High." The point of the parallelism is already clear. It is intended to exalt Jesus, born of a virgin mother, transcendentally above John, born of infertile and aged parents.

The second act is the *publicized birth* of each child. That of John is told first, but rather succinctly, in 1:57–58:

> Now the time came for Elizabeth to give birth, and she bore a son. Her neighbors and relatives heard that the Lord had shown his great mercy to her, and they rejoiced with her.

But the birth of Jesus is told much more lengthily in 2:7–14:

> And she [Mary] gave birth to her firstborn son and wrapped him in bands of cloth, and laid him in a manger, because there was no place for them in the inn. In that region there were shepherds living in the fields, keeping watch over their flock by night. Then an angel of the Lord stood before them, and the glory of the Lord shone around them, and they were terrified. But the angel said to them, "Do not be afraid; for see—I am bringing you good news of great joy for all the people: to you is born this day in the city of David a Savior, who is the Messiah, the Lord. This will be a sign for you: you will find a child wrapped in bands of cloth and lying in a manger." And suddenly there was with the angel a multitude of the heavenly host, praising God and saying, "Glory to God in the highest heaven, and on earth peace among those whom he favors!"

Parallelism, however, still emphasizes primacy. When John is born in 1:58 only "neighbors and relatives" rejoice with Elizabeth, but with Jesus in 2:13 it is "a multitude of the heavenly host, praising God."

The third act is the *circumcision and naming* of each child, of John in 1:59–63a and of Jesus in 2:21.

> On the eighth day they came to circumcise the child, and they were going to name him Zechariah after his father. But his mother said, "No; he is to be called John." They

said to her, "None of your relatives has this name." Then they began motioning to his father to find out what name he wanted to give him. He asked for a writing tablet and wrote, "His name is John." And all of them were amazed. Immediately his mouth was opened and his tongue freed, and he began to speak, praising God.

After eight days had passed, it was time to circumcise the child; and he was called Jesus, the name given by the angel before he was conceived in the womb.

The fourth act is the *public presentation and prophecy of destiny* for each child. The public presentation for John takes place in his parents' home, the reports go out through neighbors to the surrounding hill country, and the prophecy is actually more about Jesus than it is about John. In 1:65–79:

Fear came over all their neighbors, and all these things were talked about throughout the entire hill country of Judea. All who heard them pondered them and said, "What then will this child become?" For, indeed, the hand of the Lord was with him. Then his father Zechariah was filled with the Holy Spirit and spoke this prophecy: "Blessed be the Lord God of Israel, for he has looked favorably on his people and redeemed them. He has raised up a mighty savior for us in the house of his servant David, as he spoke through the mouth of his holy prophets from of old, that we would be saved from our enemies and from the hand of all who hate us. Thus he has shown the mercy promised to our ancestors, and has remembered his holy covenant, the oath that he swore to our ancestor Abraham, to grant us that we, being rescued from the hands of our enemies, might serve him without fear, in holiness and righteousness before him all our days. And you, child, will be called the prophet of the Most High; for you will go before the Lord to prepare his ways, to give knowledge of salvation to his people by the forgiveness of their sins. By the tender mercy of our God, the dawn from on high will break upon us, to give light to those who sit in darkness and in the shadow of death, to guide our feet into the way of peace."

But the public presentation of Jesus is in the Temple, not just in a home; the report goes out to all who "were looking for the redemption of Jerusalem" and not just to the nearby hill country; and the prophecy of destiny is given by both Simeon and Anna and focuses exclusively on Jesus. In 2:21–38:

> When the time came for their purification according to the law of Moses, they brought him up to Jerusalem to present him to the Lord (as it is written in the law of the Lord, "Every firstborn male shall be designated as holy to the Lord"), and they offered a sacrifice according to what is stated in the law of the Lord, "a pair of turtledoves or two young pigeons." Now there was a man in Jerusalem whose name was Simeon; this man was righteous and devout, looking forward to the consolation of Israel, and the Holy Spirit rested on him. It had been revealed to him by the Holy Spirit that he would not see death before he had seen the Lord's Messiah. Guided by the Spirit, Simeon came into the temple; and when the parents brought in the child Jesus, to do for him what was customary under the law, Simeon took him in his arms and praised God, saying, "Master, now you are dismissing your servant in peace, according to your word; for my eyes have seen your salvation, which you have prepared in the presence of all peoples, a light for revelation to the Gentiles and for glory to your people Israel." And the child's father and mother were amazed at what was being said about him. Then Simeon blessed them and said to his mother Mary, "This child is destined for the falling and the rising of many in Israel, and to be a sign that will be opposed so that the inner thoughts of many will be revealed—and a sword will pierce your own soul too." There was also a prophet, Anna the daughter of Phanuel, of the tribe of Asher. She was of a great age, having lived with her husband seven years after her marriage, then as a widow to the age of eighty-four. She never left the temple but worshiped there with fasting and prayer night and day. At that moment she came, and began to praise God and to speak about the child to all who were looking for the redemption of Jerusalem. When they had finished everything required by the law of the Lord, they returned to Galilee, to their own town of Nazareth.

The fifth act is the *description of the child's growth,* and, as in all those preceding cases, John comes first but Jesus, in second place, is exalted over him. In 1:80 and 2:40–52:

The child [John] grew and became strong in spirit, and he was in the wilderness until the day he appeared publicly to Israel.

The child [Jesus] grew and became strong, filled with *wisdom;* and the *favor of God* was upon him. . . .
And when he was twelve . . . his parents . . . found him in the temple, sitting among the teachers, listening to them and asking them questions; and all who heard him were amazed at his understanding and his answers. . . .
And Jesus increased in *wisdom* and stature, and in *favor with God* and man.

Jesus' exaltation is consummated in the story framed by the sets of italicized phrases. John is hidden in the wilderness, but Jesus is already astounding the teachers in the Temple at twelve years of age.

Luke, in that double infancy story, sends two powerful messages to hearer or reader: John is the condensation and consummation of his people's past, but Jesus is far, far greater than John.

Moses and Jesus

Matthew, like Luke, is equally interested in connecting Jesus' birth with the ancient traditions of his people's sacred writings. But instead of imagining infertile couples and miraculous conceptions, he focuses exclusively on the infancy of Moses. The background story presumes both the basic narrative from Exodus 1-2 and the popular expansions of it current in the first century of the common era. In the biblical version, Pharaoh, the ruler of Egypt, attempted to exterminate the Israelites resident in his land by commanding, in Exodus 1:22, "Every son that is born to the Hebrews you shall cast into the Nile, but you shall let every daughter live." Moses happens to be born at this time and is saved only because his mother hides him after birth and eventually leaves him in a basket near the riverbank, where he is saved by Pharaoh's own daughter. Eventually, of course, he will deliver his own people from lethal danger in Egypt and lead them to their Promised Land. Anyone who reads that story can easily see two problems with its narrative coherence. First, why did Moses just happen to be born at that wrong time? Second, why did the Israelites continue having children if their newborn sons were doomed? Both those questions are answered as the Mosaic infancy was retold in expanded popular accounts. In what follows I quote from both earlier and later versions of such popular traditions. The earlier ones, in Josephus and Pseudo-Philo, date from the first century and are very important in proving that those expansions were already available before Matthew composed his infancy account. The later ones, such as the one in the *Book of Remembrances* (or *Sefer ha-Zikronot*), an unedited medieval Hebrew manuscript in the Bodleian Library at Oxford, are more complete and allow fuller and more detailed comparisons with Matthew. Imagine, once again, a parallel drama but now in three rather than five acts. Here, however, those three acts have separate and subordinate scenes.

The first act is *the ruler's plot.* Moses does not just happen to be born after the massacre was decreed; rather, the massacre was decreed in order to kill him. Josephus, a priestly Jewish historian, who published the twenty-volume *Jewish Antiquities,* a history of his people, around 93 or 94 C.E., adds in the following details when paraphrasing the Exodus account from the Bible:

> A further incident had the effect of stimulating the Egyptians yet more to exterminate our race. One of the sacred scribes—persons with considerable skill in accurately predicting the future—announced to the king that there would be born to the Israelites at that time one who would abase the sovereignty of the Egyptians and exalt the Israelites, were he reared to maturity, and would surpass all men in virtue and win everlasting renown. Alarmed thereat, the king, on this sage's advice, ordered that every male child born to the Israelites should be destroyed by being cast into the river.

It is, in other words, precisely to kill the predestined child that Pharaoh ordered the massacre of the male children. That account is developed over four specific scenes in the much later *Book of Remembrances.*

> [1 *Sign.*] Pharaoh dreamed that he was sitting on the throne of his kingdom. He looked up and saw an old man

standing before him with a balance like those of a merchant in his hand. The old man grasped the scales and held them up before Pharaoh. Then he took all the elders of Egypt, her princes and her nobles and put them on one scale of the balance. After that he took a tender lamb and put it on the second scale and the lamb outweighed them all. Pharaoh wondered at this terrible vision, how the lamb outweighed them all and then Pharaoh awoke to find it was only a dream.

[2 *Fear.*] Next morning Pharaoh arose and when he had summoned all his courtiers and narrated his dream they were extremely frightened.

[3 *Consultation.*] Then one of the royal princes answered. "This can only mean that a great evil shall come on Egypt at the end of days." "And what is that?" the king asked the eunuch. So the eunuch replied to the king. "A child will be born in Israel who will destroy all the land of Egypt. If it pleases the king let a royal statute be written here and promulgated throughout all the land of Egypt to kill every newborn male of the Hebrews so that this evil be averted from the land of Egypt."

[4 *Massacre.*] And the king did so and he sent to call the midwives of the Hebrews. [The story here reverts to Exodus 1:15.]

That story, with its four successive scenes, is the model for Matthew's account of Jesus' birth in 2:1–18, although, of course, he has to include the pagan wise men, which have no parallel in the popular accounts of Moses' birth. For Matthew, Jesus is both *rejected* by the Herodian authority and *accepted* by pagan wisdom. The wise pagans at the start of Jesus' life look to the concluding admonition to "teach all nations" at the end, in Matthew 28:19. Here is his version, in summary format:

[1 *Sign.*] In the time of King Herod, after Jesus was born in Bethlehem of Judea, wise men from the East came to Jerusalem, asking, "Where is the child who has been born king of the Jews? For we observed his star at its rising, and have come to pay him homage."

[2 *Fear.*] When King Herod heard this, he was frightened, and all Jerusalem with him.

[3 *Consultation.*] Calling together all the chief priests and scribes of the people, he inquired of them where the Messiah was to be born. They told him, "In Bethlehem of Judea; for so it has been written by the prophet."

[4 *Massacre.*] When Herod saw that he had been tricked by the wise men, he was infuriated, and he sent and killed all the children in and around Bethlehem who were two years old or under.

The second act is *the father's decision.* While Exodus 2:1–2 simply states that after the decree of massacre, "a man from the house of Levi went and took to wife a daughter of Levi [who] conceived and bore a son," the popular versions greatly expand the story. The anonymous *Book of Biblical Antiquities,* erroneously attributed to the Jewish philosopher Philo, but dating in any case from soon after the fall of Jerusalem in 70 C.E., expands that sparse information quite considerably.

Then the elders of the people assembled the people with mourning and mourned and lamented saying . . . let us appoint us an ordinance, that no man come near his wife . . . for it is better to die childless, until we know what God will do. And Amram [father-to-be of Moses] answered and said . . . I will not abide by that which you ordain, but will go in and take my wife and beget sons, that we may be made many on the earth. . . . Now therefore I will go and take my wife, neither will I consent to the commandment of the king. . . . And the word which Amram had in his heart was pleasing to God. . . . And Amram of the tribe of Levi went forth and took a wife of his tribe, and it was so when he took her, that the residue did after him and took their wives. . . . And the spirit of God came upon Maria [Miriam] by night, and she saw a dream, and told her parents in the morning saying: I saw this night, and behold a man in a linen garment stood and said to me: Go and tell your parents: behold, that which shall be born of you shall be cast into the water, for by him water shall be dried up, and by him will I do signs, and I will save my people, and he shall have the captaincy thereof always.

In that version Amram refuses to join in the general divorce and Miriam's prophetic function is simply to proclaim the future.

But in the much later and more detailed *Book of Remembrances* Amram actually joined in the general divorce and it took Miriam's prophecy to change his mind. There are three scenes in this act.

> [1 *Divorce.*] When the Israelites heard the decree ordained by Pharaoh that their male children be thrown into the river part of the people divorced their wives but the rest stayed married to them. . . .
>
> [2 *Reassurance.*] And then at the end of three years the Spirit of God descended on Miriam and she went and prophesied in the centre of the house saying: "Behold, the son will be born to my father and my mother at this time who will save Israel from the power of Egypt."
>
> [3 *Remarriage.*] So when Amram had heard the words of the child he went and remarried his wife whom he had divorced after the decree of Pharaoh ordering the destruction of every male of the house of Jacob. And in the third year of the divorce he slept with her and she conceived by him.

Those three scenes reappear in Matthew 1:18–25, although the virgin conception greatly changes the actual content. Notice especially the resemblances between Miriam's prophetic and Gabriel's angelic reassurance concerning the destined *savior*.

> [1 *Divorce.*] When his mother Mary had been engaged to Joseph, but before they lived together, she was found to be with child from the Holy Spirit. Her husband Joseph, being a righteous man and unwilling to expose her to public disgrace, planned to dismiss her quietly.
>
> [2 *Reassurance.*] But just when he had resolved to do this, an angel of the Lord appeared to him in a dream and said, "Joseph, son of David, do not be afraid to take Mary as your wife, for the child conceived in her is from the Holy Spirit. She will bear a son, and you are to name him Jesus, for he will save his people from their sins.". . .
>
> [3 *Remarriage.*] When Joseph awoke from sleep, he did as the angel of the Lord commanded him; he took her as his wife, but had no marital relations with her until she had borne a son; and he named him Jesus.

The third act is *the child's escape,* and here the popular traditions wisely refrain from tampering with the Exodus account, which is already perfect. Moses escapes from Pharaoh's massacre and eventually leads his people from Egypt to their Promised Land. But here Matthew introduces a terrible irony: Jesus escapes from Herod, but now it is *to* rather than *from* pagan Egypt that he must flee. This underlines another Matthean theme not present in the Mosaic parallel: it is pagan wisdom from abroad, not civil power at home, that accepts and worships the newborn Jesus.

It is not the bare biblical account but the expanded popular versions of Moses' birth that served Matthew as the model for the birth of Jesus. Just as Pharaoh heard of the predestined child's arrival and sought to kill him by killing all the infant males, so did Herod the Great with Jesus. And just as Moses' father refused to accept the general decision of divorce and received a heavenly message through Miriam announcing his child's destiny, so Joseph considered but rejected divorce from Mary upon receiving an angelic message announcing his child's destiny. Moses would "save my people" from Egypt, but Jesus would "save his people from their sins." There are, of course, ironic reversals as well as parallel details in Matthew's account. Pagan wise men read the stars and come from afar to accept Jesus, while Herod reads the Jewish Scriptures and seeks to kill him. And, above all, Jesus flees for refuge to Egypt, the very land from which Moses finally escaped. But once again Matthew, like Luke, sends a strong and powerful message by his very structure. Jesus is the new and greater Moses.

∞ Searching the Scriptures

On the surface, then, Luke and Matthew created completely different infancy stories about Jesus, the former composing, with emphasis on the mothers, a detailed comparison between Jesus and John as the consummation of the Old Testament, the latter composing, with emphasis on the fathers, a detailed comparison between Jesus and Moses as the pinnacle of the Old Testament. But on a more profound level they adopted exactly the same strategy. The past was used to ground the present and found the future, but in the process Jesus became incomparably greater than any predecessor on which he was being modeled. That similarity in general procedure was not coincidental but represented divergent examples of an even earlier Christian tradition, that of searching the scriptures as foundational, and not just apologetical or polemical, texts to understand Jesus, his movement, his destiny, and the lives and hopes of his first followers. Other and more specific examples of that search can be seen behind three incidents that Matthew and Luke have in common and that must therefore have preceded their own individual compositions: the virginal conception, the Davidic ancestry, and the Bethlehem birth of Jesus.

A Virgin Shall Conceive

Both Matthew and Luke agree on the virginal conception of Jesus. The former account focuses on Joseph as he considers divorce from Mary, his betrothed wife, who became pregnant before they ever had intercourse. This potential divorce is, as we have just seen, modeled on that of Moses' parents in the contemporary popular accounts of that birth and, as in that inaugural story, is prevented by a prophetic message from God. In Matthew 1:20–23:

> "Joseph, son of David, do not be afraid to take Mary as your wife, for the child conceived in her is from the Holy Spirit. She will bear a son, and you are to name him Jesus, for he will save his people from their sins." All this took place to fulfill what had been spoken by the Lord through the prophet: "Look, the virgin shall conceive and bear a son, and they shall name him Emmanuel," which means, "God is with us."

That cited prophet is Isaiah 7:14, and the original situation for the prophecy in 734 or 733 B.C.E. was a failed attempt to persuade Ahaz, king of the southern Jewish kingdom of Judah, which was under attack from the combined forces of Syria and the northern Jewish kingdom of Israel, to trust in God rather than appeal to the Assyrian emperor for assistance. Since Ahaz refused assurance of divine assistance, he received instead a prophecy of doom, in Isaiah 7:14–25. Before *any* "young woman shall conceive and bear a son" and that child "knows how to refuse the evil and choose the good"—that is, grows to maturity—both the two attacking kingdoms and Ahaz's own kingdom would lie devastated. God will indeed be "Immanuel," that is, "God with him"—but in judgment, not salvation. The prophecy in Isaiah says nothing whatsoever about a virginal conception. It speaks in Hebrew of an *almah,* a virgin just married but not yet pregnant with her first child. In the Greek translation of the Hebrew Scriptures the term *almah* was translated as *parthenos,* which in that context meant exactly the same thing—namely, a newly married virgin. Both Isaiah's Immanuel prophecy and Virgil's *Fourth Eclogue* looked to the short period between the birth and maturing of a child, but where the latter promised absolute peace, the former promised absolute devastation within that same short period of time. Matthew, in any case, read the prophecy of Isaiah as one of hope rather than despair and took its term *virgin* to apply not only to the prior state of the mother but to her continuing state even during and after conception.

Luke agrees with Matthew that Mary was engaged to be married when the conception took place, but he emphasizes that it is a virginal conception by divine power, in 1:31–35:

> "And now, you will conceive in your womb and bear a son, and you will name him Jesus. He will be great, and will be called the Son of the Most High, and the Lord God will give to him the throne of his ancestor David. He will reign over the house of Jacob forever, and of his kingdom there will be no end." Mary said to the angel, "How can this be, since I am a virgin?" The angel said to her, "The Holy Spirit will come upon you, and the power of the Most High will overshadow you; therefore the child to be born will be holy; he will be called Son of God."

You will notice immediately that Luke, unlike Matthew, has no explicit reference to Isaiah 7:14. It is, however, implicitly present. Matthew 1:21 says that "the child conceived in her is from the Holy Spirit. She will bear a son, and you are to name him Jesus." Luke 1:31 says, "You will conceive in your womb and bear a son, and you will name him Jesus." But those are remarkably similar verses from two sources independent of one another. Both, however, are closely modeled on Isaiah 7:14 itself: "The young woman is with child and shall bear a son, and shall name him Immanuel." Indeed, in the Greek, Luke is even closer than Matthew to Isaiah.

Thus, with the substitution of *Jesus* for *Immanuel*, the common Christian tradition independently inherited by Matthew explicitly and by Luke implicitly derived the virginal conception from an interpretation of Isaiah 7:14. Clearly, somebody went seeking in the Old Testament for a text that could be interpreted as prophesying a virginal conception, even if such was never its original meaning. Somebody had already decided on the transcendental importance of the adult Jesus and sought to retroject that significance onto the conception and birth itself. It is not necessary, by the way, to presume that all early Christian traditions viewed Isaiah 7:14 as prophesying a virginal conception for Jesus. Indeed, it cannot be found anywhere outside that tradition independently known to Matthew and Luke and used only in their divergent infancy narratives.

Once opponents of Christianity heard claims of virginal conception and divine generation for Jesus, they would reply with instant and obvious rebuttal: his having no known human father means he was a bastard! The pagan philosopher Celsus, writing in the last quarter of the second century, declares, in the name of both Judaism and paganism, that a cover-up for bastardy must have been the real reason for such claims. The illegitimate father was, he claims, a Roman soldier named Panthera, in whose name we catch a mocking and reversed allusion to *parthenos*, the Greek word for the young woman from Isaiah 7:14.

Born in David's Village

Both Matthew and Luke agree that Jesus was born in Bethlehem, a village south of Jerusalem in the Judean hills. But once again we are in mythology rather than history. In the Hebrew Scriptures at 1 Samuel 17:12, "David was the son of an Ephrathite of Bethlehem in Judah, named Jesse, who had eight sons." But David was more than just a monarch from the past: he was, like

Arthur, the once and future king. As waves of social injustice, foreign domination, and colonial exploitation swept over Jewish territory, people imagined a future Davidic leader who would bring back the peace and glory of a bygone age hallowed by longstanding nostalgia and suffused with utopian idealism. Among the prophecies gathered into the book of Micah, a younger contemporary of Isaiah in the late eighth century B.C.E. but, unlike him, from the lower classes, there is this fervent hope in 5:2:

> But you, O Bethlehem of Ephrathah, who are one of the little clans of Judah, from you shall come forth for me one who is to rule in Israel, whose origin is from of old, from ancient days.

That prophecy is explicitly cited by Matthew 2:6 in explaining why the Expected One, the Messiah or Christ or Anointed One, would be born at Bethlehem. He seems to take it for granted that Joseph and Mary had always been resident there and moved to Nazareth only after the birth of Jesus and flight into Egypt.

For Luke, like Matthew, Jesus is clearly the Davidic Messiah, that figure expected within certain circles of Judaism as the hope of the future, a figure as magnificent in general promise as he is unclear in precise detail. As we saw earlier, the angelic messenger told Mary, in Luke 1:32, that Jesus "will be great, and will be called the Son of the Most High, and the Lord God will give to him the throne of his ancestor David." But, unlike Matthew, Luke starts his story with Joseph and Mary resident at Nazareth. So he must have them at Nazareth before the birth. Here is why they go to Bethlehem, in Luke 2:1–7:

> In those days a decree went out from Emperor Augustus that all the world should be registered. This was the first registration and was taken while Quirinius was governor of Syria. All went to their own towns to be registered. Joseph also went from the town of Nazareth in Galilee to Judea, to the city of David called Bethlehem, because he was descended from the house and family of David. He went to be registered with Mary, to whom he was engaged and who was expecting a child. While they were there, the time came for her to deliver her child. And she gave birth to her firstborn son and wrapped him in bands of cloth,

and laid him in a manger, because there was no place for
them in the inn.

Three problems. First, there was no such worldwide census under Octavius Augustus. Second, there was indeed a census
of Judea, Samaria, and Idumea, the territories ruled by Herod
the Great's son Archelaus until the Romans exiled him to Gaul
and annexed his lands in 6 C.E. Publius Sulpicius Quirinius,
imperial legate for Syria in 6–7 C.E., would have been in charge
of that census. But that was ten years after the death of Herod
the Great, although Luke 1:5 starts the story of John and Jesus
"in the days of Herod, King of Judea." Third, we know from census and taxation decrees in Roman Egypt that individuals were
usually registered where they were living and working. They had
to return *there* if they were absent elsewhere. The idea of everyone going back to their ancestral homes for registration and
then returning to their present homes would have been then, as
now, a bureaucratic nightmare. What was important then, as
now, was to get you registered where you could be taxed. It is a
little sad to have to say so, because it has always been such a cap-
tivating story, but the journey to and from Nazareth for census
and tax registration is a pure fiction, a creation of Luke's own
imagination, providing a way of getting Jesus' parents to
Bethlehem for his birth. Notice, however, that the Bethlehem
birth, like the virginal conception, is linked to Old Testament
prophecy explicitly by Matthew but only implicitly by Luke.
Finally, recall this interchange in John 7:41–42, where people are
arguing whether Jesus is or is not the Davidic Messiah or Christ.

Others said, "This is the Messiah." But some asked,
"Surely the Messiah does not come from Galilee, does he?
Has not the scripture said that the Messiah is descended
from David and comes from Bethlehem, the village where
David lived?"

There is no indication that anyone in that argument or, for that
matter, in any other text of the New Testament knows about
claims of a Bethlehem birth for Jesus. Both virginal conception
and Bethlehem birth seem unique to whatever common tradition was available to Matthew and Luke for their infancy stories.
The confessions of faith that lie beneath them—that Jesus was
the Son of God and that Jesus was the Davidic Messiah—are, of

course, much more deeply imbedded within the early Christian traditions.

In the Days of King Herod

There is one final point common to Matthew and Luke's infancy stories, and, since they are mutually independent, this is indicative of an even earlier tradition that both of them were using. Luke 1:5, as we have just seen, starts the parallel infancies of John and Jesus with the rather vague chronological notation that they happened "in the days of Herod, king of Judea." Similarly, Matthew 2:1 dates the arrival of the Magi "in the days of Herod the king." But that common phrase could refer to any time in a period of over thirty years.

For about a hundred years before the Romans arrived, the Jewish state had been ruled by its own native kings of the Hasmonean dynasty. But as Jewish royal civil war interacted disastrously with Roman aristocratic civil war, it was the Idumean Herod who finally won out. The Roman Senate declared him king of Judea, and he ruled with political shrewdness and ruthless cruelty from 37 to 4 B.C.E.

To say, therefore, that Jesus was born "in the days of Herod" the Great gives us a span of over thirty years. Two indications, of equally dubious validity, point toward a date at the end of that period. As you will recall, Luke 2:2 had connected Jesus' birth at Bethlehem to the taxation census under Quirinius, in about 6–7 C.E. That, unfortunately, is about ten years after the death of Herod the Great, but it might be argued that Luke's mistake indicates a date later rather than earlier in Herod's reign. And as you will also recall, Matthew 2:13–23, following his Pharaoh and Moses model, had Herod the Great kill all the infant males at Bethlehem, had Jesus flee into Egypt, and, after the death of Herod but while Jesus was still a child, had Jesus, instead of returning to Bethlehem, go to Nazareth. Once again, a date toward the end of Herod's reign is indicated. Both of those items are, however, so dictated by compositional creativity that even their combination hardly offers historical security.

The death of Herod the Great caused massive social and political rebellion in all regions of his territories. Its magnitude may be measured, as may that of all such revolts, by the level of force needed to suppress it. Local disturbances could be contained by local auxiliary forces, since there were no legions stationed within the Jewish state. But deeper unrest or wider rebellion needed the Syrian legate and his legions to come south and restore Roman imperial control. Josephus, the Jewish historian whom I shall describe in greater detail in the next chapter, speaks of three lower-class leaders who sought the kingship vacated by Herod's death, in continuity with the ancient messianic and military models of Saul and David. There was Judas, to the north in Galilee; Simon, to the east in Perea, beyond the Jordan; and Athronges, to the south in Judea. Judas was tall and handsome, as was Saul of old, and Athronges was a shepherd, just like David. That triad indicates not only armed revolt in all major areas of the country but armed revolt arising from the peasant classes and based on the ancient models of Saul and David, those nostalgically idealized and unrealistically remembered paradigms for just kingship under divine mandate and true royalty under heavenly control. In that situation, then, the Syrian governor, Publius Quinctilius Varus, had to bring three legions, apart from numerous auxiliary troops, all the way to Jerusalem and had to crucify two thousand rebels outside its walls before Roman dominion was once again securely established. The stage was then set to divide up Herod's domains among three of his sons, with Archelaus getting Idumea, Judea, and Samaria in the south and middle, Antipas getting Galilee to the north and Perea beyond the Jordan to the east, and Philip getting territories beyond the Jordan to the north. But all of that would insure that the death of Herod would be a date that those who had experienced its effects could not easily forget. Throughout the entire country, and even on the most basic peasant level, where the coming and going of dynasties might be otherwise irrelevant, the ending of "the days of King Herod" would have been etched in the popular memory for a long time afterward. It is thus at least possible that early Christian traditions might have been able to recall that Jesus was born before or even just before that terrible period. A birth date, therefore, soon before 4 B.C.E. is at least an educated guess.

Judging from extant burial inscriptions, the life expectancy of Jewish males in the Jewish state was then twenty-nine years. Since we are certain that Jesus died between 26 and 36 C.E. when Pontius Pilate was prefect of Judea, his age at death would have been almost exactly the statistical average.

∞ Is Not This the Carpenter?

Christians believe that Jesus is, according to John 1:14, the Word of God made flesh, but they seldom ask to what social or economic class that flesh belonged. Confronted with Jesus' adult reputation, neighbors in his native village of Nazareth ask a double question, according to Mark 6:3:

> "Is not this the carpenter, the son of Mary and brother of James and Joses and Judas and Simon, and are not his sisters here with us?"

Matthew 13:55–56 is dependent on Mark 6:3 but expands it to three questions and changes the opening:

> "Is not this the carpenter's son? Is not his mother called Mary? And are not his brothers James and Joseph [Joses] and Simon and Judas? And are not all his sisters with us? Where then did this man get all this?"

Luke 4:22 is also dependent on Mark 6:3 but shortens it to a single question: "Is not this Joseph's son?" John 6:42, in a presumably independent text, has Galileans ask, "Is not this Jesus, the son of Joseph, whose father and mother we know? How can he now say, 'I have come down from heaven'?" Only Mark, therefore, mentions Jesus' being a carpenter. What does that admittedly single independent source tell us about family and carpentry?

I understand the virginal conception of Jesus to be a confessional statement about Jesus' status and not a biological statement about Mary's body. It is later faith in Jesus as an adult retrojected mythologically onto Jesus as an infant, but that understanding has two important consequences. First, those four named brothers and at least two unnamed sisters are Jesus' natural siblings. Second, he is not necessarily the firstborn child of Joseph and Mary. He could just as easily be their youngest, for all we know. I wonder, in fact, if the emphasis given to James, who is known to both Paul and Josephus as Jesus' "brother," might indicate that James was the eldest in the family and that his prominence after the death of Jesus was due not just to his renowned piety but to his leadership position in a family whose father, Joseph, may well have been long dead. That is, of course, sheer speculation, but I mention it to remind us that Jesus as Mary's firstborn child is secure only in combination with Jesus' virginal conception taken literally, factually, and historically.

Whether we read "carpenter" with Mark or "carpenter's son" with Matthew makes little difference in a world where sons usually followed their father's professions in any case. But what exactly was the social or economic class of a *tektōn*, here translated as "carpenter"? The immediate problem is to avoid interpreting a term like *carpenter* in modern terms as a skilled, well-paid, and respected member of the middle class. But the only way to do that effectively is to discipline our imagination with both social history and cross-cultural anthropology.

Ramsay MacMullen has noted that one's social pedigree would easily be known in the Greco-Roman world and that a description such as "carpenter" indicated lower-class status.* At the back of his book he gives a "Lexicon of Snobbery" filled with terms used by literate and therefore upper-class Greco-Roman authors to indicate their prejudice against illiterate and therefore lower-class individuals. Among those terms is *tektōn*, or "carpenter," the same term used for Jesus in Mark 6:3 and for Joseph in Matthew 13:55. One should not, of course, ever presume that upper-class sneers dictated how the lower classes actually felt about themselves. But, in general, the great divide in the Greco-Roman world was between those who had to work with their hands and those who did not.

An earlier study by Gerhard Lenski helps put all of that in a wider cross-cultural frame of reference.** He divides human societies, by technology and ecology, into hunting and gathering, simple horticultural, advanced horticultural, agrarian, and industrial societies. The Roman Empire was an agrarian society, characterized by the forging of iron plows, the harnessing of

---

* Ramsay MacMullen, *Roman Social Relations: 50 B.C. to A.D. 384* (New Haven, CT, and London: Yale Univ. Press, 1974), pages 17–18, 107–108, 139–140, 198 note 82.

** Gerhard Lenski, *Power and Privilege: A Theory of Social Stratification* (New York: McGraw-Hill, 1966), pages 189–296.

animal traction, and the use of wheel and sail to move goods. It was also characterized by an abysmal gulf separating the upper from the lower classes. On one side of that great divide were the Ruler and the Governors, who together made up 1 percent of the population but owned at least half of the land. Also on that same side were three other classes: the Priests, who could own as much as 15 percent of the land; the Retainers, ranging from military generals to expert bureaucrats; and the Merchants, who probably evolved upward from the lower classes but who could end up with considerable wealth and even some political power as well. On the other side were, above all, the Peasants—that vast majority of the population about two-thirds of whose annual crop went to support the upper classes. If they were lucky they lived at subsistence level, barely able to support family, animals, and social obligations and still have enough for the next year's seed supply. If they were not lucky, drought, debt, disease, or death forced them off their own land and into share-cropping, tenant farming, or worse. Next came the Artisans, about 5 percent of the population, below the Peasants in social class because they were usually recruited and replenished from its dispossessed members. Beneath them were the Degraded and Expendable classes—the former with origins, occupations, or conditions rendering them outcasts; the latter, maybe as much as 10 percent of the population, ranging from beggars and outlaws to hustlers, day laborers, and slaves. Those Expendables existed, as that terrible title suggests, because, despite mortality and disease, war and famine, agrarian societies usually contained far more of the lower classes than the upper classes found it profitable to employ. Expendables were, in other words, a systemic necessity.

If Jesus was a carpenter, therefore, he belonged to the Artisan class, that group pushed into the dangerous space between Peasants and Degradeds or Expendables. I emphasize that any decision on Jesus' socioeconomic class must be made not in terms of Christian theology but of cross-cultural anthropology, not in terms of those interested in exalting Jesus but in terms of those not even thinking of his existence. Furthermore, since between 95 and 97 percent of the Jewish state was illiterate at the time of Jesus, it must be presumed that Jesus also was illiterate, that he knew, like the vast majority of his contemporaries in an oral culture, the foundational narratives, basic stories, and general expectations of his tradition but not the exact texts, precise citations, or intricate arguments of its scribal elites. Scenes, in other words, such as Luke 2:41–52, where Jesus' youthful wisdom astonishes the learned teachers in the Temple at Jerusalem, or Luke 4:1–30, where his adult skill in finding and interpreting a certain Isaiah passage astonishes his fellow villagers in the synagogue at Nazareth, must be seen clearly for what they are: Lukan propaganda rephrasing Jesus' oral challenge and charisma in terms of scribal literacy and exegesis.

∞　A Question of Class

Ruler and Artisan bring us back to Octavius and Jesus. For Octavius all the dates were well known, but fervent followers preferred mythology. For Jesus, even if the dates had been remembered rather than forgotten, followers would probably have opted likewise for mythology. Believers, in a similar but of course quite separate process, went back to their respective foundational texts, one to the *Iliad* and the *Odyssey* of the Homeric tradition, the other to the Law and the Prophets of the Hebraic tradition, and each found exactly what was needed, one to exalt Italy over Greece, the other to exalt Christianity over Judaism. Jesus, in terms of history's best guess, was born, *possibly* just before 4 B.C.E., to Joseph and Mary at Nazareth, a tiny hamlet whose population has been estimated at anything from twelve hundred to two hundred people, and although I earlier accepted that former assessment, I am now more inclined to presume the latter. He was born into but not necessarily as the first of a large family and had at least six siblings. The rest is mythology, telling us much about Jesus' later followers but nothing about Jesus' earlier origins, telling us how future history might be founded but not at all how past history had happened.

　　In one sense, however, that is all beside the point. The pious pastor and the village atheist who argue for and against the historicity of Jesus' birth stories miss a far more fundamental issue. The divine origins of Jesus are, to be sure, just as fictional or mythological as those of Octavius. But to claim them for Octavius surprised nobody in that first century. What was incredible was that anyone at all claimed them for Jesus.

Sometime between 177 and 180 C.E., with the emperor Marcus Aurelius already persecuting Christians, the pagan philosopher Celsus wrote his *True Doctrine* as an intellectual attack on their religion. When he discusses Jesus' virgin birth, for example, he never says that such an event is incredible in itself. What is incredible is that it could happen to a member of the lower classes, a Jewish peasant nobody like Jesus.

> What absurdity! Clearly the Christians have used the myths of the Danae and the Melanippe, or of the Auge and the Antiope in fabricating the story of Jesus' virgin birth.... After all, the old myths of the Greeks that attribute a divine birth to Perseus, Amphion, Aeacus and Minos are equally good evidence of their wondrous works on behalf of mankind—and are certainly no less lacking in plausibility than the stories of your followers. What have you done by word or deed that is quite so wonderful as those heroes of old?

It is not absurd, in Celsus's mind, to claim that Jesus was *divine*, but it is absurd to claim that *Jesus* was divine. Who is *he* or what has *he* done to deserve such a birth? Class snobbery is, in fact, very close to the root of Celsus's objection to Christianity:

> First, however, I must deal with the matter of Jesus, the so-called savior, who not long ago taught new doctrines and was thought to be a son of God. This savior, I shall attempt to show, deceived many and caused them to accept a form of belief harmful to the well-being of mankind. Taking its root in the lower classes, the religion continues to spread among the vulgar: nay, one can even say it spreads because of its vulgarity and the illiteracy of its adherents. And while there are a few moderate, reasonable, and intelligent people who are inclined to interpret its beliefs allegori-cally, yet it thrives in its purer form among the ignorant.

It is not enough, therefore, to keep saying that Jesus was not born of a virgin, not born of David's lineage, not born in

Bethlehem, that there was no stable, no shepherds, no star, no Magi, no massacre of the infants, and no flight into Egypt. All of that is quite true, but it still begs the question of who he was and what he did that caused his followers to make such claims. That is a historical question, and it cannot be dismissed with Celsus's sneer.

TWO

The Jordan Is Not Just Water

THE Near East and Mediterranean types of apocalypticism are certainly the most literarily elaborated. . . . However, if we widen our scope, we will find striking phenomenological parallels in the cultures of the Americas, Africa and Oceania, which can hardly be explained with reference to early historical connections with the above area, or by way of diffusion. . . . The revitalization of mythic material and its reinterpretation with reference to the contemporaneous situation is a recurrent feature in these movements.

Tord Olsson, in *Apocalypticism in the
Mediterranean World and the Near East,*
David Hellholm, ed. (Tübingen: Mohr,
Siebeck, 1979)

To the purist the millennium can properly refer only to the fixed period of 1000 years that is found in the Judaic-Christian tradition. In our perspective, however, the term may be applied figuratively to any conception of a perfect age to come, or a perfect land to be made accessible. The picture will vary according as time is fitted into the scheme of the cosmos. The perfect age may come by an act of regeneration, time being bent back, as it were, to recapture some state of harmony in which the world began. It may have some of this quality of early freshness and yet come as time is running out. It will then last for a period that is fixed, variable, or indeterminate, and it may even form part of a cycle of ages. Or it may be an age to last indefinitely, with no doom ahead.

> Sylvia L. Thrupp, in *Millennial Dreams in Action: Studies in Revolutionary Religious Movements* (New York: Shocken, 1970)

∞   God Now Rested over Italy

In the previous chapter the Jewish historian Josephus was mentioned in passing. It is now time to meet him more formally and consider him more fully. He was born into the priestly aristocracy of Jerusalem in 37 C.E. and appeared in Rome before the emperor Nero to defend some fellow priests in 64 C.E. In the First Roman-Jewish War of 66 to 73 C.E. he was in charge of the revolt in Galilee but eventually surrendered to the Roman general Vespasian in 67 C.E. Having foretold that his captor would become emperor, he was released when that prophecy was accomplished in 69 C.E. He observed the siege and fall of Jerusalem as interpreter for Vespasian's son Titus and returned to Rome under patronage of the new Flavian dynasty of Vespasian, emperor in 69–79, Titus in 79–81, and Domitian in 81–96 C.E. He died probably around the end of the first century. So, at least for the First Roman-Jewish War, he was a participant and eyewitness on both the Jewish and Roman sides. Josephan accuracy, however, cannot always be taken for granted. How, then, does one learn to read Josephus between the extremes of either noncritical paraphrase or total skepticism?

Josephus's first work was the *Jewish War*, written between the mid-seventies and early eighties C.E. It not only described the period from 66 to 74 C.E. but prefaced that primary subject with a review of the preceding period from 175 B.C.E. to 66 C.E. His second work was the much longer but not nearly as well written *Jewish Antiquities*, with a completed first edition published in 93–94 C.E. It detailed the period from the creation of the world until the outbreak of the war in 66 C.E. He wrote, therefore, two separate accounts for the years between 175 B.C.E. and 66 C.E., twin versions that must be carefully compared to understand Josephan emphases, prejudices, and purposes. Two of his major presuppositions are of significance for the present chapter.

First, in keeping with the traditional conjunction of biblical prophecy and imperial history, whatever happens to the Jews in the contemporary world empire is interpreted in terms of God's punitive and salvific designs. That applies to the Romans, just as it had earlier to the Egyptians, Assyrians, Babylonians, Persians, Greeks, and Syrians. Thus, concerning the Roman Empire in general and the Flavian dynasty in particular, Josephus's theological position is absolutely clear, as in *War* 5.367, 378, and 412:

> Fortune, indeed, had from all quarters passed over to them [the Romans], and God who went the round of the nations, bringing to each in turn the rod of empire, now rested over Italy. . . . You are warring not against the Romans only, but also against God. . . . The Deity has fled from the holy places and taken His stand on the side of those with whom you are now at war.

God, according to Josephus, wants the Jews to be politically obedient to Rome; thus, those in revolt during that First Roman-Jewish War are actually revolting against God.

A second prejudice is, however, even more important. Recall, from the preceding chapter, that powerfully evocative hope for a future ideal ruler, an Anointed One or Messiah, who would bring back justice and peace to a Jewish homeland overpowered by social discrimination, cultural domination, and imperial oppression. As that control became more and more total and that hope became more and more desperate, individuals or groups often turned apocalyptic and began to imagine some massive and world-shaking divine intervention bringing heaven down to earth or earth up to heaven. Details could be vague, and all the more powerful for that vagueness, but God, with or without human military force, must soon, surely soon, act to restore a terribly disordered world. Here is how that hope sounded, from one group around the middle of the first century B.C.E., in the *Psalms of Solomon* 17:21, 29, 32–33, and 35:

> *See, Lord, and raise up for them their king,*
> *the son of David, to rule over your servant Israel*
> *in the time known to you, O God. . . .*
> *And he will have gentile nations serving under his yoke. . . .*
> *There will be no unrighteousness among them in his days,*
> *for all shall be holy,*
> *and their king shall be the Lord Messiah.*
> *[For] he will not rely on horse and rider and bow,*
> *nor will he collect gold and silver for war.*
> *Nor will he build up hope in a multitude for a day of war. . . .*
> *He will strike the earth with the word of his mouth forever.*

But that is not at all the way Josephus understood Jewish messianic and apocalyptic expectations. Here, from *War* 6.312–313, is his interpretation:

> What more than all else incited them to the war [even as the Temple burned in 70 C.E.] was an ambiguous oracle . . . found in their sacred scriptures, to the effect that at that time one from their country would become ruler of the world. This they understood to mean someone of their own race, and many of their wise men went astray in their interpretation of it. The oracle, however, in reality signified the sovereignty of Vespasian who was proclaimed emperor in Jewish soil.

A word of background. The emperor Nero, saved from assassination by suicide in June of 68 C.E., had brought the Julio-Claudian dynasty down to its ignominious end. For a year, with three rival imperial claimants, there was danger of another prolonged period of civil war, but in July of 69 C.E. Vespasian, then waging war in Judea, was proclaimed emperor. The new Flavian dynasty needed all the prophecies it could find and all the victories it could win, even over a tiny nation like the Jewish homeland. The captured Josephus's stunning application of Jewish apocalyptic messianism to Vespasian in 67 C.E. during the Galilean portion of the First Roman-Jewish War saved his life when first uttered and made his career when later verified. It is hardly likely, against that background, that Josephus would explain too clearly or underline too sharply the existence of alternative apocalyptic or messianic fulfillments before or apart from Vespasian himself.

Besides, therefore, a first Josephan prejudice in favor of Roman imperial power as a heavenly mandate, there is also this second prejudice in favor of the Flavian dynasty as decreed by God, foretold by the Bible, and prophesied by Josephus himself. And all of that must be kept in mind in reviewing his account of John the Baptist.

∞   In Chains to Machaerus

Recall what was said in the preceding chapter about Herod the Great's three sons assuming different portions of their father's domains after his death in 4 B.C.E. Around the year 30 C.E., Herod Antipas, who received Galilee and Perea, had rejected his first wife in order to marry Herodias, wife of his half-brother Herod, and thereafter had been defeated in battle by his rejected father-in-law, Aretas, king of the Nabateans. Josephus frames his account of the Baptist by the suggestion that divine vengeance for John's execution lay behind that military defeat. His account of John is suffused with theological apologetics and becomes, in fact, less comprehensible the more one thinks about it. I give the text from *Antiquities* 18.116–119 in two parts, the better to comment on its strangeness.

> Herod had put him [John, surnamed the Baptist] to death, though he was a good man and had exhorted the Jews to lead righteous lives, to practice justice towards their fellows and piety towards God, and so doing to join in baptism. In his view this was a necessary preliminary if

baptism was to be acceptable to God. They must not employ it to gain pardon for whatever sins they committed, but as a consecration of the body implying that the soul was already thoroughly cleansed by right behaviour.

Josephus insists that baptism was not a magical or ritual act that removed sin but rather a physical and external cleansing available *only after* an already effected spiritual and internal purification. It is certainly difficult to see anything worthy of death in a bodily rite primarily intended for those already saints, and from that description alone one would not expect *crowds* coming to John for such a baptism. But one already senses, behind Josephus's careful exposition, a somewhat different understanding of baptism, one in which body and soul were united and in which the rite removed sin just as surely as did the actions of the priests in Jerusalem's Temple. It was, in fact, as Josephus so carefully denies, a calculated alternative to that salvific system.

He continues his story about John:

> When others too joined the crowds about him, because they were aroused to the highest degree by his sermons, Herod became alarmed. Eloquence that had so great an effect on mankind might lead to some form of sedition, for it looked as if they would be guided by John in everything that they did. Herod decided therefore that it would be much better to strike first and be rid of him before his work led to an uprising, than to await for an upheaval, get involved in a difficult situation and see his mistake. . . . John, because of Herod's suspicions, was brought in chains to Machaerus . . . and there put to death.

Suddenly everything changes, but without any explanation. Who are those *others,* why are they so *aroused,* what is the content of those *sermons,* whither would John lead those who obeyed him *in everything that they did,* and how might it all *lead to some form of sedition* or even to an *uprising?* After reading that second section, one is not surprised that Antipas moved swiftly to eliminate John. The problem is how that second section can be reconciled with the first one; how did ritual piety get misinterpreted as potential revolt? The answer demands a detour through what the New Testament gospels say about John and then a return once more to Josephus.

∞ The Wilderness of Jordan

Antipas's execution of John cannot be explained by a simple appeal to Mark 6:17–29, even if one took that marvelous fiction as historical fact:

> Herod himself had sent men who arrested John, bound him, and put him in prison on account of Herodias, his brother Philip's wife, because Herod had married her. For John had been telling Herod, "It is not lawful for you to have your brother's wife." And Herodias had a grudge against him, and wanted to kill him. But she could not, for Herod feared John, knowing that he was a righteous and holy man, and he protected him. When he heard him, he was greatly perplexed; and yet he liked to listen to him. But an opportunity came when Herod on his birthday gave a banquet for his courtiers and officers and for the leaders of Galilee. When his daughter Herodias came in and danced, she pleased Herod and his guests; and the king said to the girl, "Ask me for whatever you wish, and I will give it." And he solemnly swore to her, "Whatever you ask me, I will give you, even half of my kingdom." She went out and said to her mother, "What should I ask for?" She replied, "The head of John the baptizer." Immediately she rushed back to the king and requested, "I want you to give me at once the head of John the Baptist on a platter." The king was deeply grieved; yet out of regard for his oaths and for the guests, he did not want to refuse her. Immediately the king sent a soldier of the guard with orders to bring John's head. He went and beheaded him in the prison, brought his head on a platter, and gave it to the girl. Then the girl gave it to her mother. When his disciples heard about it, they came and took his body, and laid it in a tomb.

Mark's account is best seen as his own creation, allowing him to emphasize certain parallels between the fate of John and Jesus, especially how both were put to death at the insistence of others by a reluctant and almost guiltless civil authority—Antipas for one, Pilate for the other. In life, death, and even burial by disciples, John is, for Mark, the precursor of Jesus. And, probably, he was deliberately recalling an earlier and well-known Mediterranean horror story. When, in 184 B.C.E., Cato was one of the two official censors at Rome, he had Lucius Quinctius Flaminius expelled from the senate despite his consular rank. His crime is described by the orator Cicero, who died in 43 B.C.E.; again by the historian Livy, who died in 17 C.E.; and finally by the rhetorician Seneca the Elder, who died in 40 C.E. Here is one of the two versions in Livy's history of Rome, Book 39.43:3–4.

> At Placentia a notorious woman, with whom Flaminius was desperately in love, had been invited to dinner. There he was boasting to the courtesan, among other things, about his severity in the prosecution of cases and how many persons he had in chains, under sentence, whom he intended to behead. Then the woman, reclining below him, said that she had never seen a person beheaded and was very anxious to behold the sight. Hereupon, he says, the generous lover, ordering one of the wretches to be brought to him, cut off his head with his sword. This deed . . . was savage and cruel: in the midst of drinking and feasting, where it was the custom to pour libations to the gods and to pray for blessings, as a spectacle for a shameless harlot, reclining in the bosom of a consul, a human victim sacrificed and bespattering the table with his blood!

The point was not that the man was innocent; he was going to be executed in any case. But it should still not be done just to please a mistress, and not at a banquet. The story was clearly a well-known example of how *not* to exercise power. Mark's creation intends, most likely, to recall that classic model.

Even if one took John's criticism of Antipas's marital rearrangements as fact, it would hardly be warrant for execution. Some more serious threat must have motivated Antipas's action. One could, indeed, almost guess what that threat must have been, since Josephus gets most oblique, devious, and defensive whenever Jewish messianism or apocalypticism is in question. It would hardly do, after all, to show too clearly that what Josephus had applied to the Roman emperor Vespasian could also be applied by others to anti-Roman Jewish patriots, especially to ones of a class far, far beneath the imperial purple. And it is precisely as an apocalyptic prophet that John appears in the New Testament gospels, although there too one sees a tendency to smother politics in piety and rebellion in religion.

Josephus never mentioned anything about the wilderness or the Jordan in relation to John, and he protested too much that John's baptism was *not* to remit sins. Mark records wilderness, Jordan, and remission of sins, a contradiction to Josephus that warns us that those elements hang somehow together, that their omission served Josephan interests, and that we will have to return to them below. Here is Mark 1:4–5:

> John the baptizer appeared in the wilderness, proclaiming a baptism of repentance for the forgiveness of sins. And people from the whole Judean countryside and all the people of Jerusalem were going out to him, and were baptized by him in the river Jordan, confessing their sins.

Geographically that area extends on either side of the southern Jordan Valley. It included most of Antipas's Perean territories and was protected on its southern borders by the palace-fortress of Machaerus.

From another gospel source we even get a sample of one of John's sermons that had, according to Josephus, so *aroused* those unidentified *others*. John said, according to the *Q Gospel* in Matthew 3:7–12 or Luke 3:7–9 and 16b–17:

> "You offspring of vipers! Who warned you to flee from the coming fury? Change your ways if you have changed your mind. Don't say, 'We have Abraham as our father.' I am telling you, God can raise up children for Abraham from these stones. Even now the ax is aimed at the root of the trees. Every tree that does not bear good fruit is cut down and thrown into the fire. . . . I am plunging you in water; but one who is stronger than I is coming, one whose sandals I am not worthy to touch. He will overwhelm you with holy spirit and fire. His winnowing fork is in his hand

to clear his threshing floor and gather the wheat into his granary. The chaff he will burn with a fire that no one can put out."

In the present sequence of the gospel narrative, that prophecy of the Coming One refers to Jesus, although, to be sure, it hardly serves as a very good description of Jesus' activity. It is only, however, in John 1:26–31 that the Baptist rephrases his prophecy and then explicitly applies it to Jesus:

John answered them, "I baptize with water. Among you stands one whom you do not know, the one who is coming after me; I am not worthy to untie the thong of his sandal." This took place in Bethany, across the Jordan, where John was baptizing. The next day he saw Jesus coming toward him and declared, "Here is the Lamb of God who takes away the sin of the world! This is he of whom I said, 'After me comes a man who ranks ahead of me because he was before me.' I myself did not know him; but I came baptizing with water for this reason, that he might be revealed to Israel."

That explicit rephrasing and direct application underlines what is evident in John the Baptist's sermon when it is taken by itself and apart from its present location in the gospel sequence. John was not talking about Jesus at all but rather about the imminent advent of the avenging apocalyptic God. That cataclysmic advent is imagined with two powerful images, behind both of which stands the threat of fire. God as the Coming One is first like a forester with an ax separating good trees from bad and then like a thresher separating grain from chaff. For John's fiery vision there are only two categories, the good and the bad, and the time is very short to decide in which category one intends to live and die.

Exactly what Josephus predictably suppresses about John the Baptist is what we find about him in the gospel stories despite their own rather different theological interests in turning John into the herald of Jesus. John was an apocalyptic preacher announcing, in classical Jewish tradition, the imminent advent of an avenging God and not, like Josephus, the imminent advent of an imperial conqueror. But we still need to know more about the wilderness, the Jordan, and the connection between baptizing and remitting sins. For that we go back to Josephus once more.

∞ The Apocalyptic Drummer

I have already mentioned something about the mythological trappings of the Augustan age as great poetry wrapped the new imperial reality in a mantle of ancient glory and manifest destiny. Recall those famous lines from Virgil's *Aeneid* 6.851–853:

> *Roman, remember by your strength to rule*
> *Earth's peoples—for your arts are to be these:*
> *To pacify, to impose the rule of law,*
> *To spare the conquered, battle down the proud.*

Now think, for a moment, how that looked from the other side, from below, from the viewpoint of the pacified, the conquered, and the battled down. Read the magnificent speech created, to his great and abiding honor, by the aristocratic Roman historian Tacitus in the *Agricola* 30, a biography of his father-in-law, Gnaeus Julius Agricola, governor of Britain between 77 and 84 C.E. The rebel general Calgacus describes the Roman Empire just before his fatal encounter with its military might in northeastern Scotland:

> Robbers of the world, now that earth fails their all-devastating hands, they probe even the sea: if their enemy have wealth, they have greed; if he be poor, they are ambitious; East nor West has glutted them; alone of mankind they covet with the same passion want [poor lands] as much as wealth [rich lands]. To plunder, butcher, steal, these things they misname empire: they make a desolation and they call it peace.

How do oppressed people react to overbearing cultural seductiveness, overpowering military superiority, overwhelming economic exploitation, and overweening social discrimination? One way is simply to fight and lose, fight and lose, again and again and again. But, as we already saw with regard to the messianic uprisings after the death of Herod the Great in

4 B.C.E., such military struggles may often be fought under leaders who invoke the memory of ancient indigenous victories and who expect the supernatural assistance of ancestors or angels, gods or God. Those *messianic claimants* must be distinguished from *apocalyptic prophets*. The latter do not presume any military rebellion but announce instead that transcendental power will soon effect what human resistance cannot imagine—a total victory of good over evil, of us over them, and a world of justice and goodness where earth and heaven coalesce forever.

Apocalypticism, which is usually called millennialism or millenarianism within the wider scope of comparative anthropology, comes in two main types, one stemming, according to Lenski's stratification of classes described in the previous chapter, from the Retainers, who support the Governors with their brains and their pens; and the other from the Peasants, who support it with their brawn and their bodies. We already saw an example of the former resistance in the *Psalms of Solomon* from some highly literate scribal or sacerdotal group within Judaism in the century before John the Baptist or Jesus. That is also the type of apocalypticism found within the Bible in the book of Daniel and the book of Revelation. I focus now, however, on peasant apocalypticism within Jesus' century, because that is the most immediate background for an understanding of John the Baptist. But, just as those peasant messianic claimants invoked the ancient models of Saul and David, so would these peasant apocalyptic prophets invoke the ancient models of Moses and Joshua.

Throughout the thirties, forties, fifties, and sixties of that first century, resistance repeatedly erupted in the Jewish homeland not only among Jews but even among Samaritans as well, and Josephus speaks, with scathing contempt, of impostors, deceivers, charlatans, and false prophets who led the people astray during that time. But despite such name-calling, he also gives us a clear idea of what they were doing. One general description and one specific illustration, both from the fifties, will suffice. Both occurred when Felix was Roman governor over the entire country, the Herodian princelings had mostly passed from the scene, and the country was on the brink of total insurrection. This is the summary statement about such apocalyptic prophets in the parallel texts of *War* 2.258–260 and *Antiquities* 20.167b–168:

> (1) Besides these [the Sicarii, Retainer terrorists assassinating Jewish collaborators in Jerusalem] there arose another body of villains, with purer hands but more impious intentions, who no less than the assassins ruined the peace of the city. Deceivers and imposters, under the pretence of divine inspiration fostering revolutionary changes, they persuaded the multitude to act like madmen, and led them out into the desert under the belief that God would there give them *tokens of deliverance*.

> (2) Imposters and deceivers called upon the mob to follow them into the desert. For they said that they would show them unmistakable marvels and *signs* that would be wrought in harmony with *God's design*.

Felix moved immediately against the unarmed multitude, and a massacre swiftly followed. But the phrases that I have italicized are of special importance in understanding what the apocalyptic prophets were attempting to do. They were reenacting, as it were, the ancient model of Moses and Joshua leading the Israelites out of the desert and into the Promised Land around twelve hundred years before. Thus, for example, *tokens or signs of deliverance* is the same expression used for the plagues that Moses invoked upon Egypt before the Exodus in *Antiquities* 2.327. And *God's design or providence* is the same phrase used for the miracle with his staff that Moses performed against his Egyptian competitors before the Exodus in *Antiquities* 2.286. So, despite himself, Josephus puts these prophets in Mosaic continuity. Their expectation was that such an unarmed ritual operation would persuade or compel God to reenact that inaugural deliverance, now against the Romans as long ago against the Canaanites.

The specific illustration makes the typology of Moses and Joshua, of wilderness and Jordan, of crossing and victory, of human impotence and divine violence, even more clear. Once again I give the parallel texts from *War* 2.261–262 and *Antiquities* 20.169–170, as each contains significant elements missing from the other.

(1) A still worse blow was dealt at the Jews by the Egyptian false prophet. A charlatan, who had gained for himself the reputation of a prophet, this man appeared in the country, collected a following of about thirty thousand dupes, and led them by a circuitous route from the desert to the mount called the Mount of Olives. From there he proposed to force an entrance into Jerusalem and, after overpowering the Roman garrison, to set himself up as tyrant of the people, employing those who poured in with him as his bodyguard.

(2) At this time there came to Jerusalem from Egypt a man who declared that he was a prophet and advised the masses of the common people to go out with him to the mountain called the Mount of Olives, which lies opposite the city at a distance of five furlongs. For he asserted that he wished to demonstrate from there that at his command Jerusalem's walls would fall down, through which he promised to provide them an entrance into the city.

Once again, of course, Felix moved swiftly, and a massacre ensued, although the Egyptian himself escaped. In the Acts of the Apostles 21:38, by the way, Claudius Lysias, tribune of the Jerusalem forces under Felix, mistook Paul for the escaped Egyptian prophet and asked him, "Then you are not the Egyptian who recently stirred up a revolt and led the four thousand assassins out into the wilderness?" What the Egyptian and his followers did was go out into the wilderness, cross the Jordan into the Promised Land, and circle the walls of Jerusalem as Joshua had done at Jericho, hoping thus to conquer by divine power what they could not conquer by mere human strength.

Apocalyptic prophets led large crowds into the wilderness so that they could recross the Jordan into the Promised Land, which God would then restore to them as of old under Moses and Joshua. God didn't, and they died. But the desperation of their hope surely deserves better treatment than Josephus accords it. Prophecy was, for Josephus, however, something to be exercised only by scribal and sacerdotal classes, by Retainers talking to Governors, by himself talking to Vespasian, and not by peasant marchers who could only talk with their bodies, write with their lives, and die with their hopes unfulfilled.

I place John the Baptist among those Jewish and peasant apocalyptic prophets appearing, according to Josephus, from the thirties through the sixties of that terrible first common-era century. But that claim draws two immediate objections.

Why did Josephus not hurl against John those same disparaging and contemptuous epithets he reserved for the other apocalyptic prophets? Recall, from above, his insistence that the Jews considered Antipas's military defeat a divine punishment for his execution of John. That means that John was remembered, and remembered by sufficient numbers to have that interpretation retained by Josephus over sixty years later. My suspicion is that there were some such Jewish people alive in Rome at the time Josephus was writing the *Antiquities* and he, nothing if not prudent, sanitized John for Jewish and Roman consumption. But that very process is so obvious that we could almost guess what John must have been doing by reading between the lines, even without anything else. No wonder Josephus never mentioned the wilderness or the Jordan when speaking of John; for, as every Jew would know, the wilderness was not just sand and the Jordan was not just water. If all baptism required was water, even flowing water, that could be found in lots of places apart from the Jordan itself. John did not, in other words, *baptize* in the Jordan; he baptized in the *Jordan*.

Why, second, if John was an apocalyptic prophet, do we have no evidence of him *leading* masses of people anywhere, and why did Antipas move, as far as we can tell, only against John and not against his assembled followers? Josephus used the phrase "come together in baptism," but John's strategy was not to gather an ever-growing crowd east of the Jordan in Antipas's Perea pending mass movement westward. When people came to him, he kept sending them back *from* the wilderness, *through* the Jordan, which washed away their sins, and, purified and ready, *into* the Promised Land, there to await the imminent coming of the redeeming and avenging God. What he was forming, in other words, was a giant system of sanctified individuals, a huge web of apocalyptic expectations, a network of ticking time bombs all over the Jewish homeland. Its magnitude insured a lasting memory, but its diffusion made it both possible and necessary for Antipas to strike precisely at John himself and at John alone. John was the first of those many large-movement and peasant-based first-century apocalyptic prophets centered on wilderness and Jordan, Moses and Joshua, but he also went a way particularly his own.

∞   John Baptizes Jesus

That Jesus was baptized by John is as historically certain as anything about either of them ever can be. The reason is that the theological apologetics exercised by Josephus in telling about John are nothing compared with those exercised by the gospels in telling about John and Jesus. The Christian tradition is clearly uneasy with the idea of John baptizing Jesus, because that seems to make John superior and Jesus sinful.

Mark 1:9 tells about the baptism without any defensive commentary, but immediately overshadows it with the heavenly voice in 1:10–11.

> In those days Jesus came from Nazareth of Galilee and was baptized by John in the Jordan. And just as he was coming up out of the water, he saw the heavens torn apart and the Spirit descending like a dove on him. And a voice came from heaven, "You are my Son, the Beloved; with you I am well pleased."

That would seem quite adequately to exalt revelation over baptism and Jesus over John. But it is not enough for Luke 3:21, which, before telling about the divine voice, hurries past Jesus' baptism to emphasize his prayer; or for Matthew 3:13–15, which has John protest to Jesus; or for the *Gospel of the Nazoreans* 2, a text found outside the New Testament. Here are those three increasingly defensive texts:

> (1) Now when all the people were baptized, and when Jesus also had been baptized and was praying, the heaven was opened [and so forth].

> (2) Then Jesus came from Galilee to John at the Jordan, to be baptized by him. John would have prevented him, saying, "I need to be baptized by you, and do you come to

me?" But Jesus answered him, "Let it be so now; for it is proper for us in this way to fulfill all righteousness." Then he consented.

(3) Behold, the mother of the Lord and his brethren said to him: John the Baptist baptizes unto the remission of sins, let us go and be baptized by him. But he said to them: Wherein have I sinned that I should go and be baptized by him? Unless what I have said is ignorance [a sin of ignorance].

Finally, two sources never even mention the baptism of Jesus, although both know about John's baptizing activity. The *Q Gospel* is much more interested in John's preaching than in John's baptism, and it may have had nothing at all about Jesus' baptism at his hands. And neither does John 1:32–34 give any account of Jesus' baptism, although it is quite ready to tell of the epiphany:

And John testified, "I saw the Spirit descending from heaven like a dove, and it remained on him. I myself did not know him, but the one who sent me to baptize with water said to me, 'He on whom you see the Spirit descend and remain is the one who baptizes with the Holy Spirit.' And I myself have seen and have testified that this is the Son of God."

John, who is probably dependent on the other three New Testament gospels for his Baptist traditions, never mentions a word about Jesus' baptism in all of 1:19–34 and instead emphasizes John the Baptist's witness concerning Jesus. With John's gospel, then, the baptism of Jesus is gone forever, and only the revelation about Jesus remains.

∞ From Fasting to Feasting

John was, then, an apocalyptic prophet like, but also somewhat unlike, many others to follow in the decades leading up to the First Roman-Jewish War in 66 C.E. Jesus was baptized by him in the Jordan. John went, in other words, out into the Trans-Jordanian Desert and submitted himself to the Jewish God and Jewish history in a ritual reenactment of the Moses and Joshua conquest of the Promised Land. He became part, thereafter, of a network within the Jewish homeland awaiting, no doubt with fervent and explosive expectation, the imminent advent of God as the Coming One. Presumably, God would do what human strength could not do—destroy Roman power—once an adequate critical mass of purified people were ready for such a cataclysmic event. The major question is not whether Jesus *began* as an apocalyptic believer but whether he *continued* as such and whether, when he began his own mission, he did so by picking up the fallen banner of the Baptist.

There are three sets of sayings that seem, especially in their conjunction and cumulative effect, to indicate that Jesus broke with John's vision and developed quite a different message for his own program. The first set is found in both the *Gospel of Thomas* 78 and the *Q Gospel* in Matthew 11:7b–9 or Luke 7:24b–26. The former version has changed the ending toward criticism of the powerful rather than praise of the prophet.

> (1) Jesus said: "Why have you come out to the countryside? To see a reed shaken by the wind? And to see a person dressed in soft clothes, [like your] rulers and your powerful ones? They are dressed in soft clothes, and they cannot understand truth."

> (2) Jesus began to speak to the crowds about John: "What did you go out into the wilderness to see? A reed shaking in the wind? [The implied answer is no.] Then tell me what you went out to see? A man in soft clothes? Look, those who wear soft clothes live in palaces. So what did you expect? A prophet? Yes, of course, and much more than a prophet.

In terms of format the saying is set up as an implicit dialogue; it is addressed to those presumably sympathetic to John. In terms of content the saying sets up a contrast between desert and palace and between their appropriate and expected inhabitants. But, while a prophet is clearly named as the one you expect to find in the desert, the palace dweller is not defined as king or courtier, ruler or minister. He is simply described, metaphorically, as one who bends to the prevailing wind and, literally, is dressed in soft or luxurious garments. But, even if that is a correct reading, why is the saying set up like that? Why compare and contrast the desert-dwelling prophet with, precisely, the palace-dwelling "man." The only answer I can imagine is that the saying intends a comparison between John and Antipas and that it arose, directly and immediately, from the crisis engendered among his followers by John's incarceration and execution. It reads like an attempt to maintain faith in John's apocalyptic vision despite John's own execution. What do you prefer: a dead Baptist or a living Antipas? Maybe Jesus was still with John when Antipas struck and that saying correctly summarized his initial defense of John despite the shock of his arrest.

The second set is also found both in the *Gospel of Thomas* 46 and in the *Q Gospel* in Matthew 11:11 or Luke 7:28. Once again I give both versions, in that order.

(1) Jesus said, "From Adam to John the Baptist, among those born of women, no one is so much greater than John the Baptist that the person's eyes should not be averted [before him out of respect]. But I have said that whoever among you becomes a child will know the kingdom and will become greater than John."

(2) "I am telling you, no one born of a woman is greater than John; yet the least in God's realm is greater than he."

But that set seems to contradict the preceding one. The first set exalts John above Antipas, but the second set concludes by exalting anyone in the Kingdom of God above even John. That expression—the Kingdom of God—will require much more discussion in the next chapter, but for now I accept the second set of sayings as a startlingly paradoxical juxtaposition of greatest and least. Not John in the desert but the child in the Kingdom is the beginning of the future.

Both those sets of sayings about John derive from the historical Jesus, and that leaves only one conclusion—namely, that between those twin assertions Jesus changed his view of John's mission and message. John's vision of awaiting the apocalyptic God, the Coming One, as a repentant sinner, which Jesus had originally accepted and even defended in the crisis of John's death, was no longer deemed adequate. It is not enough to await a future kingdom; one must enter a present one here and now. By the time Jesus emerged from John's shadow with his own vision and his own program, they were quite different from John's, but it may well have been John's own execution that led Jesus to understand a God who did not and would not operate through imminent apocalyptic restoration.

The third and final set is composed of sayings by friends or enemies contrasting John and Jesus, and these indicate a recognition that the two individuals were somehow very different from one another. Notice, for example, how John as fasting and Jesus as feasting are contrasted in the following two units, the former from Mark 2:18–20 and the latter from the *Q Gospel* in Matthew 11:18–19 or Luke 7:33–34:

> (1) Now John's disciples and the Pharisees were fasting; and people came and said to him, "Why do John's disciples and the disciples of the Pharisees fast, but your disciples do not fast?" Jesus said to them, "The wedding guests cannot fast while the bridegroom is with them, can they? As long as they have the bridegroom with them, they cannot fast. The days will come when the bridegroom is taken away from them, and then they will fast on that day."

> (2) John did not come eating and drinking, and they are saying, "He is demon possessed." The son of man [that is, Jesus] has come eating and drinking, and they say, "Look at him, a glutton and a drunkard, a friend of tax collectors and sinners."

Behind the positive metaphors of that former unit and the negative ones of that latter there is present a similar contrast between a *fasting John* and a *feasting Jesus*. John, in other words, lived in apocalyptic asceticism, and Jesus did the opposite. But, of course, to say that Jesus was not an apocalyptic ascetic does not at all tell us what he was. All that has been established so far is what John was, where Jesus began, and how eventually, in his own words and in the eyes of others, Jesus became something very different—indeed, almost the exact opposite of the Baptist.

∞ One Like a Son of Man

There is, it would seem, an immediate and crippling objection to those preceding conclusions. Did not Jesus repeatedly foretell the coming of the Son of Man, a figure clearly apocalyptic? Was not Jesus, in other words, just as apocalyptic as John the Baptist? The question thus presses: Did Jesus speak of himself or any other protagonist as the coming Son of Man?

The Hebrew or Aramaic term translated as "son of man" is simply, like *mankind* in English, a chauvinistic way to describe all of humanity, a patriarchal way for the part to describe the whole in its own exclusive image. An example is Psalm 8:4, where the poetic parallelism makes the meaning redundantly clear. I give it first in the old Revised Standard Version and then in the new one.

What is man that thou art mindful of him,
and the son of man that thou dost care for him?

What are human beings that you are mindful of them,
mortals that you care for them?

The change from older to newer translation involves not just the elimination of the anachronistic *thou art* and *thou dost* but the replacement of the chauvinistic *man* and *son of man* in the former translation by *human beings* and *mortals* in the latter translation. That is, of course, what those former terms actually meant.

Another example, of exactly that same usage, is in Daniel 7, an apocalyptic vision intended to reassure faithful Jews, persecuted between 167 and 164 B.C.E. by the Syrian monarch Antiochus IV Epiphanes, that, just as Babylonians, Medes, Persians, and Greeks had come and gone, so also would the Syrian onslaught swiftly pass. Thereafter and in their places, God would create a perfect and everlasting kingdom for those who had been persecuted and had remained faithful despite everything. And just as those evil empires were described as "like a lion . . . like a bear . . . like a leopard"—that is, like wild beasts here below—so also, but in deliberate contrast, was the holy kingdom described as "like a son of man"—that is, like a human being from heaven above. That is certainly not a title but rather a literary contrast: as those evil kingdoms could be incarnated as beasts, so can the perfect kingdom be incarnated as a human being. But, especially in Greek translation, where the Hebrew or Aramaic expression sounds as strange as it does in English, "a son of man" could easily become a title, "the Son of Man." That title would then indicate some specific individual as the designated agent for God's imminent apocalyptic judgment on an evil world. In other words, a generic usage for all human beings together became a titular usage for some single human being alone.

It is absolutely clear that Jesus as presented in the canonical gospels uses "Son of Man" in such a titular sense and that he is thereby imagining himself or some other transcendental figure as the future agent of God's judgment. The question, however, is whether the historical Jesus himself ever used such an expression or whether it represents an interpretation from within earliest Christianity.

My main reason for denying that Jesus ever historically used the titular expression is that in the entire Son of Man tradition *there is only a single instance where two independent sources have the expression in more than a single version.* Wherever it is found, except for that one case, it is in one but not the other version, and it always looks as if it is coming in later rather than having been there from the start. My argument is not at all that Jesus should not or could not have spoken about the coming Son of Man. It is simply that in every single case where we have him so speaking, it seems a later rather than an earlier presence.

I look only at that single exception because it may be extremely significant in understanding why titular Son of Man expressions were later placed on Jesus' own lips. The saying is found in both the *Gospel of Thomas* 86 and the *Q Gospel* in Matthew 8:19–20 or Luke 9:57–58.

> (1) Jesus said, "[Foxes have] their dens and birds have their nests, but the child of humankind [*literally:* son of man] has no place to lay his head and rest."

(2) When someone said to him, "I will follow you wherever you go," Jesus answered, "Foxes have dens, and birds of the sky have nests, but the son of man has nowhere to lay his head."

That is an example of the generic, not the titular, usage. Jesus comments that the birds have their homes *above* the earth, the foxes have their homes *below* the earth, but human beings, who should have their homes *upon* the earth, find that they have no place of their own even to lie down and sleep. That generic statement hardly applies, of course, to aristocratic elites, but Jesus was presumably not addressing them. He was speaking to the poor and the destitute, who would easily recognize themselves as the human beings in question. That interpretation will require further proof in the next chapter, but for now my point is that here "the son of man" certainly does not mean the imminent or future agent of divine judgment. Jesus used the generic term "son of man" to identify himself with those he was addressing, to emphasize that he shared with them a common destiny as *we* poor or destitute human beings. It was thereafter easier to create and place upon his lips certain titular "Son of Man" sayings as the tradition of his words grew after his death.

At the dawn of this century, Albert Schweitzer insisted that John and Jesus were both apocalyptic preachers, each attempting in his own way to force the advent of the avenging God. This is his description, toward the end of his classic study, *The Quest of the Historical Jesus:*

There is silence all around. The Baptist appears, and cries: "Repent, for the Kingdom of Heaven is at hand." Soon after that comes Jesus, and in the knowledge that He is the coming Son of Man lays hold of the wheel of the world to set it moving on that last revolution which is to bring all ordinary history to a close. It refuses to turn, and He throws Himself upon it. Then it does turn; and crushes Him. Instead of bringing in the eschatological conditions, He has destroyed them. The wheel rolls onward, and the mangled body of the one immeasurably great Man, who was strong enough to think of Himself as the spiritual ruler of mankind and to bend history to His purpose, is hanging upon it still. That is His victory and His reign.*

Notice, however, that he uses the term *eschatological* where I have consistently used the word *apocalyptic*. He explains what he means by *eschatological* a few pages later on:

That which is eternal in the words of Jesus is due to the very fact that they are based on an eschatological world-view, and contain the expression of a mind for which the contemporary world with its historical and social circumstances no longer had any existence. They are appropriate, therefore, to any world, for in every world they raise the man who dares to meet their challenge, and does not turn and twist them into nothingness, above his world and his time, making him inwardly free, so that he is fitted to be, in his own world and in his own time, a simple channel of the power of Jesus. . . . Why spare the spirit of the individual man its appointed task of fighting its way through the world-negation of Jesus, of contending with Him at every step over the value of material and intellectual goods—a conflict in which it may never rest?**

There is a confusion in Schweitzer's text between a wider or generic and a narrower or specific term. Both terms are absolutely necessary, and so is their careful distinction from one another. The wider term is *eschatology* or *world-negation*. It indicates a radical criticism of culture and civilization and thus a fundamental rejection of this world's values and expectations. It describes those who have turned profoundly away from normal life in disappointment or anger, in sorrow or pain, in contempt or abandonment. They imagine another and more perfect world whose alluring vision trivializes the one all around them. But that wider term must cover all sorts of ideas and programs and all types of ideal or perfect worlds. Examples are mystical, utopian, ascetic, libertarian, or anarchistic eschatologies or world-negations. Those are all narrower or more specific

---

* Albert Schweitzer, *The Quest of the Historical Jesus: A Critical Study of Its Progress from Reimarus to Wrede,* trans. W. Montgomery (New York: Macmillan, 1968; first published 1906), pages 370–371.
** Schweitzer, *The Quest of the Historical Jesus,* page 402.

terms. They extend from ascetics who stalk away from the world into caves, deserts, or monasteries, to nihilists who destroy it with words, deeds, or bombs. Another such specific term is *apocalyptic eschatology*. It presumes a world judged so catastrophically evil and deemed so irrevocably beyond human remedy that only immediate divine intervention can rectify it. It furnishes, therefore, a special revelation about the imminent ending of that evil world, about the liberation and exaltation of *us* and the conversion, punishment, or annihilation of *them*, and about a new situation in which *we* are taken up to heaven or heaven descends to embrace *us*.

Schweitzer was both superficially wrong and profoundly right. Jesus was not an apocalyptic prophet like John the Baptist, but he was an eschatological or world-negating figure, as I shall argue in the next chapter. Still, any discussion of Schweitzer should include the last lines of his great book:

> He comes to us as One unknown, without a name, as of old, by the lake-side, he came to those men who knew Him not. He speaks to us the same word: "Follow thou me!" and sets us to the tasks that He has to fulfil for our time. He commands. And to those who obey, whether they be wise or simple, He will reveal Himself in the toils, the conflicts, the sufferings that they shall pass through in his fellowship, and, as an ineffable mystery, they shall learn in their own experience Who He is.*

* Schweitzer, *The Quest of the Historical Jesus,* page 403.

THREE

A Kingdom of Nuisances and Nobodies

Discourse about *basileia* ("rule") during the Greco-Roman period was not limited to circles of Jewish apocalypticists, nor, for that matter, to those with specifically Jewish interests. *Basileia* was a common topic of far-reaching significance throughout Hellenistic culture. . . . But in the post-Alexander age . . . kings, tyrants, and generals were much too much in evidence . . . [and] the critical issues now centered on power and privilege, and on the rights and duties of those who had it. . . . It was therefore *basileia* that was most under discussion, though other terms could be used as well. . . . *Basileia* is what kings and rulers had: sovereignty, majesty, dominion, power, domain. How to guarantee the just and beneficent exercise of power was a very big question throughout this period. . . .

As happens, moreover, the abstract models constructed in order to imagine the practical issues inherent in the political structures of society could be used as well to think through basic questions about social ethos in general. . . . "King" no longer needed to refer to the actual king of a city or kingdom. "King" became an abstract representation of *anthropos* ("human being") at the "highest" level imaginable, whether of endowment, achievement, ethical excellence, or mythical ideal.

Burton Mack, "The Kingdom Sayings in Mark," *Forum* 3, no. 1 (1987)

∞ The Now or Future Kingdom

I am not particularly happy with the word *kingdom* as a translation of the Greek word *basileia,* but it is so traditional that any alternative might be confusing. It is not only that *king-* is chauvinistic but that *-dom* sounds primarily local, as if we were talking about some specific site or some geographically delineated location on earth. But what we are actually talking about, as the preceding epigraph reminds us, is power and rule, a process much more than a place, a way of life much more than a location on earth. The basic question is this: How does human power exercise its rule and how, in contrast, does divine power exercise its rule? The Kingdom of God is people under divine rule—and that, as ideal, transcends and judges all human rule. The focus of discussion is not on kings but on rulers, not on kingdom but on power, not on place but on process. The Kingdom of God is what the world would be if God were directly and immediately in charge.

But even within that understanding of the phrase, it is both possible and necessary to imagine a basic fourfold typology of the Kingdom of God in Jewish usage contemporary with Jesus. Imagine four quadrants or types created by the intersection of two axes. One axis is a *time* distinction, with the future or present at either end. The other axis is a *class* distinction, based once again on Lenski's model, with Retainers or scribal elites at one end and Peasants or ordinary people at the other.

The future or apocalyptic Kingdom of God is dependent on the overpowering action of God moving to restore justice and peace to an earth ravished by injustice and oppression. Believers can, at the very most, prepare or persuade, implore or assist its arrival, but its accomplishment is consigned to divine power alone. And despite a serene vagueness about specifics and details, its consummation would be objectively visible and tangible to all, believers and unbelievers alike, but with appropriately different fates for each group. We have already seen examples of both the Retainer and Peasant applications of this apocalyptic vision. The Retainers, or scribal bureaucrats, are exemplified in whatever group wrote the *Psalms of Solomon,* cited earlier, with their hope for the imminent coming of "their king, the Son of David" or "their king . . . the Lord Messiah." The Peasants are exemplified in those apocalyptic prophets like John the Baptist who modeled their ritual actions on the inaugural victories of Moses and Joshua. The scribal elites wrote and proclaimed, because that was what they could do, and the peasant leaders marched and performed, because that was what they could do. I do not presume that either mode is in any way better than the other. Those two groups furnish, however, only two parts of the fourfold typology.

An alternative to the future or apocalyptic Kingdom is the present or sapiential vision. The term *sapiential* underlines the necessity of wisdom—*sapientia* in Latin—for discerning how, here and now in this world, one can so live that God's power, rule, and dominion are evidently present to all observers. One enters that kingdom by wisdom or goodness, by virtue, justice, or freedom. It is a style of life for now rather than a hope of life for the future. This is therefore an ethical kingdom, but it could be just as eschatological as was the apocalyptic kingdom. Its ethics could, for instance, challenge contemporary morality to its depths. It would be incorrect to presume that, in my terminology, a sapiential Kingdom of God was any less world-negating than an apocalyptic one.

The present or sapiential Kingdom of God has, like its future or apocalyptic alternative, two types, one for Retainers and another for Peasants. Here are three examples of the former type.

The first is from the Jewish philosopher Philo of Alexandria, a contemporary of Jesus who lived between 10 B.C.E.

and 45 C.E., writing in the *Special Laws* 4.135–136. There a human monarch, meditating on the laws he makes for his people, states that the only valid political or earthly kingdom is modeled on the transcendental or heavenly Kingdom of God:

> Other kings carry rods in their hands as sceptres but my sceptre is the book of the Sequel to the Law, my pride and my glory, which nothing can rival, an ensign of sovereignty which none can impeach, formed in the image of its archetype, the kingship of God.

For Philo, therefore, the wise and the virtuous already partake in the kingdom or kingship of God, and only political dominions with laws modeled on God's are worthy even of the title of kingdom.

The second example is also a Jewish work, the *Wisdom of Solomon,* written, most likely, during the reign of the emperor Caligula, between 37 and 41 C.E. The true and lasting rule is not that which the kings of the earth now exercise but that which they would receive if they submitted themselves to wisdom's own rule. They are kings without the real kingdom. The biblical Jacob, on the other hand, possessed the true kingdom, although he was not a king, in 10:10.

> *When a righteous man fled from his brother's wrath,*
> *she [Wisdom] guided him on straight paths;*
> *she showed him the kingdom of God.*

The Kingdom of God is the Kingdom of Wisdom eternally present—available, on the one hand, to anyone who heeds her call, and transcendent, on the other, to all the evil rulers of the world.

The third example is from the *Sentences of Sextus* 307–311, a pagan work, probably from the second century, with later Christian adaptations, whose moral teaching is intensely ascetic and highly concerned with sexuality.

> *A wise man presents God to humanity.*
> *Of all his works God is most proud of a sage.*
> *Next to God, nothing is as free as a wise man.*
> *Whatever God possesses belongs also to the sage.*
> *A wise man shares in the kingdom of God.*

Thus, even for a pagan sage, let alone a Jewish or a Christian one, an ethical or sapiential Kingdom of God was as clear a possibility as an apocalyptic one.

Those three examples all imagine a present Kingdom of God that wise, just, and virtuous sages—that is, the precise class to which all three writers belonged—could enter into here and now. But what of the remaining quadrant or type? What would a present or sapiential Kingdom of God, a life-style under God's direct dominion, look like to peasants, and especially to a peasant talking to peasants? It is, as no doubt you have guessed by now, in that fourth quadrant or type that I am locating Jesus.

He was an illiterate peasant, but with an oral brilliance that few of those trained in literate and scribal disciplines can ever attain. When today we read his words in fixed and frozen texts we must recognize that the oral memory of his first audiences could have retained, at best, only the striking image, the startling analogy, the forceful conjunction, and, for example, the plot summary of a parable that might have taken an hour or more to tell and perform. I give several examples of what the here-and-now Kingdom of God meant for Jesus, from each of the major genres in which that oral memory preserved, developed, but also created such traditions.

∞ Tearing the Family Apart

If the supreme value for the twentieth-century American imagination is *individualism*, based on economics and property, that for the first-century Mediterranean imagination can be called, to the contrary, *groupism*, based on kinship and gender. And there were really only two groups—the familial and the political, kinship and politics—to be considered. But we have, precisely against both those groups, biting aphorisms and dialogues from the historical Jesus. There is, first of all, an almost savage attack on family values, and it happens very, very often. Here are four quite different examples. Each has different versions available, but I give only one version for each example. The first one is from the *Gospel of Thomas* 55, the second from Mark 3:31–35, the third from the *Q Gospel* in Luke 11:27–28 but with no

Matthean parallel, and the final one from the *Q Gospel* in Luke 12:51–53 rather than in Matthew 10:34–36.

(1) Jesus said, "Whoever does not hate father and mother cannot be a follower of me, and whoever does not hate brothers and sisters . . . will not be worthy of me."

(2) Then his mother and his brothers came; and standing outside, they sent to him and called him. . . . And he replied, "Who are my mother and my brothers?" And looking at those who sat around him, he said, "Here are my mother and my brothers! Whoever does the will of God is my brother and sister and mother."

(3) A woman from the crowd spoke up and said to him, "How fortunate is the womb that bore you, and the breasts that you sucked!" But he said, "How fortunate, rather, are those who listen to God's teaching and observe it!"

(4) "Do you think that I have come to bring peace to the earth? No, I tell you, but rather division! From now on five in one household will be divided, three against two and two against three; they will be divided: father against son and son against father, mother against daughter and daughter against mother, mother-in-law against her daughter-in-law and daughter-in-law against mother-in-law."

The family is a group to which one is irrevocably assigned, but in those first two units, that given grouping is negated in favor of another one open to all who wish to join it. And the reason those groups are set in stark contrast becomes more clear by the third example. A woman declares Mary blessed because of Jesus, presuming, in splendid Mediterranean fashion, that a woman's greatness derives from mothering a famous son. But that patriarchal chauvinism is negated by Jesus in favor of a blessedness open to anyone who wants it, without distinction of sex or gender, infertility or maternity.

Finally, it is in the last aphorism that the point of Jesus' attack on the family becomes most clear. Imagine the standard Mediterranean family with five members: mother and father, married son with his wife, and unmarried daughter, a nuclear extended family all under one roof. Jesus says he will tear it apart. The usual explanation is that families will become divided as some accept and others refuse faith in Jesus. But notice where and how emphatically the axis of separation is located. It is precisely *between the generations*. But why should faith split along that axis? Why might faith not separate, say, the women from the men or even operate in ways far more random? *The attack has nothing to do with faith but with power.* The attack is on the Mediterranean family's axis of power, which sets father and mother over son, daughter, and daughter-in-law. That helps us to understand all of those examples. The family is society in miniature, the place where we first and most deeply learn how to love and be loved, hate and be hated, help and be helped, abuse and be abused. It is not just a center of domestic serenity; since it involves power, it invites the abuse of power, and it is at that precise point that Jesus attacks it. His ideal group is, contrary to Mediterranean and indeed most human familial reality, an open one equally accessible to all under God. It is the Kingdom of God, and it negates that terrible abuse of power that is power's dark specter and lethal shadow.

∞   Blessed Are (We?) Beggars

Turning from familial to political groupings, it is hard to imagine an aphorism initially more radical but eventually more banal than Jesus' conjunction of blessed poverty and the Kingdom of God. Here are four versions of the same saying, from the *Gospel of Thomas* 54, from the *Q Gospel* in both Luke 6:20 and Matthew 5:3, and from James 2:5, respectively. The first example is in Coptic translation and the last three are in Greek. As you read from first to last you can see the process of normalization at work:

> (1) "Blessed are the poor, for yours is the kingdom of heaven."

> (2) "Blessed are you who are poor, for yours is the kingdom of God."

(3) "Blessed are the poor in spirit, for theirs is the kingdom of heaven."

(4) Has not God chosen those who are poor in the world to be rich in faith and heirs of the kingdom which he has promised to those who love him?

In the third example, Matthew's *in spirit* diverts interpretation from economic to religious poverty, and James's emphasis on faith and love points toward a promised rather than a present Kingdom of God. But the stark and startling conjunction of blessed poverty and divine Kingdom is still there for all to see in the first two versions. We can no longer tell, of course, whether Jesus meant *the* or *you* or *we* poor.

There is, however, a very serious problem when the Greek word *ptōchos* is translated as "poor" in the last three examples. The Greek word *penēs* means "poor," and *ptōchos* means "destitute." The former describes the status of a peasant family making a bare subsistence living from year to year; the latter indicates the status of such a family pushed, by disease or debt, draught or death, off the land and into destitution and begging. One can see this distinction most clearly in the *Plutus* of Aristophanes, the last play of that great comic dramatist, produced probably in the Athens of 388 B.C.E. The key section is in *Plutus* 535–554, with Chremylus arguing for the advantages of the god Plutus (or Wealth) and declaring that Penia (or Poverty) and Ptōcheia (or Destitution) are both the same in any case. Poverty, appearing here as a goddess, immediately denies her equation with Destitution:

CHREMYLUS:
Well, Poverty [penian] and Destitution [ptōcheias], truly the two to be sisters we always declare.

POVERTY:
It's the beggar [ptōchou] alone who has nothing his own, nor even a penny possesses.
My poor [penētos] man, it's true, has to scrimp and to scrape, and his work he must never be slack in;
There'll be no superfluity found in his cot;
but then there will nothing be lacking.

The *poor* man has to work hard but has always enough to survive, while the *beggar* has nothing at all. Jesus, in other words, did not declare blessed the poor, a class that included, for all practical purposes, the entire peasantry; rather, he declared blessed the destitute—for example, the beggars.

Now, what on earth does that mean, especially if one does not spiritualize it away, as Matthew immediately did, into "poor [or destitute] in spirit"—that is, the spiritually humble or religiously obedient? Did Jesus really think that bums and beggars were actually blessed by God, as if all the destitute were nice people and all the aristocrats correspondingly evil? Is this some sort of naive or romantic delusion about the charms of destitution? If, however, we think not just of personal or individual evil but of social, structural, or systemic injustice—that is, of precisely the imperial situation in which Jesus and his fellow peasants found themselves—then the saying becomes literally, terribly, and permanently true. In any situation of oppression, especially in those oblique, indirect, and systemic ones where injustice wears a mask of normalcy or even of necessity, the only ones who are innocent or blessed are those squeezed out deliberately as human junk from the system's own evil operations. A contemporary equivalent: only the homeless are innocent. That is a terrifying aphorism against society because, like the aphorisms against the family, it focuses not just on personal or individual abuse of power but on such abuse in its systemic or structural possibilities—and there, in contrast to the former level, none of our hands are innocent or our consciences particularly clear.

∞ If It Is a Girl, Cast It Out

Another striking conjunction is that between infant children and divine Kingdom. Once again we can move easily from aphorism to dialogue as the tradition creates situations and settings for sayings it has retained in memory. And, once again, earliest oral memory would not have been in the form of exact syntactical arrangements recalling precisely what Jesus saw or said, but rather of a startling combination, children/Kingdom, which could then be articulated as needed in various forms and versions. Although there are four independent versions of that conjunction, I give only one, for the sake of brevity. From Mark 10:13–16:

> People were bringing little children to him in order that he might touch them; and the disciples spoke sternly to them. But when Jesus saw this, he was indignant and said to them, "Let the little children come to me; do not stop them; for it is to such as these that the kingdom of God belongs. *Truly I tell you, whoever does not receive the kingdom of God as a little child will never enter it.*" And he took them up in his arms, laid his hands on them, and blessed them.

What was, first of all, the immediate connotation of children or infants to the ancient Mediterranean as distinct from the modern American mind? Read this ancient papyrus letter, discovered around the turn of the century on the west bank of the Nile about 120 miles south of Cairo in the excavated rubbish dumps of ancient Oxyrhynchus, the modern El Bahnasa. The worker Hilarion writes to his wife, Alis, addressed in Egyptian fashion as sister, on 18 June in the year 1 B.C.E. From the *Oxyrhynchus Papyri* 4.744:

> Hilarion to his sister Alis many greetings, likewise to my lady Berous [his mother-in-law?] and to Apollonarion [their first and male child]. Know that we are even yet in Alexandria. Do not worry if they all come back [except me] and I remain in Alexandria. I urge and entreat you, be concerned about the child [Apollonarion] and if I should receive my wages soon, I will send them up to you. If by chance you bear a son, if it is a boy, let it be, if it is a girl, cast it out [to die]. You have said to Aphrodisias, "Do not forget me." How can I forget you? Therefore I urge you not to worry. 29 [year] of Caesar [Augustus], Payni [month] 23 [day].

Hilarion and some companions had left their home at Oxyrhynchus and traveled north to work in Alexandria. His wife, Alis, pregnant with their second child, having heard nothing nor received anything from him, transmitted her concern through Aphrodisias, who was also traveling to the capital. The letter is Hilarion's response to her concern, and, tender to his pregnant wife but terrible to his unborn daughter, it shows us with stark clarity what an infant meant in the Mediterranean. It was quite literally a nobody unless its father accepted it as a member of the family rather than exposing it in the gutter or rubbish dump to die of abandonment or to be taken up by another and reared as a slave. To be like an infant child is interpreted by Matthew 18:1–4 as meaning to have appropriate humility, by the *Gospel of Thomas* 22 as meaning to practice sexual asceticism, and by John 3:1–10 as meaning to have recently received baptism. Those three readings avoid the horrifying meaning of a child as a nothing, a nobody, a nonperson in the Mediterranean world of paternal power, absolute in its acceptance or rejection of the newly born infant.

In giving Mark's version above I italicized the core aphorism, whose basic conjunction of children/Kingdom is all that certainly came from Jesus. Concentrate, for a moment, on the framing situation created by Mark himself. This indicates the situation not from the historical Jesus but from the historical Mark. Notice those framing words: *touch, took in his arms, blessed, laid hands on.* Those are the official bodily actions of a father designating a newly born infant for life rather than death, for accepting it into his family rather than casting it out with the garbage. And the disciples do not want Jesus to act in this positive and accepting way. There must, therefore, have been a debate within the Markan community on whether it should adopt such abandoned infants, and Mark has Jesus say yes even though other authorities—the disciples themselves—say no. Once again we are forced to face ancient Mediterranean realities, and Mark's later application helps us to see more clearly what was there from Jesus in the beginning: that a Kingdom of Children is a Kingdom of Nobodies.

∽ Who Needs a Mustard Plant?

There is another rather startling conjunction, but in a parable rather than in an aphorism or dialogue—the conjunction between the mustard seed and the Kingdom. The parable is, by the way, the only one attributed to Jesus that has triple independent attestation. I give only one version, from Mark 4:30–32:

And he said, "With what can we compare the kingdom of God, or what parable shall we use for it? It is like a grain of mustard seed, which, when sown upon the ground, is the smallest of all the seeds on earth; yet when it is sown it grows up and becomes the greatest of all shrubs, and puts forth large branches, so that the birds of the air can make nests in its shade."

Once again, a word about Mediterranean mustard plants and nesting birds helps us to understand the startling nature of that conjunction. The Roman author Pliny the Elder, who was born in 23 C.E. and died when scientific curiosity brought him too close to an erupting Vesuvius in 79 C.E., wrote about the mustard plant in his encyclopedic *Natural History* 19.170–171:

Mustard . . . with its pungent taste and fiery effect is extremely beneficial for the health. It grows entirely wild, though it is improved by being transplanted: but on the other hand when it has once been sown it is scarcely possible to get the place free of it, as the seed when it falls germinates at once.

There is, in other words, a distinction between the wild mustard and its domesticated counterpart, but even when one deliberately cultivates the latter for its medicinal or culinary properties, there is an ever-present danger that it will destroy the garden. The mustard plant is dangerous even when domesticated in the garden, and is deadly when growing wild in the grain fields. And those nesting birds, which may strike us as charming, represented to ancient farmers a permanent danger to the seed and the grain. The point, in other words, is not just that the mustard plant starts as a proverbially small seed and grows into a shrub of three, four, or even more feet in height. It is that it tends to take over where it is not wanted, that it tends to get out of control, and that it tends to attract birds within cultivated areas, where they are not particularly desired. And that, said Jesus, was what the Kingdom was like. Like a pungent shrub with dangerous take-over properties. Something you would want only in small and carefully controlled doses—if you could control it. It is a startling metaphor, but it would be interpreted quite differently by those, on the one hand, concerned about their fields, their crops, and their harvests, and by those, on the other, for whom fields, crops, and harvest were always the property of others.

∞ Open Commensality

Let that title stand unexplained for a moment. Its meaning and necessity will soon become clear. At the end of the preceding chapter, a comparison was made between John and Jesus in terms of fasting and feasting. The contrast was made both in neutral terms by Jesus himself and in very inimical terms by opponents: John fasted and they called him demonic; Jesus ate and drank and they said he was "a glutton and a drunkard, a friend of tax collectors and sinners." It is obvious why John, as an apocalyptic ascetic, was fasting, but what was Jesus doing? It is not enough to say that those opponents are simply accusing him of social deviancy through nasty name-calling. That is, of course, quite true, but why precisely those names rather than any of the others easily available?

Here is another parable of Jesus, which helps answer that question and will serve to ground all of those aphorisms, dialogues, and parables concerning the Kingdom of God. It is found in the *Q Gospel,* but with widely divergent versions in Matthew 22:1–13 and Luke 14:15–24. It is also found in the *Gospel of Thomas* 64, as follows:

> Jesus said, "A person was receiving guests. When he had prepared the dinner, he sent his servant to invite the guests. The servant went to the first and said to that one, 'My master invites you.' That person said, 'Some merchants owe me money; they are coming to me tonight. I must go and give them instructions. Please excuse me from dinner.' The servant went to another and said to that one, 'My master has invited you.' That person said to the servant, 'I have bought a house and I have been called away for a day. I shall have no time.' The servant went to another and said to that one, 'My master invites you.' That person said to the servant, 'My friend is to be married and I am to arrange the banquet. I shall not be able to come. Please excuse me from dinner.' The servant went to another and said to that one, 'My master invites you.' That

person said to the servant, 'I have bought an estate and I am going to collect the rent. I shall not be able to come. Please excuse me.' The servant returned and said to his master, 'The people whom you invited to dinner have asked to be excused.' The master said to his servant, 'Go out on the streets and *bring back whomever you find* to have dinner.' Buyers and merchants [will] not enter the places of my father."

This is one of those rare cases where the *Gospel of Thomas* interprets a parable. It appends, as commentary: "Buyers and merchants [will] not enter the places of my father." Jesus, not the host, speaks that judgment. For my present purpose, I leave aside that interpretation to focus closely on the replacement guests, the reference to which I have italicized above. Compare how they are described by Jesus in Luke 14:21b–23 and in Matthew 22:9–10, respectively:

(1) "'Go out quickly to the streets and lanes of the city, and bring in the poor and maimed and blind and lame.'" And the servant said, 'Sir, what you commanded has been done, and still there is room.' And the master said to the servant, 'Go out to the highways and hedges, and *compel people to come in,* that my house may be filled.'"

(2) "'Go therefore to the thoroughfares, and invite to the marriage feast *as many as you find.'* And those servants went out into the streets and gathered all whom they found, both bad and good; so the wedding hall was filled with guests."

In both those cases, separate interpretations have divergently specified the replacement guests. Luke mentions the outcasts and Matthew mentions the good and the bad, but the italicized phrases indicate the more original and unspecified command to bring in whomever you can find.

I leave aside, therefore, individual interpretations inserted around or within the three texts to underline the common structural plot discernible behind them all. It tells the story of a person who gives a presumably unannounced feast, sends a servant to invite friends, but finds by late in the day that each has a quite valid and very politely expressed excuse. The result is a dinner ready and a room empty. The host replaces the absent guests with anyone off the streets. But if one actually brought in *anyone off the street,* one could, in such a situation, have classes, sexes, and ranks all mixed up together. Anyone could be reclining next to anyone else, female next to male, free next to slave, socially high next to socially low, and ritually pure next to ritually impure. And a short detour through the cross-cultural anthropology of food and eating underlines what a social nightmare that would be.

Think, for a moment, if beggars came to your door, of the difference between giving them some food to go, of inviting them into your kitchen for a meal, of bringing them into the dining room to eat in the evening with your family, or of having them come back on Saturday night for supper with a group of your friends. Think, again, if you were a large company's CEO, of the difference between a cocktail party in the office for all the employees, a restaurant lunch for all the middle managers, or a private dinner party for your vice presidents in your own home. Those events are not just ones of eating together, of simple table fellowship, but are what anthropologists call *commensality*— from *mensa,* the Latin word for "table." *It means the rules of tabling and eating as miniature models for the rules of association and socialization.* It means table fellowship as a map of economic discrimination, social hierarchy, and political differentiation. This is how Peter Farb and George Armelagos summarized commensality at the beginning and end of their book on the anthropology of eating:

> In all societies, both simple and complex, eating is the primary way of initiating and maintaining human relationships. . . . Once the anthropologist finds out where, when, and with whom the food is eaten, just about everything else can be inferred about the relations among the society's members. . . . To know what, where, how, when, and with whom people eat is to know the character of their society.*

---

* Peter Farb and George Armelagos, *Consuming Passions: The Anthropology of Eating* (Boston: Houghton Mifflin, 1980), pages 4 and 211.

Similarly, Lee Edward Klosinski reviewed the significant cross-cultural anthropological and sociological literature on food and eating and concluded:

> Sharing food is a transaction which involves a series of mutual obligations and which initiates an interconnected complex of mutuality and reciprocity. Also, the ability of food to symbolize these relationships, as well as to define group boundaries, surfaced as one of its unique properties. . . . Food exchanges are basic to human interaction. Implicit in them is a series of obligations to give, receive and repay. These transactions involve individuals in matrices of social reciprocity, mutuality and obligation. Also, food exchanges are able to act as symbols of human interaction. Eating is a behavior which symbolizes feelings and relationships, mediates social status and power, and expresses the boundaries of group identity.*

What Jesus' parable advocates, therefore, is an open commensality, an eating together without using table as a miniature map of society's vertical discriminations and lateral separations. The social challenge of such equal or egalitarian commensality is the parable's most fundamental danger and most radical threat. It is only a story, of course, but it is one that focuses its egalitarian challenge on society's miniature mirror, the table, as the place where bodies meet to eat. Since, moreover, Jesus lived out his own parable, the almost predictable counteraccusation to such open commensality would be immediate: Jesus is a glutton, a drunkard, and a friend of tax collectors and sinners. He makes, in other words, no appropriate distinctions and discriminations. And since women were present, especially unmarried women, the accusation would be that Jesus eats with whores, the standard epithet of denigration for any female outside appropriate male control. All of those terms—tax collectors, sinners, whores—are in this case derogatory terms for those with whom, in the opinion of the name callers, open and free association should be avoided.

---

* Lee Edward Klosinski, *The Meals in Mark* (Ann Arbor, MI: University Microfilms, 1988), pages 56–58.

The Kingdom of God as a process of open commensality, of a nondiscriminating table depicting in miniature a nondiscriminating society, clashes fundamentally with honor and shame, those basic values of ancient Mediterranean culture and society. Most of American society in the twentieth century is used to *individualism*, with guilt and innocence as sanctions, rather than to *groupism*, with honor and shame as sanctions. Here is a description of Mediterranean honor and shame, from a 1965 cross-cultural anthology; Pierre Bourdieu is speaking on the basis of his field work among the Berber tribesmen of Algerian Kabylia in the late fifties:

> The point of honour is the basis of the moral code of an individual who sees himself always through the eyes of others, who has need of others for his existence, because the image he has of himself is indistinguishable from that presented to him by other people. . . . Respectability, the reverse of shame, is the characteristic of a person who needs other people in order to grasp his own identity and whose conscience is a kind of interiorization of others, since these fulfil for him the role of witness and judge. . . . He who has lost his honour no longer exists. He ceases to exist for other people, and at the same time he ceases to exist for himself.*

The key phrase here is *through the eyes of others*, and the more we understand that process, the more radically challenging Jesus' Kingdom of God starts to appear. We might see Jesus' message and program as quaintly eccentric or charmingly iconoclastic (at least at a safe distance), but for those who take their very identity from the eyes of their peers, the idea of eating together and living together without any distinctions, differences, discriminations, or hierarchies is close to the irrational and the absurd. And the one who advocates or does it is close to the deviant and the perverted. He has no honor. He has no shame.

---

* Pierre Bourdieu, "The Sentiment of Honour in Kabyle Society," in *Honour and Shame: The Values of Mediterranean Society*, ed. John G. Peristiany (Chicago: Univ. of Chicago Press, 1966; Midway Reprints, 1974), pages 211–212.

∞ Radical Egalitarianism

Open commensality is the symbol and embodiment of radical egalitarianism, of an absolute equality of people that denies the validity of any discrimination between them and negates the necessity of any hierarchy among them. To all of this there is an obvious objection: you are just speaking of contemporary democracy and anachronistically retrojecting that back into the time and onto the lips of Jesus. I look, in reply and defense, both to general anthropology and to specific history during the first century.

Those who, like peasants, live with a boot on their neck can easily envision two different dreams. One is quick revenge—a world in which they might get in turn to put their boots on those other necks. Another is reciprocal justice—a world in which there would never again be any boots on any necks. Thus, for example, the anthropologist James C. Scott, moving from Europe to Southeast Asia, notes the popular tradition's common reaction to such disparate elite traditions as Christianity, Buddhism, and Islam, and argues very persuasively that peasant culture and religion are actually an anticulture, criticizing alike both the religious and political elites that oppress it. It is, in fact, a reactive inversion of the pattern of exploitation common to the peasantry *as such:*

> The radical vision to which I refer is strikingly uniform despite the enormous variations in peasant cultures and the different great traditions of which they partake. . . . At the risk of over generalizing, it is possible to describe some common features of this reflexive symbolism. It nearly always implies a society of brotherhood in which there will be no rich and poor, in which no distinctions of rank and status (save those between believers and non-believers) will exist. Where religious institutions are experienced as justifying inequities, the abolition of rank and status may well include the elimination of religious hierarchy in favor of communities of equal believers. Property is typically, though not always, to be held in common and shared. All unjust claims to taxes, rents, and tribute are to

> be nullified. The envisioned utopia may also include a self-yielding and abundant nature as well as a radically transformed human nature in which greed, envy, and hatred will disappear. While the earthly utopia is thus an anticipation of the future, it often harks back to a mythic Eden from which mankind has fallen away.*

That is the ancient peasant dream of radical egalitarianism. It does not deny the other dream, that of brutal revenge, but neither does that latter negate the former's eternal thirst for reciprocity, equality, and justice.

One instance from the first century shows both those dreams coming together in the last days of the doomed Temple during the First Roman-Jewish War. As Vespasian's forces moved steadily southward and tightened the noose around Jerusalem in the fall of 67 and winter of 68 C.E., groups of peasant rebels under bandit leaders were forced repeatedly into the capital for refuge. They became known, collectively or in coalition, as the Zealots, and one of their first actions was to install a new High Priest. According to ancient tradition, the High Priest was chosen from the family of Zadok, as had been true since at least the time of Solomon. But when, in the second century B.C.E., the Jewish dynasty of the Hasmoneans wrested control of their country from the Syrians, they had simply appointed themselves High Priests. And thereafter, from Herod the Great to the outbreak of the revolt against Rome, the High Priests were selected from four families, likewise not of legitimate Zadokite origins. What the Zealots did was return to the legitimate high-priestly line, but within it they elected by lot rather than by choice. Josephus, telling the story in *Antiquities* 4.147–207, as an aristocratic priest is almost inarticulate with anger at what he considers an impious mockery. Here is the key section, in 155–156:

> They accordingly summoned one of the high-priestly clans, called Eniachin, and cast lots for a high priest. By chance the lot fell to one who proved a signal illustration of their depravity; he was an individual named Phanni,

---

* James C. Scott, "Protest and Profanation: Agrarian Revolt and the Little Tradition," *Theory and Society* 4 (1977): 225–226.

son of Samuel, of the village of Aphthia, a man who not only was not descended from high priests, but was such a clown that he scarcely knew what the high priesthood meant. At any rate they dragged their reluctant victim out of the country and, dressing him up for his assumed part, as on the stage, put the sacred vestments upon him and instructed him how to act in keeping with the occasion.

Lottery is what egalitarianism looks like in practice. If all members of some group are eligible for office, then the only fair human way to decide is by lot, leaving the choice up to God. That was how Saul, the first Jewish king, was elected from "all the tribes of Israel," according to 1 Samuel 10:21. And that was how the early Christians chose a replacement for the traitor apostle Judas from among "the men who have accompanied us" since the beginning, according to Acts of the Apostles 1:21–26. Obviously, of course, as in the implicit and presumed male exclusivity of the former case and the explicit and very deliberate male exclusivity of the latter one, discriminations can be present even in a lottery. They are there, too, in electing a High Priest only from a certain family. But granting that, a lottery attempts to deal equally among all candidates accepted as appropriate within a given context. Despite all of Josephus's tendentious rhetoric, what the Zealots did is quite clear and consistent. They restored the ancient Zadokite line according to selection by lot, and one presumes, of course, that such was to be the future mode of selection as well. Furthermore, this was probably more than just a new or legitimate High Priest. It was also, at least as far as the Zealots were concerned, a new and legitimate government of the city and the country. For those peasants, then, the idea of egalitarianism, even if not in its most radical form, was quite understandable and practicable.

Radical egalitarianism is not contemporary democracy. In the United States, for example, every appropriate person has a vote *in electing* the president, but although every appropriate person has also a legitimate right *to be* president, we are not yet ready for a national lottery instead of a presidential campaign. The open commensality and radical egalitarianism of Jesus' Kingdom of God are more terrifying than anything we have ever imagined, and even if we can never accept it, we should not explain it away as something else. I conclude, then, by putting Jesus' vision and program back into the matrix from which it sprang, the ancient and universal peasant dream of a just and equal world. These are the words of an unnamed peasant woman from Piana dei Greci, in the province of Palermo, Sicily, speaking to a northern Italian journalist during an 1893 peasant uprising:

> We want everybody to work, as we work. There should no longer be either rich or poor. All should have bread for themselves and for their children. We should all be equal. I have five small children and only one little room, where we have to eat and sleep and do everything, while so many lords have ten or twelve rooms, entire palaces. . . . It will be enough to put all in common and to share with justice what is produced.*

---

* Cited in Eric J. Hobsbawm, *Primitive Rebels: Studies in Archaic Forms of Social Movement in the 19th and 20th Centuries* (New York: Norton, 1965), page 183.

CHAPTER 4

In the Beginning Is the Body

MEN may seek salvation from evil conceived in many forms—from anxiety; illness; inferiority feelings; grief; fear of death; concern for the social order. What they seek may be healing; the elimination of evil agents; a sense of access to power; the enhancement of status; increase of prosperity; the promise of life hereafter, or reincarnation, or resurrection from the grave, or attention from posterity; the transformation of the social order (including the restoration of a real or imagined past social order). . . . Of the various theodicies that organize appropriate promises and command the appropriate activities to cope with these specific apprehensions of evil, two responses are widely found among the less-developed peoples—the thaumaturgical [the magical or miracle-working] and the revolutionist. . . . Of all the forms of religious response to the world, [the revolutionist or millennialist] alone is incapable, in its own terms, of attaining any measure of success. . . . Only millennialism stakes all on a prophesied external

75

event to occur cataclysmically, suddenly, and soon, and proceeding from the action of an external agency. Thaumaturgical belief is not only the pristine religious orientation, it is also more persistent than millennialism. The many little failures of magic are less disturbing to believers than the one big periodic failure of the millennium, and are more easily explained away.

Bryan R. Wilson, *Magic and the Millennium:
A Sociological Study of Religious Movements of
Protest Among Tribal and Third-World Peoples*
(New York: Harper & Row, 1973)

∞ The Politic Body

Was Jesus' message about the Kingdom of God all talk, or did it involve action as well? And if it was only talk, even marvelous or terrifying talk, why did peasants listen to it? The discussion in the preceding chapter made it clear that it was more than talk. It was not the open commensality in the Parable of the Feast but rather the open commensality in Jesus' active practice that generated those nasty accusations of gluttony, drunkenness, and eating with tax collectors or sinners (with Commies, as it were, in the American fifties). We have also seen that table was and is a miniature model for society. But now, before discussing Jesus as an exorcist and healer, as practicing and not just preaching the Kingdom, I need to take another short detour through cross-cultural and especially medical anthropology.

Table as a map of society, and commensality as a cartography of socialization, derive at their most basic level from the *human body* as a microcosm for the macrocosm of *political society.* We are quite used to calling society the body politic, but it is equally important to reverse the process and speak as well of the politic body. It is not just that society is body writ large; body is society writ small. Every adolescent knows that how one cuts or colors one's hair, marks or ornaments one's face, adorns or dresses one's body can, especially in traditional situations, challenge group quite fundamentally, all the way from inner family to outer society. No one has emphasized that body-society interaction more repeatedly or mined it more productively than the anthropologist Mary Douglas:

> The body is a model which can stand for any bounded system. Its boundaries can represent any boundaries which are threatened or precarious. The body is a complex structure. The functions of its different parts and their relations afford a source of symbols for other complex structures. We cannot possibly interpret rituals concerning excreta, breast milk, saliva, and the rest unless we are prepared to see in the body a symbol of society, and to see the powers and dangers credited to social structure reproduced in small on the human body.*

> The human body is common to us all. Only our social condition varies. The symbols based on the human body are used to express different social experiences.**

That extremely fruitful hypothesis explains why eating, in the previous chapter, and healing, in this one, are not simply private operations between individuals but social miniatures that can support or challenge, affirm or negate a culture's behavioral rules or a society's customary codes. Indeed, *body to society as microcosm to macrocosm* undergirds not only those chapters but my entire understanding of the historical Jesus. There is always and ever the politic body as well as the body politic. Note the interaction of body and society as Jesus heals diseases or exorcizes demons in the following two sections.

∞ ## To Touch a Leper

The healing of the leper in Mark 1:40–44 exemplifies both the significance of Jesus' miracles in their first-century Mediterranean Jewish environment and also the process by which a tradition is changed from its *original situation* in the life of Jesus through its *oral transmission* within the earliest Christian

---

* Mary Douglas, *Purity and Danger: An Analysis of Concepts of Pollution and Taboo* (London: Routledge & Kegan Paul, 1966), page 115.

** Mary Douglas, *Natural Symbols: Explorations in Cosmology* (New York: Random House, Pantheon Books, 1970), page xiv.

communities into its final *written formulation* in the canonical gospels.

> A leper came to him begging him, and kneeling he said to him, "If you choose, you can make me clean." Moved with pity [or, in some manuscripts: with anger], Jesus stretched out his hand and touched him, and said to him, "I do choose. Be made clean!" Immediately the leprosy left him, and he was made clean. After sternly warning him he sent him away [literally: cast him out] at once, saying to him, "See that you say nothing to anyone; but go, show yourself to the priest, and offer for your cleansing what Moses commanded, as a testimony to them [literally: to or against them (presumably, the Temple priests)]."

My interpretation of that scene is very indebted to a series of articles by John J. Pilch that appeared in the periodical *Biblical Theology Bulletin* during the 1980s. They show most clearly how important medical anthropology is for understanding Jesus' miracles of healing.

Lepra *and Leprosy*

It is certain, first of all, that to translate the Hebrew word *ṣāraʿat* or the Greek word *lepra* by the modern term "leprosy" is flatly wrong. What we call leprosy is caused by *Mycobacterium leprae*, a bacillus discovered in 1868 by the Norwegian physician Gerhard Henrik Armauer Hansen. That disease was, in fact, known in New Testament times but was then called *elephas* or *elephantiasis*. Ancient *ṣāraʿat* or *lepra*, on the other hand, covered several diseases, all of which involved a rather repulsive scaly or flaking skin condition—for example, psoriasis, eczema, or any fungus infection of the skin. Hereafter, I use the word *leprosy* with implicit quotation marks to mean such diseases and not ancient *elephas* or modern leprosy, But, in any case, who cares what the disease was? Is not the healing what counts? Yes and no. And that no brings us back to the politic body, the individual body as microcosm of the whole society.

In a society whose leadership is intensely concerned with the danger of being absorbed by a more powerful culture, an emphasis on *social*-boundary protection may well be symbolized by an emphasis on *bodily*-boundary protection. In ancient times, for example, tiny Israel, constantly overpowered by imperial absorption on the political and military level and constantly withstanding imperial absorption on the cultural and religious level, had, in the Jewish Scriptures, a massive priestly legislation concerning bodily boundaries. I quote once more from Mary Douglas:

> When rituals express anxiety about the body's orifices, the sociological counterpart of this anxiety is a care to protect the political and cultural unity of a minority group. The Israelites were always in their history a hard-pressed minority.... The threatened boundaries of their body politic would be well mirrored in their care for the integrity, unity, and purity of the physical body.*

That meant an especial concern with orifices, with what should and should not enter or exit from the body's standard openings. Thus Leviticus 11 legislates about food going into the body and Leviticus 12 about babies coming out. But Leviticus 13–14, on leprosy, raises an even more dangerous boundary problem. The standard bodily orifices can be clearly delineated and their incomings and outgoings categorized as clean or unclean. And that establishes, as it was meant to do, an intense concentration on boundary establishment. When, however, would-be orifices start to appear where no orifices are meant to be, then, unable to tell orifice from surface, or with all boundaries rendered porous, the entire system breaks down. That is why biblical leprosy applies not only to *skin*, as in Leviticus 13:1–45 and 14:1–32, but to *clothes*, as in 13:46–59, and to house *walls*, as in 14:33–53, and it renders each surface ritually unclean—that is, socially inappropriate. The leprous person is not a social threat because of medical contagion, threatening infection or epidemic, as we might imagine, but because of symbolic contamination, threatening in microcosm the very identity, integrity, and security of society at large. And so, in Leviticus 13:45–46:

> The person who has the leprous disease shall wear torn clothes and let the hair of his head be disheveled; and he

---

* Douglas, *Purity and Danger*, page 113.

shall cover his upper lip and cry out, "Unclean, unclean." He shall remain unclean as long as he has the disease; he is unclean. He shall live alone; his dwelling shall be outside the camp.

Those sufferers are in mourning for their lost lives, because in an honor-and-shame society, where, as we have seen earlier, one's existence is in the eyes of others, they are now quite dead. In such societies, with strict distinctions of clean and unclean—not, of course, as clinical or medical but as social or symbolic categories—the heartbreak of psoriasis was not funny. It was tragic. If, by the way, such practices strike you as archaic and pathetic, you might ask yourself whether you or your group has ever been militarily defeated, socially marginalized, or culturally absorbed. Probably for better, our social boundaries are very open, and so, possibly for worse, are our bodily boundaries.

Illness and Disease

What would we have seen, then, if we had been there when the leper was healed? What exactly happened, granted all that body-society interaction just explained? Once again, a swift detour into cross-cultural anthropology prevents us from projecting some current American presuppositions back into the ancient Mediterranean world.

Medical anthropology or comparative ethnomedicine has proposed a basic distinction between *curing a disease* and *healing an illness.* Here are two basic formulations of that difference. The first is from Leon Eisenberg.

> Patients suffer "illnesses"; physicians diagnose and treat "diseases.". . . Illnesses are *experiences* of disvalued changes in states of being and in social function; diseases, in the scientific paradigm of modern medicine, are *abnormalities* in the *structure* and *function* of body organs and systems. . . . The very limitations of their technology kept indigenous healers more responsive to the extra-biological aspects of illness, for it was chiefly those aspects they could manipulate. Our success in dealing with certain disease problems

breeds then ideological error that a technical fix is the potential solution to all. It would be absurd to suggest that we should forego the power of Western medicine in deference to shamanism. It is essential to enquire how we can expand our horizons to incorporate an understanding of illness as a psychological event. Indeed, our worship of restricted and incomplete disease models can be viewed as a kind of ritual or magical practice in itself.*

A *disease* is, to put it bluntly, between me, my doctor, and a bug. Something is wrong with my body, and I take it to a doctor to be fixed. What is lacking in that picture is not just the entire psychological but, much more important, the entire social dimension of the phenomenon. How have I been trained to think of my body, modern medicine, and doctors? How does my dysfunction involve my family, my job, or, in some cases, wider and wider levels of society? *Disease* sees the problem, unrealistically, on the minimal level; *illness,* realistically, on the wider level. Think, for example, of the difference between curing the disease or healing the illness known as AIDS. A cure for the disease is absolutely desirable, but in its absence, we can still heal the illness by refusing to ostracize those who have it, by empathizing with their anguish, and by enveloping their sufferings with both respect and love.

A second formulation of that distinction comes from Arthur Kleinman.

A key axiom in medical anthropology is the dichotomy between two aspects of sickness: disease and illness. *Disease* refers to a malfunctioning of biological and/or psychological processes, while the term *illness* refers to the psychosocial experience and meaning of perceived disease. Illness includes secondary personal and social responses to the primary malfunctioning (disease) in the individual's physiological or psychological status (or both). . . . Viewed from this perspective, illness is the shaping of disease into

---

* Leon Eisenberg, "Disease and Illness: Distinctions Between Professional and Popular Ideas of Sickness," *Culture, Medicine and Psychiatry* 1 (1977): 11.

behavior and experience. It is created by personal, social, and cultural reactions to disease.*

Seen from those perspectives, the leper who met Jesus had both a *disease* (say, psoriasis) and an *illness*, the personal and social stigma of uncleanness, isolation, and rejection. And as long as the disease stayed or got worse, the illness also would stay or get worse. In general, if the disease went, the illness went with it. What, however, if the disease could not be cured but the illness could somehow be healed?

This is the central problem of what Jesus was doing in his healing miracles. Was he curing the disease through an intervention in the physical world, or was he healing the illness through an intervention in the social world? I presume that Jesus, who did not and could not cure that disease or any other one, healed the poor man's illness by refusing to accept the disease's ritual uncleanness and social ostracization. Jesus thereby forced others either to reject him from their community or to accept the leper within it as well. Since, however, we are ever dealing with the politic body, that act quite deliberately impugns the rights and prerogatives of society's boundary keepers and controllers. By healing the illness without curing the disease, Jesus acted as an alternative boundary keeper in a way subversive to the established procedures of his society. Such an interpretation may seem to destroy the miracle. But miracles are not changes in the physical world so much as changes in the social world, and it is society that dictates, in any case, how we see, use, and explain that physical world. It would, of course, be nice to have certain miracles available to change the physical world if we could, but it would be much more desirable to make certain changes in the social one, which we can. We ourselves can already make the physical world totally uninhabitable; the question is whether we can make the social world humanly habitable.

---

* Arthur Kleinman, *Patients and Healers in the Context of Culture: An Exploration of the Borderland Between Anthropology, Medicine, and Psychiatry*, in the series *Comparative Studies of Health Systems and Medical Care* (Berkeley: Univ. of California Press, 1980), page 72.

Event and Tradition

In terms of the *original* situation, therefore, Jesus' action puts him on a direct collision course with priestly authority in the Temple. After touching a leper he can hardly turn around and tell him to observe the purity code that he himself has just broken. This is not, by the way, a case of divine law against human law, compassion against legalism, gospel against law, let alone Christianity against Judaism. It is more likely a case within Judaism of Galilean peasants against Jerusalem priests. But what we see at the *transmissional* level is intense apologetics seeking to bring Jesus into line with traditional biblical and legal practice—to show him, in terms of purity regulations, as an observant Jew. That explains those emotional expressions such as "anger . . . sternly . . . cast him out" in Mark 1:41 and 43 and, especially, that terminal injunction in 1:44 to "go, show yourself to the priest, and offer for your cleansing what Moses commanded." In other words, at the second or transmissional level, the story was adapted to make Jesus legally observant, something that creates a war of interpretation within the narrative itself. Finally, at the third or *redactional* level, as Mark records the story in his gospel, he makes one very significant final change. He himself is much more in sympathy with that legally unobservant Jesus at the story's original level, so he adds, after the injunction to go to the Temple, a phrase translated above as "as a testimony to them." It could be better translated with, "as a witness against them"—in other words, "to show them who's boss." But in either case, for Mark, Jesus is enjoining the visit to the Temple not as legal observance but as confrontational witness.

Those three layers—the original, transmissional, and redactional—are constantly laminated within our gospels, but this is a classic case of all three rather clearly visible within a single text. Yet no amount of theological apologetics at the second level or even their undoing at the third level can ever obliterate the first or original level in which Jesus heals by refusing to accept traditional and official sanctions against the diseased person. Jesus heals him, in other words, by taking him into a community of the marginalized and disenfranchised—into, in fact, the Kingdom of God. If one actually wanted to make up a story about Jesus and a leper in which Jesus was portrayed from the inception as an observant Jew, here is how to do it, from Luke 17:11–19:

> On the way to Jerusalem he was passing along between Samaria and Galilee. And as he entered a village, he was met by ten lepers, who stood at a distance and lifted up their voices and said, "Jesus, Master, have mercy on us." When he saw them he said to them, "Go and show yourselves to the priests." And as they went they were cleansed. Then one of them, when he saw that he was healed, turned back, praising God with a loud voice; and he fell on his face at Jesus' feet, giving him thanks. Now he was a Samaritan. Then said Jesus, "Were not ten cleansed? Where are the nine? Was no one found to return and give praise to God except this foreigner?" And he said to him, "Rise and go your way; your faith has made you well."

That story is found only in Luke's gospel, and, whether created totally by him or not, it shows how a leper and a legally observant Jesus should behave. First, the lepers keep their distance and never approach too close to Jesus. Second, he sees them but never comes close enough to touch. Third, he tells them immediately to go to the Temple. Finally, they are healed on their way there so that both Jesus' power and legal observance are in conjunction rather than confrontation. That Jesus is an observant Jew is not the point of that story, of course, just its basic presupposition. But it serves, in contrast, to underline the fact that a story that starts with Jesus touching a leper will never be able to get either of them safely back inside official and traditional legality.

❧ To Expel a Demon

To talk of disease and illness or curing and healing, even to propose a fundamental distinction between them or to emphasize not just mind over matter but society over mind, is still to move in a world relatively easy to understand. But now we turn to spirits, good and bad, or to trance and possession, and that seems like another world. I myself, for example, do not believe that there are personal supernatural spirits who invade our bodies from outside and, for either good or evil, replace or jostle for place with our own personality. But the vast, vast majority of the world's people have always so believed, and according to one recent cross-cultural survey, about 75 percent still do. So while I may not accept their *explanation,* I tread very carefully in discussing the *phenomenon* that leads them to that diagnosis. What are they seeing, and why are they seeing it that way? Am I seeing something completely different or simply the same through different eyes? I am sure, in any case, that it is absolutely not acceptable to say, "I don't believe in demons," and think that explains everything. To disagree on a diagnosis is not the same as denying a symptom; to debate an interpretation is not the same as negating a phenomenon. Nevertheless, even if we agree that there is something real, as distinct from faked or simulated, behind events understood by participants as possession, the interpretations may also be very significant.

Let me explain why I cannot simply say that these are but different names for the same event and that, for example, whether we talk of demonic possession or of a special form of multiple personality disorder, it is all just the same event in any case. Two examples will suffice.

E. Mansell Pattison tells the story of Mary, a thirteen-year-old girl on the Yakima Indian Reservation in central Washington.* Her hysterical symptoms were diagnosed as paranoid schizophrenia by the local medical doctor, who prescribed Chlorpromazine, an antipsychotic drug. Pattison was, fortunately for the girl, a psychiatrist with cross-cultural sensitivity, and, having learned not only that her dying shaman grandfather had prophesied that his power would descend to her but that she herself wanted to acculturate to majority American society, he advised exorcism of the unwanted shamanistic spirits. Thereafter the girl recovered completely.

Compare that with Felicitas D. Goodman's terrifying account of what happened to a young university student from

---

* E. Mansell Pattison, "Psychosocial Interpretations of Exorcism," *Journal of Operational Psychiatry* 8, no. 2 (1977): 11–15.

Klingenberg, in rural Bavaria, between 1968 and 1976.* The student was being simultaneously treated by psychiatrists and priests, the former prescribing anticonvulsant drugs such as Dilantin and Tegretol, the latter practicing repeated exorcistic rituals. Since the patient herself, as well as family and friends, believed she was possessed, the priests had the far better chance of success. But for the exorcisms to work, she had to become entranced, and the drugs impeded that possibility. The two systems fought against one another within her tortured body. For example, at one awful moment during the taped exorcisms the demons, forced by the priest to admit their names, admit also that there are other, newer demons present whose names even they do not know. The diabolical met the chemical, and the chemical won. Anneliese died in the summer of 1976.

Recall that exorcism ritual shown on prime-time American television a few years ago. The participants all believed that the young girl was possessed, and when the priest came away from confrontation with the screaming, cursing patient, he said he had looked into the face of evil. Two problems. One is the trivialization of evil, which stalks our world in far more terrible and far more covert forms than a puking adolescent. Another is the possibility that, if some special type of multiple personality disorder had been hidden behind and under that diagnosed diabolical possession, the face of evil might in fact have been sitting in the next room in the form of, say, an older male who had sexually tortured her in infancy and shattered her unformed personality into defensive shreds. The idea of demonic possession implies blame for the patient, who must surely have done something to cause—or at least omitted doing something that would have prevented—such an occurrence. The diagnosis of multiple personality disorder involves no further victimization of the victim, and evil is sought where it actually is or was. Names matter. Diagnoses differ, and the differences count. In what follows, therefore, we must speak carefully and tentatively, because here we move toward the delicate interface between the psychological and the physical in medical anthropology.

---

* Felicitas D. Goodman, *The Exorcism of Anneliese Michel* (Garden City, NY: Doubleday, 1981).

Trance and Possession

Erika Bourguignon led a five-year cross-cultural study of dissociational states, funded by the National Institute of Mental Health at Ohio State University; she published the results in various books from the late sixties to the early seventies. For what follows I am deeply indebted to her research and to that of her doctoral students, such as Felicitas Goodman, mentioned earlier. If one were to read only one short example of Bourguignon's work, the chapter on "Altered States of Consciousness" in her 1979 textbook would be representative.* In what follows, I am presuming her conclusions but also adapting them for my own use.

There seems to be a normal range for physical or mental activity and for the brain chemistry that mediates between them and blurs their difference. Anything critically above *or* below that range can create *trance,* which I shall use as the single term for states variously called *ecstasy, dissociation,* or *altered states of consciousness.* Trance, therefore, can be produced by any critical change, be it decrease *or* increase, in the external stimulation of the senses, internal concentration of the mind, or chemical composition of the brain's neurobiology. It must, therefore, be accepted as a human universal, as another gift of neurobiological evolution, a possibility open, like language, to each and every human being. But, also like language, its actualization is specified by psychosocial patterning—by cultural training, control, and expectation. Little children who grow up in Portugal will, in language, speak Portuguese with local or regional accents and will, in trance, see the Virgin Mary with blue and white robes. They will not see the god Krishna or the prophet Muhammad. They will not learn anything they do not already know in their fondest hopes or deepest fears, but they may well know it thereafter with an intensity unobtainable in other ways. Good news, therefore, and bad, at least for ideological claims. The good news is that trance's form, the *that* of trance, is absolutely cross-culturally and trans-temporally universal. The bad news is that

---

* Erika Bourguignon, *Psychological Anthropology: An Introduction to Human Nature and Cultural Differences* (New York: Holt, Rinehart & Winston, 1979), pages 233–269.

trance's content, the *what* of trance, is absolutely psychosocially conditioned and psychoculturally determined. But that could be, of course, *either for or against* that specific society or culture. And whether that against is good or bad is for destiny to decide and history to record.

Trance is susceptible to a natural or a supernatural explanation, but it is also possible to overlay these explanations on top of one another—not just to discard one in favor of the other, but to let them interact with one another on the presumption that they are *different interpretations of the same psychosomatic phenomenon.* In either explanation, for example, there is a clear distinction between good and bad states, and what is hidden behind that polarity is, in every case, control or noncontrol— whether the phenomenon is under psychosocial control or is not. Consider the phenomenon of entranced speaking in tongues; it does not interrupt the sermons in Pentecostal churches and does not happen to people en route to or from the services. It happens only at certain marked times within the service. It is, in other words, under ritual control. Trance is, therefore, a perfectly natural human experience, but its control is a perfectly natural human necessity. Societies that have such processes do not need to apologize for themselves. Societies that have no such procedures may have to consider whether there is such a thing as unhealthy trance deprivation or pathological trance substitution within their borders. It may well be the absence rather than the presence of trance that is pathological.

Legion and Swine

Granted that uncontrollable trance may be considered negatively as an undesirable condition, and may be interpreted as demonic possession in certain cultures, why was there so much of it in the first-century Jewish homeland? It seems as if Jesus encountered demoniacs around every corner. Could there be a connection between colonial oppression and forms of mental illness easily interpreted as demonic possession?

Ioan M. Lewis has argued forcibly for the close connection between possession and oppression, whether that subjugation be the sexual and familial one of women by men or the racial and imperial one of some people by other people. In that first case, "women's possession cults are . . . thinly disguised protest movements directed against the dominant sex. . . . In its primary social function, peripheral possession thus emerges as an oblique aggressive strategy." In the second, "those societies in which central possession cults persist are usually those composed of small, fluid, social units exposed to particularly exacting physical conditions, or conquered communities lying under the yoke of alien oppression." Lewis calls such possession groups "protest cults" or "ritual rebellions," and he describes them as using "oblique redressive strategies."* But notice that he is talking of situations where the possessed are organized into cults that have both a personally therapeutic and a socially subversive role. An occupied country has, as it were, a multiple-personality disorder. One part of it must hate and despise the oppressor, but the other must envy and admire its superior power. And, once again, if body is to society as microcosm to macrocosm, certain individuals may experience exactly the same split within themselves.

Take, then, the case of the Gerasene demoniac in Mark 5:1–17. It is independently attested only in Mark, and the story was almost certainly created long after Jesus' life, maybe even in the context of the First Roman-Jewish War of 66 to 73 C.E. I use it here for two reasons. One is that, despite all the mention of exorcisms in the gospels, there are no examples of independently attested *stories* about demonic expulsions. The reason is not that they did not happen during the life of the historical Jesus but that they may have been too commonplace for oral memory to record in any save the most general descriptions. Another reason I use the Markan account is to show that, in the first-century mind, there was a connection between demonic possession and colonial oppression.

> They came to the other side of the sea, to the country of the Gerasenes. And when he had come out of the boat, there met him out of the tombs a man with an unclean spirit, who lived among the tombs; and no one could bind

---

* Ioan M. Lewis, *Ecstatic Religion: An Anthropological Study of Spirit Possession and Shamanism*, Penguin Anthropology Library (Baltimore: Penguin Books, 1971), pages 31, 32, 35, 88, and 127.

him any more, even with a chain; for he had often been bound with fetters and chains, but the chains he wrenched apart, and the fetters he broke in pieces; and no one had the strength to subdue him. Night and day among the tombs and on the mountains he was always crying out, and bruising himself with stones. And when he saw Jesus from afar, he ran and worshiped him; and crying out with a loud voice, he said, "What have you to do with me, Jesus, Son of the Most High God? I adjure you by God, do not torment me." For he had said to him, "Come out of the man, you unclean spirit!" And Jesus asked him, "What is your name?" He replied, "My name is Legion; for we are many." And he begged him eagerly not to send them out of the country. Now a great herd of swine was feeding there on the hillside; and they begged him, "Send us to the swine, let us enter them." So he gave them leave. And the unclean spirits came out, and entered the swine; and the herd, numbering about two thousand, rushed down the steep bank into the sea, and were drowned in the sea. The herdsmen fled, and told it in the city and in the country. And people came to see what it was that had happened. And they came to Jesus, and saw the demoniac sitting there, clothed and in his right mind, the man who had had the legion; and they were afraid. And those who had seen it told what had happened to the demoniac and to the swine. And they began to beg Jesus to depart from their neighborhood.

An individual is, of course, being healed, but the symbolism is also hard to miss or ignore. The demon is both one and many; is named Legion, that fact and sign of Roman power; is consigned to swine, that most impure of Judaism's impure animals; and is cast into the sea, that dream of every Jewish resister. And it may be left open whether the exorcist is asked to depart because a cured demoniac is not worth a herd of swine or because the people see quite clearly the political implications of the action. As I said, I do not think this is an actual scene from Jesus' life, but it openly characterizes Roman imperialism as demonic possession and shows that, in linking colonial domination with demonic possession, we are not simply retrojecting modern sensibilities back into first-century minds. There is for us a modern equivalent among the Lunda-Luvale tribes of the Barotse in what was then Northern Rhodesia. They always had, according to Barrie Reynolds, traditional ailments called *mahamba,* which resulted from possession by ancestral spirits.* But they then developed a special modern version called *bindele,* the Luvale word for "European," which necessitated a special exorcistic church and a lengthy curative process for its healing. *Legion,* I think, is to colonial Roman Palestine as *bindele* was to colonial European Rhodesia, and in both cases colonial exploitation is incarnated individually as demonic possession.

In discussing Jesus' exorcisms, therefore, two factors must be kept in mind. One is the almost split-personality position of a colonial people. If they submit gladly to colonialism, they conspire in their own destruction; if they hate and despise it, they admit that something more powerful than themselves, and therefore to some extent desirable, is hateful and despicable. And what does that do to them? Another is that colonial exorcisms are at once less and more than revolution; they are, in fact, individuated symbolic revolution.

Jesus and Beelzebul

One final point. Jesus both healed diseases and expelled demons, and quite often illness and possession are considered to be simultaneous states. An example is the following incident from the *Q Gospel* at Luke 11:14–15, where Satan is named as Beelzebul, the name of an ancient Canaanite god:

> Now he was casting out a demon that was dumb; when the demon had gone out, the dumb man spoke, and the people marveled. But some of them said, "He casts out demons by Beelzebul, the prince of demons."

My focus here is on that accusation, which, unconnected with any specific cure, is also found in Mark 3:22 and must therefore be taken very seriously. But why did anyone make such

* Barrie Reynolds, *Magic, Divination and Witchcraft Among the Barotse of Northern Rhodesia,* Robins Series 3 (Berkeley: Univ. of California Press, 1963), pages 133–138.

an accusation? It might be enough to say that it is just standard name-calling, the type of rhetorical assassination we know so well from political campaigns. That it simply intends to dismiss Jesus as a deviant. But, once again, as earlier with accusations of gluttony, drunkenness, or eating with tax collectors and sinners, name-calling is usually based on something that makes the naming at least possibly believable. Is there anything similar behind this attack?

I have one very tentative suggestion to explain that specific accusation, tentative not because the answer is anything unexpected, but simply because there is so little other evidence for it. *Did Jesus sometimes, or always, heal while he himself was in a state of trance?*

In an anthology on trance and possession, Arnold M. Ludwig discussed the maladaptive and adaptive expressions of altered states of consciousness, and gave healing as the first of that latter category.

> Throughout history, the production of ASC's [altered states of consciousness] has played a major role in various healing arts and practices. The induction of these states has been employed for almost every conceivable aspect of psychological therapy. Thus, shamans may lapse into trance or possession states in order to determine the etiology of their patients' ailments, or to learn of specific remedies or healing practices. Moreover, the shaman, hungan, medicine man, priest, preacher, physician, or psychiatrist may regard the production of an ASC in the patient as a crucial prerequisite for healing and an essential prelude to treatment. There are countless instances of healing practices designed to take advantage of the heightened suggestibility, the tendency to attribute increased meaning to ideas, the propensity for emotional catharsis, and the feelings of rejuvenation associated with ASC's. The early Egyptian and Greek practices of "incubation" in sleep temples, the faith cures at Lourdes and other religious shrines, healing through prayer and meditation, cures by the "healing touch," the laying on of hands, encounters with religious relics, spiritual healing, spirit-possession cures, exorcism, mesmeric or magnetic treat-

ment, and modern day hypnotherapy—all are obvious instances of the role of ASC's in treatment.*

I am quite aware that there is not much evidence for Jesus as an *entranced healer* using contagious trance as a therapeutic technique, but I am also aware that the talky, preachy, speechy side of religion is often not too much at home with the touchy, feely, squealy side. It is possible, therefore, that the tradition ignored it even if it was present there originally. In any case, since trance is so trans-temporally and cross-culturally universal and since there is that pointed accusation of possession against Jesus, I prefer to leave the question open for the future.

I emphasize as strongly as possible that Jesus was not just a teacher or a preacher in purely intellectual terms, not just part of the history of ideas. He not only discussed the Kingdom of God; he enacted it, and said others could do so as well. If all he had done was talk about the Kingdom, Lower Galilee would probably have greeted him with a great big peasant yawn. But you cannot ignore the healings and the exorcisms, especially in their socially subversive function. You cannot ignore the pointedly political overtones of the very term *Kingdom of God* itself. It is, unfortunately, one of the abiding temptations of pastors and scholars to reduce Jesus to words alone, to replace a lived life with a preached sermon or an interesting idea. To remove, however, that which is radically subversive, socially revolutionary, and politically dangerous from Jesus' *actions* is to leave his life meaningless and his death inexplicable.

∞   Back from the Dead

If some of Jesus' healings and exorcisms can and should be understood against the basic background in cross-cultural anthropology ranging from the interaction of body and society (Mary Douglas) to the interface of medicine and psychiatry

---

* Arnold M. Ludwig, "Trance and Possession States," in *Proceedings of the Second Annual Conference of the R. M. Bucke Memorial Society, 4-6 March 1968*, ed. Raymond Prince (Montreal: R. M. Bucke Memorial Society, 1968), page 87.

(Erika Bourguignon), what of others such as the raising of the dead and the stilling of the storm? I leave aside for now all those actions usually called nature miracles, where Jesus is involved with objects rather than persons; I will consider them in detail in this book's final chapter. But what, for example, about Lazarus? As a cover illustration for my book *The Historical Jesus: The Life of a Mediterranean Jewish Peasant* I chose an early and very popular Christian carving of the raising of Lazarus. I chose it because, while I do not think this event ever did or could happen, I think it is absolutely true. Let me explain.

We are back to, in fact we have never left, the individual's politic body as the microcosm of society's body politic. Let me call the microcosm or body side of that interaction an *event*, an actual and historical healing of an afflicted individual at a moment in time. And let me call the macrocosmic or society side of that interaction a *process*, some wider socioreligious phenomenon that is symbolized by such an individual happening. But just as event can give rise to process, so process can give rise to event. The case of the Galilean leper shows us how an action performed on one single body reaches out to become an action performed on society at large. And it would happen with or without Jesus' intention, since body/society symbolism is a permanent given. As all the theological apologetics exercised on that story emphasize, Jesus is making claims about who regulates social boundaries, who determines cultural norms, who defines religious authority, and who decides political power. In that case, *event becomes process.* But the case of the Gerasene demoniac indicates the opposite phenomenon. I do not think there ever was an event such as that. It is, of course, possible that there was such a happening, but the event is just too perfect an embodiment of every Jewish revolutionary's dream. In that case, most likely, *process becomes event.* For example, if in front of a hypothetical Lincoln High School in America there stands a statue of that president with upraised ax ready to smash through the chains binding a slave's feet, is that true or false? Do we not have to respond that it is not true as event but is quite accurate as process?

There is nothing very surprising in all of this. The basic symbolic interaction postulated by Mary Douglas's body/

society parallelism means that social symbolism is always latent in bodily miracle and that bodily miracle always has social signification. It is very easy and indeed inevitable to move in both directions—from body to society or event to process, and from society to body or process to event. And it is very possible not to be certain at times which way one is moving.

I understand, therefore, the story of Lazarus as process incarnated in event and not the reverse. I do not think that anyone, anywhere, at any time brings dead people back to life. But when I read John 11:21–27 I can see very clearly what the process was for that writer:

> Martha said to Jesus, "Lord, if you had been here, my brother would not have died. And even now I know that whatever you ask from God, God will give you." Jesus said to her, "Your brother will rise again." Martha said to him, "I know that he will rise again in the resurrection at the last day." Jesus said to her, "I am the resurrection and the life; he who believes in me, though he die, yet shall he live, and whoever lives and believes in me shall never die. Do you believe this?" She said to him, "Yes, Lord; I believe that you are the Christ, the Son of God, he who is coming into the world."

For John's gospel, the process of general resurrection is incarnated in the event of Lazarus's resuscitation. That is one such movement from process to event. But I can imagine peasants all over Lower Galilee who would have said with equal intensity that Jesus brought life out of death and would not have been thinking of the heavenly future but the earthly present. Life out of death is how they would have understood the Kingdom of God, in which they began to take back control over their own bodies, their own hopes, and their own destinies.

∞   How Not to Be a Patron

I consider finally one special facet of Jesus' activity, his itinerancy, and I do so against the background of Greco-Roman patronage and clientage. You will recall from the earlier discussion that, in speaking of Jesus' open commensality, I mentioned honor and shame as a pivotal set of values in Mediterranean culture. Another pivotal set is patronage and clientage; and, if Jesus' eating program directly negated distinctions of honor and shame, so did his healing program deny processes of patronage and clientage.

Patron and Client

Recall, from Chapter 1, that there were only two classes in ancient society, a very small upper class and a very large lower class. With no middle class in between, what kept such a society from breaking absolutely apart? What kept it together were multiple ligatures of patronage and clientage. Those without power could be *clients* to the *patrons* above them, and those patrons might even be themselves clients to others far more powerful still. *Brokers* were clients to those above them and patrons to those below. In a patronal society such as the ancient Roman one, and unlike modern American society, influence was a moral duty: the emperors needed it, the moralists praised it, and countless inscriptions publicly proclaimed it. Patronage and clientage, at their best, gave some hope or chance to individuals among the lower classes, but at their worst they confirmed dependency, maintained hierarchy, sustained oppression, and stabilized domination. This is Thomas F. Carney's description of patronal society:

> This was a society based on patronage, not class stratification; so little pyramids of power abounded. . . .
>
> Thus society resembled a mass of little pyramids of influence, each headed by a major family—or one giant pyramid headed by an autocrat—not the three-decker sandwich of upper, middle, and lower classes familiar to us from industrial society. . . .
>
> The client of a power wielder thus becomes a powerful man and himself in turn attracts clients [that is, he becomes a broker]. Even those marginal hangers-on to power attract others, more disadvantageously placed, as their clients. So arise the distinctive pyramids of power—patron, then first order clients, then second and third order clients and so on—associated with a patronage soci-

ety. It is quite different from the three-layer sandwich of a class society.*

It is easiest to give examples of patronal society as it works horizontally between equals taking turns in playing patron or client to one another. The Romans called that *amicitia* or "friendship"—but in our sense of cronyism, good old boys, or the old-school-tie network. Examples of such patronal friendship can be seen in the surviving letters of any important or aristocratic Roman. It is of course much, much harder to see the vertical processes of patronage, *especially from the viewpoint of lower-class clients.* Even if we had such letters—written, say, for illiterates by the alley scribes of Egypt—they would have to be carefully deferential and politely respectful. There is, however, one place to catch a glimpse of what it must have been like to be such a dependent, and that is in Juvenal's *Fifth Satire,* which I cite from Hubert Creekmore's translation. But it must be read with care, not only because it is savage satire but also because Juvenal, who lived around 60 to 127 C.E., was banished from Rome by the emperor Domitian and returned later, impoverished, dependent, fearful, and, above all, bitingly scornful of a rich world in which he, unlike Epictetus, described in the next chapter, longed mostly to participate more fully.

He describes a dinner in which the rich host, Virro, invites some poor clients to a meal and then deliberately insults them by giving good bread, food, wine, and service to himself and his friends but bad equivalents to them. We are back again with commensality, but now as calculated insult and intentional humiliation. Juvenal addresses Trebius, one of those hangers-on who sit far from the host and hope to get his scraps instead of their own bad food.

> *You appear*
> *To yourself as a free man, a tycoon's*
> *guest; he thinks you—*
> *Not bad guesswork—a slave to his*
> *kitchen's odor. For who*
> *Could be so destitute as to suffer*

---

* Thomas F. Carney, *The Shape of the Past: Models and Antiquity* (Lawrence, KS: Coronado Press, 1975), pages 63, 80, and 171.

this patron twice
If as a boy he had worn the free man's
golden device,
Or even the leather boss, the badge
poor folk would wear?
The hope to dine well deceives you:
"Look, that half-eaten hare
He'll give us now, or from the haunch
of boar some bits;
We'll get what's left of the capon
soon." So all of you sit
In silence, ready, with bread held
tight, untasted, and wait.
It's a wise man who treats you thus.
If you can tolerate
All this, you deserve it. Some day
you'll offer, with shaven pate,
Your head to be slapped [like a clown] and won't
be afraid of being skinned
By keen whips [like a slave], worthy at last of such
feasts and such a friend.

Unless you had started life as slaves, asks Juvenal, how could you take such abuse? Maybe, he concludes, you will end up as slaves. Despite his seething resentment we catch a glimpse of what lower-class clientage must have felt like in actual practice. But that is in a big city. It is hard even to imagine how the lower classes fared in rural situations within a patronal society. In the crowded city, even the poorest clients were useful to greet the patron as he appeared from his house in the morning or to accompany him on political or social visits during the day. Their presence and number proclaimed his importance. But, as Juvenal noted, clientage could be very, very close to slavery, and at times it could be much worse. Although slave societies and patronal societies have both been justified as moral associations, it is probably better not to mourn their passing from the human scene.

James and Peter

What is at stake here is the meaning of the *itinerancy* of Jesus. Why is he always going somewhere rather than being settled in one place and letting crowds come to him? Many people were permanently on the move in that first century for reasons of teaching, business, administration, or military activity. In those cases itinerancy was simply an accidental necessity of one's mission. But was the itinerancy of Jesus more than that? Was his itinerancy or even vagrancy a programmatic part of his radical message? If it was, I term it *radical itinerancy* rather than simple *functional itinerancy*—the type associated, for example, with Paul or anyone else on the move for purely practical reasons of mission. At the end of the preceding chapter, I used the term *radical egalitarianism* to summarize what the Kingdom of God meant for Jesus. I now propose that radical itinerancy was its necessary concomitant, its geographical equivalent, and its symbolic demonstration.

Two examples, each associated with one of those twin Mediterranean groups, the familial and the political, kin and associates, confirm that we are indeed dealing with programmatic rather than functional itinerancy in the case of Jesus.

We are told in Mark 6:4 that Jesus' own family did not believe in him, and yet according to Galatians 1:18–19, when Paul arrived in Jerusalem, say around 38 C.E., he found James the brother of Jesus already there along with Peter. What happened in between? How did James get from disbelief to belief, and from Nazareth to Jerusalem? My proposal is that the family believed quite fully in Jesus' power and importance, message and mission, *but not at all in the way he was carrying it out.* What Jesus should have done, as any Mediterranean family knew, was settle down at his home in Nazareth and establish there a healing cult. He would be its *patron,* the family would be its *brokers,* and as his reputation went out along the peasant grapevine, the sick would come as *clients* to be healed. That would have made sense to everyone, would have been good for everyone—for Jesus, for his family, and for little Nazareth itself. But instead Jesus kept to the road, brought healing to those who needed it, and had, as it were, to start off anew every day. That was no way to run a healing ministry and no way to treat your family, especially within the world of Mediterranean values. Of course his family believed in him, but rather in the way he *should* behave than in the way he *was* behaving. It is not surprising, therefore, once Jesus was gone, to find James firmly settled and precisely located in Jerusalem. And in charge, at least for those who accepted his authority.

My second example is even more explicit and confirms for me the preceding explanation of the change within Jesus' family from disbelief to belief. This is found in Mark 1:16–38, but it must be used with great care, for it is the only independent source for Jesus' inaugural day in Capernaum. I doubt very much if this chronicles an actual day in the life of the historical Jesus. But it shows, like the Gerasene demoniac in Mark 5:1–20 earlier, that in Jesus' society people thought this way and that I am not simply retrojecting twentieth-century prejudices back upon them.

Jesus calls Peter and others to become his disciples in 1:16–20. Next he impresses those in the synagogue with his authority both to teach and to exorcize in 1:21–28. Then he enters the house of Peter and heals his mother-in-law in 1:29–31. Finally, the whole city and all its sick are gathered together at Peter's door once the Sabbath has ended. Any Mediterranean person would recognize what should happen or is already happening. Peter's house is becoming a brokerage place for Jesus' healing, and Peter will broker between Jesus and those seeking help. What happens, according to 1:35–38?

> And in the morning, a great while before day, he rose and went out to a lonely place, and there he prayed. And Simon and those who were with him pursued him, and they found him and said to him, "Every one is searching for you." And he said to them, "Let us go on to the next towns, that I may preach there also; for that is why *I came out.*"

Matthew does not copy any of that incident. Luke does so, but at 4:43 he spoils Mark's last sentence by rephrasing it as "for I was sent for this purpose." Jesus, however, is explaining why he "came out"—that is, why he must leave Peter's house. But Peter, if Mark had granted him a reply, would have said that it made much more sense to stay right there at Capernaum, let the word go forth along the peasant grapevine, and await the crowds that would come to his door. It would also make much more sense in the psychosociology of healing. But all Jesus says is that he "came out" from Peter's house. That entire day is a Markan creation opposing Jesus to Peter and showing their, from Mark's point of view, incompatible visions of mission. I take from it only its opposition of itinerancy and brokerage and its usefulness for seeing what is radical about itinerancy.

The equal sharing of spiritual and material gifts, of miracle and table, cannot be centered in one place because that very hierarchy of place, of here *over* there, of this place *over* other places, symbolically destroys the radical egalitarianism it announces. Radical egalitarianism denies the processes of patronage, brokerage, and clientage, and demands itinerancy as its programmatic symbolization. Neither Jesus nor his followers are supposed to settle down in one place and establish there a brokered presence. And, as healers, we would expect them to stay in one place, to establish around them a group of followers, and to have people come to them. Instead, they go out to people and have, as it were, to start anew each morning. But, for Jesus, the Kingdom of God is a community of radical or unbrokered equality in which individuals are in direct contact with one another and with God, unmediated by any established brokers or fixed locations.

CHAPTER 5

No Staff, No Sandals, and No Knapsack

Most subordinate classes throughout most of history have rarely been afforded the luxury of open, organized, political activity. Or, better stated, such activity was dangerous, if not suicidal. . . . For all their importance when they do occur, peasant rebellions—let alone revolutions—are few and far between. The vast majority are crushed unceremoniously. . . . For these reasons it seemed to me more important to understand what we might call *everyday* forms of peasant resistance—the prosaic but constant struggle between the peasantry and those who seek to extract labor, food, taxes, rents, and interest from them. Most forms of this struggle stop well short of outright collective defiance. Here I have in mind the ordinary weapons of relatively powerless groups: foot dragging, dissimulation, desertion, false compliance, pilfering, feigned ignorance, slander, arson, sabotage, and so on. These . . . forms of class struggle . . . require little or no coordination or planning;

they make use of implicit understandings and informal networks; they often represent a form of individual self-help; they typically avoid any direct, symbolic confrontation with authority. . . . When such stratagems are abandoned in favor of more quixotic action, it is usually a sign of great desperation.

> James C. Scott, *Weapons of the Weak: Everyday Forms of Peasant Resistance* (New Haven, CT: Yale Univ. Press, 1985)

∾ The Arts of Resistance

Jesus was a *Mediterranean Jewish peasant.* I understand that interpretation in its three facets within cross-cultural anthropology. The process involves a composite model whose elements I will now summarize before proceeding further.

The Mediterranean basin stressed groupism based on kin and gender rather than individualism based on economics and property, and its pivotal moral values were rooted in honor and shame as well as patronage and clientage. I have already discussed how Jesus' theory and practice of *eating,* of open commensality, was a fundamental challenge to honor and shame. I have also indicated how his theory and practice of *healing* was an equally fundamental challenge to patronage and clientage. Each separately, and especially both together, challenged the Mediterranean's hierarchies, distinctions, and discriminations.

Jesus' Jewishness is particularly important in terms of the body/society interaction, the politic-body and body-politic connection, in which the former is always a microcosm of the latter. This interaction is present in every human culture and society, but it is especially significant in ones with threatened boundaries, which, because they must legislate carefully to preserve group identity, legislate just as carefully about bodily integrity. Do not get purity codes mixed up with either moral sins or medical contagions, but think, for instance, of our own military in terms of body/group interaction: a Marine with long hair and an earring is unclean and impure in the classic meaning of those terms as someone or something bodily/socially inappropriate from the viewpoint of authority. He is, as it were, symbolically contagious.

Mediterranean, Jewish, but also a peasant. With the inclusion of this chapter's epigraph, I now have in place the three main layers of a cross-cultural model for peasantry, for understanding Jesus' peasant roots.

Gerhard Lenski's *Power and Privilege* gives us the classes of social stratification and locates Peasants most clearly in that hierarchy. As he put it, bluntly and brutally, "The great majority of the political elite sought to use the energies of the peasantry to the full, while depriving them of all but the basic necessities of life."*

Bryan R. Wilson's *Magic and the Millennium* adds in a typology of peasant resistance among tribal and Third World peoples.** From among the various types he proposes, the two mentioned in his title receive maximum emphasis. They represent for me the options of, respectively, Jesus and John the Baptist. Jesus uses *magic,* or thaumaturgy, if you prefer a euphemism, but the only objective distinction between magic and religion is that *we* have religion while *they* have magic. Magic is especially a term that upper-class religion uses to denigrate its lower-class counterpart.

Finally, there is the work of James C. Scott, which I cited earlier when discussing the peasant dream of radical egalitarianism. The epigraph of the present chapter, taken from one of his books, and the title of this section, taken from another, *Domination and the Arts of Resistance,* bring up another very important component of the overall model.† The resistance of any oppressed people does not begin with revolt, although that is usually the point where oppressors first notice the problem.

---

* Gerhard Lenski, *Power and Privilege: A Theory of Social Stratification* (New York: McGraw-Hill, 1966).

** Bryan R. Wilson, *Magic and the Millennium: A Sociological Study of Religious Movements of Protest Among Tribal and Third-World Peoples* (New York: Harper & Row, 1973).

† James C. Scott, *Domination and the Arts of Resistance: Hidden Transcripts* (New Haven, CT: Yale Univ. Press, 1990).

Imagine peasant resistance like a giant iceberg. Most of it is covert, hidden below the surface, and not visible at all to the elites against which it is carefully aimed. Scott speaks of covert resistance as *material,* such as feigned dumbness or deliberate laziness; *formal,* such as tales of revenge or rituals of aggression; and *ideological,* such as millennial religions, myths of heroic banditry, or world-upside-down images.

We know, thanks to the powerful studies of Richard A. Horsley during the 1980s, that in the first-century Jewish homeland there were, on the overt level, such open reactions as the activities of unarmed protesters or armed bandits (about which more will be said in the next chapter) and of apocalyptic or millennial prophets and royal or messianic claimants; the latter two groups we have seen already. Such overt reactions, precisely because they are open and obvious, are usually recorded by elite observers, for example, the aristocratic Josephus. But overt resistance is always but the tip of the aforementioned iceberg, capping the mass of covert resistance without which oppressed individuals or peoples would have no human dignity, no reason to move or explode into the more overt types, which are all that get recorded by history. In Ireland, for instance, where the native Irish aristocracy had been forced into exile centuries before and replaced by a British ascendancy, there is the following legendary story. Lost English huntsman to Irish peasant in late-nineteenth-century Donegal: "Did the gentry pass this way, my good man?" "They did that, your honor." "How long ago?" "About three hundred years ago, your honor." That, too, is resistance—very small, relatively safe, but repeatable as story over and over again.

What Jesus was doing is located exactly on the borderline between the covert and the overt arts of resistance. It was not, of course, as open as the acts of protesters, prophets, bandits, or messiahs. But it was more open than playing dumb, imagining revenge, or simply recalling Mosaic or Davidic ideals. His eating and healing were, in theory and practice, the precise borderline between private and public, covert and overt, secret and open resistance. But it was no less surely resistance for all of that. A further question: Did Jesus have any type of organized social program for others to adopt and follow? We know already that he had a magnificent vision of the Kingdom of God here on earth and that by his own actions he already practiced what he preached. But were others only on the receiving end of that vision and program, or were they somehow empowered into it as active protagonists and not just passive recipients? Even as I ask that question I expect a positive answer, for one major reason. Mediterranean groupism would dictate some grouping around Jesus if his attack on familial and political communities was to make sense to his audience. What is the replacement for such communities? We saw, for example, that John the Baptist was organizing a discrete but united community of the baptized across the Jewish homeland, waiting for the advent of the apocalyptic God. What was Jesus doing on the group level, but with a very different message from a very different God?

∞ Into Whatever House You Enter

There are three main texts to be considered, and it is crucial to the argument that the three are independent of one another, that two of them are sources as early as any we have, and that all three mention a close conjunction between eating and healing (italicized in the following texts). I give those three texts together because I will constantly be referring to different aspects of them throughout the rest of this chapter.

(1) *Gospel of Thomas* 6:1 and *Gospel of Thomas* 14:

His followers asked him and said to him, "[a] Do you want us to fast? [b] How should we pray? [c] Should we give to charity? [d] What diet should we observe?". . .

Jesus said to them, "[a] If you fast, you will bring sin upon yourselves; and [b] if you pray, you will be condemned; and [c] if you give to charity, you will harm your spirits. [d] *When you go into any region and walk through the countryside, when people receive you, eat what they serve and heal the sick among them.* For what goes into your mouth will not defile you; rather, it is what comes out of your mouth that will defile you."

(2) *Q Gospel* in Matthew 9:37–38; 10:7, 10b, 12–14, and 16a; and Luke 10:2–11 (the following excerpt is from Luke):

He said, "The harvest is abundant, but the workers are few; beg therefore the master of the harvest to send out workers into his harvest. Go. Look, I send you out as lambs among wolves. Do not carry money, or bag, or sandals, [or staff]; and do not greet anyone on the road.

"Whatever house you enter, say, 'Peace be to this house.' And if a child of peace is there, your greeting will be received [literally, "your peace will rest upon him"]. But if not, let your peace return to you. And stay in the same house, *eating and drinking* whatever they provide, for the worker deserves his *wages* [in Luke; but in Matthew: *food*]. Do not go from house to house.

"And if you enter a town and they receive you, *eat what is set before you.* Pay attention to [literally: heal] the sick and say to them, 'God's kingdom has come near to you.' But if you enter a town and they do not receive you, as you leave, shake the dust from your feet and say, 'Nevertheless, be sure of this, the realm of God has come to you.'"

(3) Mark 6:7–13:

He called the twelve and began to send them out two by two, and gave them authority over the unclean spirits. He ordered them to take nothing for their journey except a staff; no bread, no bag, no money in their belts; but to wear sandals and not to put on two tunics.

He said to them, "Wherever you enter a house, *stay there* until you leave the place. If any place will not welcome you and they refuse to hear you, as you leave, shake off the dust that is on your feet as a testimony against them." So they went out and proclaimed that all should repent. They cast out many demons, and anointed with oil many who were sick and *cured* them.

What we have seen already about Jesus' theory and practice in eating and healing is presumed in what follows, but we are now considering how that was extended to others as both challenge and empowerment. Here is the heart of the original Jesus movement, a shared egalitarianism of spiritual (healing) and material (eating) resources. I emphasize this as strongly as possible, and I maintain that its materiality and spirituality, its facticity and symbolism, cannot be separated. The mission we are talking about is not, like Paul's, a dramatic thrust along major trade routes to urban centers hundreds of miles apart. Yet it concerns the longest journey in the Greco-Roman world, maybe in any world—the step across the threshold of a peasant stranger's home.

Person and Place

What sort of a mission are we dealing with, who goes on it, and to where? I use the term *mission* quite deliberately. We are dealing with more than a life-style, even one with a message implied by it or attached to it. Yet, on the other hand, we should be very careful not to read into it the full panoply of the Pauline mission, let alone all the implications of later Christian evangelization.

Who exactly is being sent on this mission? The *Gospel of Thomas,* with 14 as the displaced response to 6:1, simply says Jesus' followers or disciples. The *Q Gospel* is even less helpful in its present state. Whatever Luke 10:1 found there has been completely redacted to his own version, which now reads:

> After this the Lord appointed seventy others and sent them on ahead of him in pairs to every town and place where he himself intended to go.

That is a pure Lukan creation, so we can no longer tell to whom those mission instructions were addressed in the *Q Gospel.* For Mark 6:7, however, the missionaries are explicitly the Twelve Apostles, but that is found only in Mark. Is he, then, engaging in a similar act of creativity and equating those missionaries from the time of the historical Jesus specifically with the Twelve Apostles?

The point of Twelve is that Jesus' community forms a New Israel in miniature, a new People of God with twelve new patriarchs to replace the twelve sons of Jacob from the Old Testament. The question, however, is whether such an institution derives from the time of the historical Jesus or whether it was created after his death among certain early Christian groups. I accept the second alternative for two reasons. One is that I find it almost impossible to imagine thirteen men traveling around together among the small villages of Lower Galilee in the first century. Imagine that group arriving in a hamlet with all the men out working in the fields and only women and small children at home, especially in an honor-and-shame culture divided along gender lines. Bandits! Jesus surrounded by the Twelve would fit well as a sort of philosophical school in a city, but such a grouping is unthinkable moving among the tiny hamlets of rural Galilee. That, however, is a very general objection.

The second and more immediate one is that whole groups in the early church seem never to have heard of this most important and symbolic institution. Paul mentions a tradition about "the Twelve" in 1 Corinthians 15:5, but he distinguishes them from "all the apostles" in 15:7, and they never appear as any sort of authoritative source or group in his epistles. Neither the *Gospel of Thomas* nor the *Q Gospel* ever mentions them. The *Teaching* or *Didache,* a catechetical, liturgical, and disciplinary manual whose earliest sections may go back between 50 and 70 C.E., speaks of "apostles" only in the sense of itinerant missionaries who are given temporary hospitality as they pass through to found new communities elsewhere. The eleventh-century manuscript that alone contains this complete text is entitled, first, *The Teaching of the Twelve Apostles,* and, then, *The Teaching of the Lord through the Twelve Apostles to the Pagans.* Neither of those external titles reflects the text's internal understanding of "apostles" and must be considered as later additions. Neither do the Twelve Apostles appear in *First Clement,* a letter written around 96 or 97 C.E. from the church at Rome to that at Corinth. Finally, they are not mentioned in the letters that Ignatius of Antioch, traveling under guard to martyrdom in Rome between 110 and 117 C.E., wrote to various Christian communities along his route. If the institution of Twelve Apostles, with all its profound symbolic connotations, had been established by Jesus during his lifetime, it would have been more widely known and noted. I conclude, therefore, that the connection between Jesus' missionaries and the Twelve in Mark 6:7 is due to Mark himself and not to the historical Jesus.

The missionaries were not some specific and closed group sent out on one particular mission at one particular time. They were predominantly *healed healers,* part of whose continuing healing was precisely their empowerment to heal others. I propose, in other words, a network of shared healing with Jesus, just as I proposed a network of apocalyptic expectation with John. And it must be seriously considered how those networks interwove with each other.

One final point regarding those who were sent out as missionaries. In Mark 6:7 "the twelve," and in Luke 10:1 the "seventy others," are sent out "in pairs." Why? We know that the rabbis often traveled on official business in twos, but that was much later, after the destruction of Jerusalem's Temple in 70 C.E. There is no evidence of such a procedure at the time of Jesus. There are two other texts that may clarify what is happening. One is a highly symbolic story, one that we will look at in greater detail in the final chapter of this book, in which two followers of Jesus travel from Jerusalem to Emmaus on Easter Sunday. One of them is identified as Cleopas, a male; the other is left unidentified. I presume, in such a combination of named and unnamed pairs, especially in Mediterranean society, that the second person is a woman. She is not, however, specified as Cleopas's wife. Another text is this one in 1 Corinthians 9:5, in a context where Paul is discussing his own missionary activities:

> Do we not have the right to be accompanied by a believing wife [*adelphēn gynaika*], as do the other apostles and the brothers of the Lord and Cephas?

That translation makes the problem a simple one of support for both the missionary and his wife, as long as she, too, is a Christian. The literal Greek "sister wife" is translated into English as "believing wife." But is Paul talking about real, married, Christian wives, and, if so, how exactly are we to imagine what happened to their children in such situations? And, more specifically, how could the unmarried Paul be accompanied by his wife? My proposal is that a "sister wife" means exactly what it says: a female missionary who travels with a male missionary as if, for the world at large, she is his wife. The obvious function of such a tactic would be to furnish the best social protection for a traveling female missionary in a world of male power and violence. Was that the original purpose and focus of the "in pairs" practice—namely, to allow for and incorporate safely the possibility of female missionaries? I am utterly aware of how tentative that suggestion must remain. But I am convinced that it must be made, for two reasons. First, Paul's expression "sister wife" must be given some more adequate interpretation than "believing wife." Second, if, as suggested earlier, Jesus advocated *open* commensality, that would involve both women and men. If, then, the missionaries included women, how could that possibly have worked in the context of Galilean peasant society? I do not think women missionaries could have gone out to houses alone, and a "sister wife" relationship might have been not only the best but the only way to effect these women's work. If society got wind of this practice, its term for such women would be "whores"—the standard description for any women outside normal social convention or normal male control. Jesus, of course, would then be consorting with "whores."

Turning now from persons to places, to where exactly were those followers of Jesus sent? Notice, in the three key texts cited above, how the exact destination of the messengers changes from one text to the next or even within the same text itself. What I am watching here is the move from visiting *houses* grouped together as tiny *hamlets* near the fields, to visiting *towns* with some market capacity, and on to visiting *cities* with public buildings and possibly walls. It may be salutary to note, as a preliminary warning, that scholarly estimates of Capernaum's population at the time of Jesus vary from twenty-five thousand to seventeen hundred people.

The *Gospel of Thomas* 14:2 mentions "any region" but then specifies that as the "countryside" rather than the city. Mark specifically mentions a "house" in 6:10 and then a "place" in 6:11, but one presumes that he is speaking about the same location. The *Q Gospel* has, however, the most striking of the three versions. In the first half, at Luke 10:5–7, a "house" destination is mentioned four times, but in the second half, at Luke 10:8–11, a "town" (literally, *polis*—a city) is mentioned twice.

Recent scholarship on the *Q Gospel,* and especially the work of John S. Kloppenborg, has argued for two principal layers in the composition of that gospel. The earlier one emphasized primarily a life-style and missionary activity that, despite the expectation of opposition and even persecution, was remarkably open and hopeful. Later came a second one, far more dark and defensive, threatening dire apocalyptic vengeance against "this generation" for refusing to accept that missionary activity. What happened to change the community's vision may possibly be seen in that very change from *house* to *town,* from Luke 10:5–7 to 10:8–11. What may well have happened to the communities of the *Q Gospel* was that a relatively successful mission to the small *houses* of the villages and countryside turned into a comparatively obvious failure as the missionaries moved into *towns* such as, for example, Chorazin, Bethsaida, and Capernaum. But Jesus' earliest followers were sent to village houses rather than to urban centers.

Commensality and Payment

The move from *house mission* to *town mission* is one type of development in the history of those three key texts. Another is from *commensality* to *payment,* facilitated by the ambiguity between *food as eating together* and *food as wages in kind.* That transition was already evident in the twin versions of the *Q Gospel* in Matthew 10:10 (food) and Luke 10:7 (wages), as underlined above and below. Here are those texts again, as well as four others on the same subject from, respectively, 1 Corinthians 9:4, 9, and 14 (food); 1 Timothy 5:17–18 (wages); the *Dialogue of the Savior* 53b (food); and *Didache* 11:4–6 and 13:1–2 (food).

(1b) . . . for the worker deserves his *food.*

(1a) . . . for the worker deserves his *wages.*

(2) Do we not have the right to our *food* and drink?. . . For it is written in the law of Moses, "You shall not muzzle an ox while it is treading out the grain.". . . In the same way, the Lord commanded that those who proclaim the gospel should get their living by the gospel.

(3) Let the elders who rule well be considered worthy of double honor, especially those who labor in preaching and teaching; for the scripture says, "You shall not muzzle an ox while it is treading out the grain," and, "The worker deserves his *wages.*"

(4) Mary said [quoting Jesus], "The worker deserves his *food.*"

(5) Let every apostle who comes to you [that is, an itinerant] be received as the Lord, but let him not stay more

than one day, or if need be a second as well; but if he stays three days, he is a false prophet. . . . And when an apostle goes forth let him accept nothing but bread till he reach his night's lodging; but if he ask for money, he is a false prophet. But every true prophet who wishes to settle among you [that is, a resident] deserves his *food.* Similarly, a true teacher, like the worker, deserves his *food.*

Two of those six texts have *wages* and four have *food,* so the development is more likely from food to wages rather than vice versa. But my point is not so much the difference between food and wages, since wages could be given in kind, as food, and still be considered wages. What is at stake is the transition from *commensality* to *payment,* helped, of course, by that food/wages ambiguity. But even though the last text's decrees show the obvious problems in distinguishing between itinerant apostles and visiting panhandlers, something important was lost as open commensality developed into payment due. Maybe the mission became more efficient, better organized, and more suitable for urban rather than rural realities, but it was also becoming a different mission in the process. Commensality was not, for Jesus, merely a strategy for supporting the mission. That could have been done by alms, wages, charges, or fees of some sort. It could also have been done by simple begging. Commensality was, rather, a strategy for building or rebuilding peasant community on radically different principles from those of honor and shame, patronage and clientage. It was based on an egalitarian sharing of spiritual and material power at the most grass-roots level. For that reason any move from *food shared* to *wages due* was a momentous step in the movement's development.

∞ The Skin of My Feet for Shoes

The Kingdom of God was not, for Jesus, a divine monopoly exclusively bound to his own person. It began on the level of the body and appeared as a shared community of healing and eating—that is to say, of spiritual and physical resources available to each and all without distinctions, discriminations, or hierarchies. One entered the Kingdom as a way of life, and anyone who could live it could bring it to others. It was not just words alone, or deeds alone, but both together as life-style. So far, however, I have said nothing about the dress, equipment, or deportment codes mentioned in the texts given earlier. What do such codes have to do with the Kingdom of God? I repeat the key verses here as a reminder. They are from, respectively, the *Q Gospel* in Luke 10:4, Mark 6:8–9, and *Didache* 11:6a.

(1) "Do not carry money, or bag, or sandals, [or staff]; and do not greet anyone on the road."

(2) He ordered them to take nothing for their journey except a staff; no bread, no bag, no money in their belts; but to wear sandals and not to put on two tunics.

(3) And when an apostle goes forth let him accept nothing but bread till he reach his night's lodging.

Once again, as you read down these three texts, notice a development from a *more radical* to a *more lenient* code, just like those earlier changes from *house* to *town* and from *commensality* to *payment.* The staff and sandals forbidden in the first are allowed in the second, and the bread forbidden in the second is allowed in the third. The first verse, therefore, is the earliest: it would hardly have been necessary to allow something as normal as sandals or staff in the second verse unless somebody had forbidden them earlier in the first. Those changes serve, however, to emphasize that the commands were once real codes and not just unreal ideas, theoretical possibilities, or imaginary musings. Taking, then, the forbidding of purse, bag, sandals, staff, and salutation as basic and original, as coming from the historical Jesus, what did he mean by such a set of negations? The answer involves a look at some other radical missionaries who, in the first century, preached to the ordinary people a message both by what they said and how they lived, both by what they taught and how they dressed. Enter the Cynics.

Diogenes and Daedalus

Cynicism was a Greek philosophical movement founded by Diogenes of Sinope, who was born on the mid-southern coast of the Black Sea and lived between 400 and 320 B.C.E. The term itself means, literally, "dogism," coming from *kyon,* the Greek word for "dog," and it was used, as if quoting a well-known nickname, of Diogenes by Aristotle. It was originally a derogatory term for the provocative shamelessness with which Diogenes deliberately flouted basic human codes of propriety and decency, custom and convention. We use *cynicism* today to mean belief in nothing or doubt about everything, but what it means philosophically is theoretical disbelief *and* practical negation of ordinary cultural values and civilized presuppositions. Here is Farrand Sayre's description of the Cynics' program:

> The Cynics sought happiness through freedom. The Cynic conception of freedom included freedom from desires, from fear, anger, grief and other emotions, from religious or moral control, from the authority of the city or state or public officials, from regard for public opinion and freedom also from the care of property, from confinement to any locality and from the care and support of wives and children. . . . The Cynics scoffed at the customs and conventionalities of others, but were rigid in observance of their own. The Cynic would not appear anywhere without his *wallet, staff* and *cloak,* which must invariably be dirty and ragged and worn so as to leave the right shoulder bare. He never wore *shoes* and his *hair* and *beard* were long and unkempt.*

My italics emphasize the Cynics' dress and equipment code, which was intended as a dramatization of their refusal to accept society's material values, as a clear visualization of their countercultural position.

The classic Cynic story is that of the encounter between Diogenes and Alexander the Great at Corinth in 336 B.C.E. The latter is just setting out to conquer the world through military power; the former had already done so through disciplined indifference. This oft-told tale was already known to Cicero in his *Tusculan Disputations* 5.92 from 45 B.C.E.:

> But Diogenes, certainly, was more outspoken, in his quality of Cynic, when Alexander asked him to name anything he wanted: "Just now," he said, "stand a bit away from the

---

* Farrand Sayre, *The Greek Cynics* (Baltimore: Furst, 1948), pages 7 and 18.

sun!" Alexander apparently had interfered with his basking in the heat.

We are back, by the way, to the quotation from Burton Mack that headed Chapter 3. The story of Diogenes and Alexander involves a calculated questioning of power, rule, dominion, and kingship. Who is the true ruler: the one who wants everything, or the one who wants nothing; the one who wants all of Asia, or the one who wants only a little sunlight? If kingship is freedom, which of the two is really free, is really king? And just as Cynicism had a first flowering after the conquests of Alexander, so it had another after those of Augustus. Both times were ripe for a fundamental questioning of power, and the Cynics did so not only in abstract theory among the aristocratic elites, but in practical street theater among the ordinary people. They were populist preachers in marketplace and pilgrimage center, and their life and dress spoke as forcibly as their speech and sermons.

The Cynics' criticism was not directed, however, just at the materialism of Hellenistic culture in the wake of either the Alexandrian or Augustan empires. It was directed more fundamentally at civilization itself, advocating a self-sufficiency modeled on that of nature rather than culture. The Roman moralist Seneca the Younger, who lived between 4 B.C.E. and 65 C.E., drew the contrast, in his *Epistulae Morales* 90.14–16, not just between Alexander and Diogenes but between Daedalus and Diogenes, between the one who invented the arts of civilization and the one who refused them:

> How, I ask, can you consistently admire both Diogenes and Daedalus? Which of these two seems to you a wise man— the one who devised the saw, or the one who, on seeing a boy drink water from the hollow of his hand, forthwith took his cup from his wallet and broke it, upbraiding himself with these words: "Fool that I am, to have been carrying superfluous baggage all this time!" and then curled himself up in his tub and lay down to sleep. . . . If mankind were willing to listen to this sage, they would know that the cook is as superfluous as the soldier. . . . Follow nature, and you will need no skilled craftsmen.

Cynicism is not, in other words, just a moral attack on Greco-Roman civilization; it is a paradoxical attack on civilization itself. We are back, in fact, with that distinction seen earlier between the wider phenomenon of *eschatology* or world-negation and the narrower one of *apocalypticism* as but one of its many forms. Cynicism is the Greco-Roman form of that universal philosophy of eschatology or world-negation, one of the great and fundamental options of the human spirit. For wherever there is culture and civilization there can also be counterculture and anticivilization.

Knapsack and Staff

The Cynic missionaries and the Jesus missionaries agree about wearing no sandals and spending no time on ordinary greetings and gossip on the way. But I focus now on wallet and staff, because here they are in flat disagreement.

There is extant from around the Augustan age, before and after the time of Jesus, a series of pseudo-letters or fictional communications from revered or representative Cynics. The title of this wider section, for instance, derives from the phrase "the skin of my feet as my shoes" in *Pseudo-Anacharsis* 65, a text already known to Cicero in 45 B.C.E. These imaginary letters are now easily accessible in *The Cynic Epistles,* a collection by Abraham Malherbe. In the following excerpts from *Pseudo-Diogenes,* letters fictionally attributed to Cynicism's founder from the first century B.C.E. or even earlier, notice the constant emphasis on cloak, staff, and bag or wallet. *Cloak* refers to the single heavy or doubled outer garment worn day and night, summer and winter—the only garment used. But for now, I emphasize only bag or wallet, and staff.

> [To Hicetas] Do not be upset, Father, that I am called a dog and put on a double, coarse cloak, carry a *wallet* over my shoulders, and have a *staff* in my hand . . . living as I do, not in conformity with popular opinion but according to nature, free under Zeus.

> [To Apolexis] I have laid aside most of the things that weigh down my *wallet,* since I learned that for a plate a

hollowed out loaf of bread suffices, as the hands do for a cup.

[To Antipater] I hear that you say I am doing nothing unusual in wearing a double, ragged cloak and carrying a *wallet*. Now I admit that none of these is extraordinary, but each of them is good when undertaken out of conscious determination.

[To Anaxilaus] I have recently come to recognize myself to be Agamemnon, since for a scepter I have my *staff* and for a mantle the double, ragged cloak, and by way of exchange, my leather *wallet* is a shield.

[To Agesilaus] Life has a sufficient store in a *wallet*.

[To Crates] Remember that I started you [Crates] on your lifelong poverty. . . . Consider the ragged cloak to be a lion's skin, the *staff* a club, and the *wallet* land and sea, from which you are fed. For thus would the spirit of Heracles, mightier than every turn of fortune, stir in you.

The term *wallet* is probably a most unfortunate translation since for us it connotes money. The Greek word is always *pēra* in those letters, as it is in Luke 10:4 and Mark 6:8, and a good translation, for us, would be "knapsack" rather than "wallet" or "bag." What it symbolized for the Cynics was their complete self-sufficiency. They carried their homes with them. All they needed could be carried in a simple knapsack slung over their shoulders. Similarly with the staff. It represented their itinerant status, the fact that they had no fixed abode in any place, that they were always spiritually on the way elsewhere. The two items taken together underlined their itinerant self-sufficiency.

The Jesus missionaries, in contrast, are told precisely to carry *no* knapsack and hold *no* staff in their hands. Why this striking difference? Since a reciprocity of healing and eating is at the heart of the Jesus movement, the idea of no-staff and no-knapsack is symbolically correct for the Jesus missionaries. They are not urban like the Cynics, preaching at street corner and marketplace. They are rural, on a house mission to rebuild peasant society from the grass roots upward. Since commensality is not just a technique for support but a demonstration of message, they could not and should not dress to declare itinerant self-sufficiency but rather communal dependency. Itinerancy *and* dependency: heal, stay, move on.

Poverty and Royalty

I conclude this section with a series of quotations from the philosopher Epictetus, not to argue about who influenced whom but simply to show how poverty and royalty could be combined not just by Jesus within Judaism but by Epictetus within Greco-Roman paganism. Epictetus was born the slave son of a slave mother and lived between 55 and 135 C.E. He was allowed by his master to study philosophy, was eventually freed, and was banished from Rome along with other philosophers by the emperor Domitian in 89 C.E. Here is a justly famous passage from "On the Calling of a Cynic" in his posthumously transcribed *Discourses* 3.22.

> And how is it possible that a man who has *nothing*, who is naked, houseless, without a hearth, squalid, without a slave, without a city, can pass a life that flows easily? See, God has sent you a man to show you that it is possible. Look at me, who am without a city, without a house, without possessions, without a slave; I sleep on the ground; I have no wife, no children, no praetorium [official power], but only the earth and heavens, and one poor cloak. And what do I want? Am I not without sorrow? Am I not without fear? Am I not *free*? When did any of you see me failing in the object of my desire? or ever falling into that which I would avoid? did I ever blame God or man? did I ever accuse any man? did any of you ever see me with sorrowful countenance? And how do I meet with those whom you are afraid of and admire? Do not I treat them like slaves? Who, when he sees me, does not think that he sees his *king* and master?

Notice, in the flow of that passage, the sequence from *nothing* to *free* to *king*, the logic of poverty leading to freedom leading to royalty. Notice, also, the intense political undertones of the passage. If Epictetus represented royalty, what was the Roman emperor? And those three terms are best explained by other quotations from *Discourses* 3.22.

Poverty, first of all. Epictetus is very concerned that the externals of Cynicism may be mistaken for its internals. Since a Cynic philosopher looks much like a beggar, is not every beggar a Cynic philosopher? Do staff, knapsack, and one cloak automatically make one a Cynic? But, even while warning against that danger, he never suggests abandoning those externals. He simply insists that internal poverty must beget external and that external must not replace internal.

> So do you [would-be Cynics] also think about the matter carefully; it is not what you think it is. "I wear a rough cloak even as it is, and I shall have one then; I have a hard bed even now, and so I shall then; I shall take to myself a wallet and a staff, and I shall begin to walk around and beg from those I meet, and revile them. . . ." If you fancy the affair to be something like this, give it a wide berth; don't come near it, it is nothing for you. . . .
>
> Lo, these are words [the long quotation from 3.22 that I cited earlier] that befit a Cynic, this is his character, and his plan of life. But no, you say, what makes a Cynic is a contemptible wallet, a staff, and big jaws; to devour everything you give him, or to stow it away, or to revile tactlessly the people he meets, or to show off his fine shoulder.

It is obvious that Epictetus is speaking to an audience of the poorer classes whose normal poverty is not that different, in externals, from Cynic poverty. But, he insists, it is voluntary not necessary poverty that counts.

Freedom comes next. The one who has nothing and wants nothing is totally free. This comes not only from a physical poverty that renders one impervious to both desire and loss, but especially from a spiritual poverty that renders one oblivious to both attack and assault.

> For this too is a very pleasant strand woven into the Cynic's pattern of life; he must needs be flogged like an ass, and while he is being flogged he must love the men who flog him, as though he were the father or brother of them all. But that is not your way. If someone flogs you, go stand in the midst and shout, "O Caesar, what do I have to suf-

fer under your peaceful rule? let us go before the Proconsul." But what to a Cynic is Caesar, or a Proconsul, or anyone other than He who has sent him into the world, and whom he serves, that is, Zeus? . . .

Now the spirit of patient endurance the Cynic must have to such a degree that common people will think him insensate and a stone; nobody reviles him, nobody beats him, nobody insults him; but his body he has himself given for anyone to use as he sees fit.

It is fascinating to watch the Christian nervousness of some earlier translators in handling that passage. Does Epictetus sound too much like Jesus? In the 1910 edition of *The Moral Discourses of Epictetus,* for example, Elizabeth Carter compares that passage with Matthew 5:39–44, which speaks of turning the other cheek, giving up your garments, and going the second mile under constraint. She notes that "Christ specifies higher injuries and provocations than Epictetus doth; and requires of *all* his followers, what Epictetus describes only as the duty of one or two *extraordinary* persons, as such." Not really.

Royalty, true royalty, is the final theme, still from Epictetus. It is interesting, in this regard, that the same Greek word could be used for royal scepter and for Cynic staff:

Where will you find me a Cynic's friend? . . . He must share with him his sceptre and kingdom. . . .

See to what straits we are reducing our Cynic [if he marries], how we are taking away his kingdom from him. . . .

And yet shall the Cynic's kingship [or: kingdom] not be thought a reasonable compensation [for celibacy]?

Poverty, freedom, and royalty, then, because the Cynic "has been sent by Zeus to men, partly as a messenger . . . and partly . . . as a scout" so that he walks the earth as "one who shares in the government of Zeus." It is not my point that Jesus and Epictetus are saying or doing exactly the same thing. Difference must be respected just as much as similarity. But what Jesus called the Kingdom of God and what Epictetus might have called the Kingdom of Zeus must be compared as radical messages that taught and acted, theorized and performed against social oppression, cultural materialism, and imperial domination in the first and second centuries.

We have, in the final analysis, no way of knowing for sure what Jesus knew about Cynicism, or whether he knew about it at all. That, however, is not really the point. Maybe he had never even heard of the Cynics and was just reinventing the Cynic wheel all by himself. But the differences as well as similarities between the Jesus and the Cynic preachers are instructive even if not derivative. Both are populists, appealing to the ordinary people; both are life-style preachers, advocating their position not only by word but by deed, not only in theory but in practice; both use dress and equipment to symbolize dramatically their message. But he is rural, they are urban; he is organizing a communal movement, they are following an individual philosophy; and their symbolism demands knapsack and staff, his no-knapsack and no-staff. Maybe Jesus is what peasant *Jewish* Cynicism looked like.

CHAPTER 6

The Dogs Beneath the Cross

CRUCIFIXION as a penalty was remarkably widespread in antiquity. It appears in various forms among numerous peoples of the ancient world, even among the Greeks. . . . [It] was and remained a political and military punishment. While among the Persians and the Carthaginians it was imposed primarily on high officials and commanders, as on rebels, among the Romans it was inflicted above all on the lower classes, i.e., slaves, violent criminals, and the unruly elements in rebellious provinces, not least in Judaea. The chief reason for its use was its allegedly supreme efficacy as a deterrent; it was, of course, carried out publicly. . . . It was usually associated with other forms of torture, including at least flogging. . . . By the public display of a naked victim at a prominent place—at a crossroads, in the theatre, on high ground, at the place of his crime—crucifixion also represented his uttermost humiliation, which had a numinous dimension to it. With Deuteronomy

21.23 in the background, the Jew in particular was very aware of this. . . . Crucifixion was aggravated further by the fact that quite often its victims were never buried. It was a stereotyped picture that the crucified victim served as food for wild beasts and birds of prey. In this way his humiliation was made complete. What it meant for a man in antiquity to be refused burial, and the dishonour which went with it, can hardly be appreciated by modern man.

Martin Hengel, *Crucifixion in the Ancient World and the Folly of the Message of the Cross* (Philadelphia: Fortress Press, 1977)

∞ A Corpse for the Wild Beasts

This is the hardest chapter, for two reasons; I give one now and the other later. It is hard, for now, not only for those who have faith in Jesus, but also for those who have faith in humanity, to look closely at the terror of crucifixion in the ancient world. And when one does look closely, there is always the danger of prurient voyeurism, the vicarious thrill at another's horror. But since that world did in thousands what our century has done in millions, it is necessary to look with cold, hard eyes at what exactly such a death entailed. Nevertheless, I tread here very carefully.

In June of 1968 the only crucified skeleton ever discovered was found at Giv'at ha-Mivtar, in northeastern Jerusalem just west of the Nablus Road, in a tomb dating from the first century of the common era. There were four tombs in all, carved like small rooms into the soft limestone, each with an anteroom and then a burial chamber with niches deep enough to accommodate a human body lengthwise at burial. Such tombs were used over and over again for generations; the bones, after decomposition of their flesh within the niches, were buried together in pits dug in the floor or, as a much more costly alternative, were gathered together into ossuaries—limestone bone boxes. The niches were then reused for more recent burials. In the Giv'at ha-Mivtar complex there were fifteen such ossuaries, mostly packed to the top and containing the bones of thirty-five individuals—eleven males, twelve females, and twelve children. Of those thirty-five, one woman and her infant had died together in childbirth for lack of a midwife's help; three children, one of six to eight months, one of three to four years, and another of seven to eight years, had died of starvation; and five individuals had met violent deaths: a female and a male by burning, a female by a macelike blow, a child of three to four years by an arrow wound, and a male of twenty-four to twenty-eight years who stood five-foot-five by crucifixion. His name, inscribed on the ossuary, was then Yehochanan but now is I/4A: Tomb I, Ossuary 4 (of eight in that tomb), Skeleton A (of three in that ossuary, the other two being an incomplete adult and Yehochanan's son, another child of three to four years).

After appraisal and reappraisal by scholars from Israel's Department of Antiquities and Jerusalem's Hebrew University Hadassah Medical School, the manner of crucifixion became clear. His arms had been not nailed but tied to the bar of the cross, probably with arms to elbows over and behind it. His legs had been placed on either side of the upright beam, with separate nails holding the heelbone to the wood on each side. A small olive-wood plaque had been set between the nail's head and the heel bone lest the condemned man manage to tear his foot free from the nail. But the nail in the right heel had struck a knot in the upright and its point had become bent, so that when the man was taken down, the nail, olive wood, and heel bone all remained fixed together in burial and discovery. Finally, there was no evidence that the man's legs had been broken after crucifixion to speed his death by more instant asphyxiation.

But why, with all those thousands of people crucified around Jerusalem in the first century alone, have we found only a single skeleton, and that, of course, preserved in an ossuary? I mentioned earlier, for instance, that the Syrian governor, Publius Quinctilius Varus, needed three legions as well as auxiliary troops to quell revolts, including three major messianic uprisings, in the Jewish homeland immediately after the death of Herod the Great in 4 B.C.E. When he arrived at Jerusalem, he crucified, according to Josephus's twin accounts in *War* 2.75 and

Antiquities 17.295, "two thousand" of the rebels. Mass crucifixions also framed the beginning and ending of the First Roman-Jewish War. In the early summer of 66 C.E., Florus, then Roman governor of the Jewish homeland, ordered his troops to attack inside the city itself, according to *War* 2.306–308:

> Many of the peaceable citizens were arrested and brought before Florus, who had them first scourged and then crucified. The total number of that day's victims, including women and children, for even infancy received no quarter, amounted to about three thousand six hundred. The calamity was aggravated by the unprecedented character of the Romans' cruelty. For Florus ventured that day to do what none had ever done before, namely, to scourge before his tribunal and nail to the cross men of equestrian rank, men who, if Jews by birth, were at least invested with that Roman dignity.

Four years later, in the early summer of 70 C.E., Titus's army had completely encircled Jerusalem and the siege was being pressed toward its awful consummation, according to *War* 5.447–451:

> The majority [of those who issued from the encircled city in search of food] were citizens of the poorer class, who were deterred from deserting by fear for their families. . . . When caught, they were . . . scourged and subjected to torture of every description, before being killed, and then crucified opposite the walls . . . five hundred or sometimes more being captured daily. . . . The soldiers out of rage and hatred amused themselves by nailing their prisoners in different postures; and so great was their number, that space could not be found for the crosses nor crosses for the bodies.

Even though Roman crucifixion was, as this chapter's epigraph from Martin Hengel emphasizes, a death reserved primarily for the lower classes, it could be used, as it was by Florus, precisely to degrade and dishonor rebel members of the upper classes.

What exactly made crucifixion so terrible? The three supreme Roman penalties were the cross, fire, and the beasts. What made them supreme was not just their inhuman cruelty or their public dishonor, but the fact that *there might be nothing left to bury at the end.* That bodily destruction was involved in being cast into the fire or thrown to the beasts is obvious enough. But what we often forget about crucifixion is the carrion crow and scavenger dog who respectively croak above and growl below the dead or dying body. Martin Hengel, once again, reminds us of that terrible reality. His book, which is a catalog of the writings of Greco-Roman authors on the subject of crucifixion, quotes, for example, "fastened [and] nailed . . . [as] evil food for birds of prey and grim pickings for dogs" on page 9, "feed the crows on the cross" on page 58, and "hung . . . alive for the wild beasts and birds of prey" on page 76.

I return to the burial of the crucified later in this chapter with regard to Jesus himself, but for now I want to emphasize that Roman crucifixion was state terrorism; that its function was to deter resistance or revolt, especially among the lower classes; and that the body was usually left on the cross to be consumed eventually by the wild beasts. No wonder we have found only one body from all those thousands crucified around Jerusalem in that single century. Remember those dogs. And if you seek the heart of darkness, follow the dogs.

∞ Before the Feast of Passover

Mark says that Jesus was crucified on the first day of the Passover feast, after having celebrated the Passover Eve supper the night before. John says that it happened on Passover Eve itself and thus before that celebratory meal could have taken place. But both authors connect his death with Passover, so I accept some such connection, although this is much less certain than the fact of the crucifixion.

Passover celebrated the deliverance of the Jews from bondage in Egypt and their departure to conquer the Promised Land. It was obviously a rather dangerous festival in a colonized country with imperial overlords, with Romans replacing Egyptians, as it were—especially as it brought together very large crowds in a very concentrated space. After the death of Herod the Great, for example, and just before his son Archelaus departed for Rome to obtain the southern part of his father's kingdom in April of 4 B.C.E., there was a massacre in the Temple itself during Passover, according to Josephus's twin accounts in *War* 2.10–13 and *Antiquities* 17. 213–218:

> At this time there came round the festival during which it is the ancestral custom of the Jews to serve unleavened bread. It is called Passover, being a commemoration of their departure from Egypt. They celebrate it with gladness, and it is their custom to slaughter a greater number of sacrifices at this festival than at any other, and an innumerable multitude of people come down from the country and even from abroad to worship God.

When the assembled crowds resisted his troops, Archelaus unleashed his full force against them and, according to *War* 2.13,

> the soldiers falling unexpectedly upon the various parties busy with their sacrifices slew about three thousand of them and dispersed the remainder among the neighboring hills.

That incident reminds us of how explosive a situation Passover could be as crowds gathered in the Temple to celebrate, amid later imperial oppression, deliverance from an earlier one. With Jewish police within the Temple courts and Roman auxiliary troops overlooking them from the Antonia fortress to the north, force was poised to stop any trouble before it could even begin. But what did Jesus do to get himself crucified? It is clear that his words and deeds involved social even if not military revolution, but it was not Antipas in Galilee but Pilate in Jerusalem that crucified him. So what happened there, at that time and that place? Here are three separate incidents from the days immediately before his death. Let us see which best explains what happened.

First, the *Triumphal Entrance*. In Mark 11:1–10 there appears the story of the triumphal—or, better, antitriumphal— entry of Jesus into Jerusalem on what is now called Palm Sunday.

> And they brought the colt to Jesus, and threw their garments on it; and he sat upon it. And many spread their garments on the road, and others spread leafy branches which they had cut from the fields. And those who went before and those who followed cried out, "Hosanna! Blessed is he who comes in the name of the Lord! Blessed

is the kingdom of our father David that is coming! Hosanna in the highest."

Implicit behind that scene is a prophecy from the fourth or third century B.C.E. now included in Zechariah 9:9 that sharply contrasts Alexander the Great's entrance into a conquered city with that of the messianic deliverer coming in the future to save God's people:

> Lo, your king comes to you;
> triumphant and victorious is he,
> humble and riding on an ass,
> on a colt the foal of an ass.

And what is left implicit in Mark is rendered explicit by the parallel texts in Matthew 21:4–5 and John 12:15, both of which cite Zechariah 9:9 as being fulfilled in Jesus' entry into Jerusalem. An action such as that could certainly have provoked reaction from the authorities in a Passover situation. But its status of prophetic fulfillment, while not disproving that it could have occurred, renders it much too suspect for me to build on it as a historical event. Notice also that this incident is not based on general Davidic or Mosaic models known to every Jew but on a very precise verse in one single prophecy. It seems more what scribes look backward to find rather than what people look forward to see. I do not think, in other words, that it ever actually happened, except as later symbolic retrojection.

Next, what about the *Last Supper?* In Mark 14:22–25 Jesus celebrates the Passover Eve meal with his disciples and prophecies his impending death.

> And as they were eating, he took bread, and blessed and broke it and gave it to them, and said, "Take; this is my body." And he took the cup, and when he had given thanks he gave it to them, and they all drank of it. And he said to them, "This is my blood of the covenant, which is poured out for many. Truly, I say to you, I shall not drink again of the fruit of the vine until the day when I drink it new in the kingdom of God."

This incident is not of course public like the preceding one, but does it indicate that Jesus knew he had done or was about to do something that could bring about this death? Once again, however, the historical question comes first. Did Jesus, before his death, institute a new Passover meal in which his martyrdom with its separation of body and blood was symbolized by the meal with its separation of bread and wine? On the one hand, Paul certainly knows about such an institution in 1 Corinthians 11:23–25. But, on the other, John 13–17 has a last supper with Jesus and his disciples that is neither the Passover meal nor any type of institutionalized symbolic commemoration of his death. Neither the *Gospel of Thomas* nor the *Q Gospel* exhibits any awareness of a Last Supper tradition. Finally, the case of *Didache* 9–10 is especially significant. It describes a communal and ritual eating together, from the second half of the first century, with absolutely no hint of Passover meal, Last Supper, or passion symbolism built into its origins or development. I cannot believe that those specific Christians knew all about those elements and yet studiously avoided them. I can only presume that those elements were not there for everyone from the beginning—that is, from solemn, formal, and final institution by Jesus himself. What Jesus created and left behind was the tradition of open commensality seen so often earlier, and what happened was that, after his death, certain Christian groups created the Last Supper as a ritual that combined that commensality from his life with a commemoration of his death. It spread to other Christian groups only slowly. It cannot be used as a historical event to explain anything about Jesus' own death.

Finally, there is the *Temple Cleansing,* a most unfortunate term for what was actually a symbolic destruction of the Temple. Here we are on much more solid historical ground, because there are three independent sources for this incident.

The first version is in the *Gospel of Thomas* 71, but it contains only a *saying* without any *action,* a *word* without an accompanying *deed:*

> Jesus said, "I shall [destroy this] house, and no one will be able to build it."

That is to say, I shall utterly destroy this house. For the Temple as (God's) house, consider these verses from the Jewish *Sibylline Oracles* 4:8–11, of around 100 C.E.:

> For [the great God] does not have a house, a stone set up as a temple,
> dumb and toothless, a bane which brings many woes to men,

but one which it is not possible to see from earth nor to measure with mortal eyes, since it was not fashioned by mortal hands.

God's house or Temple is not on earth but in heaven. And that use of *house* as in the *Gospel of Thomas* 71 shows up differently in the two other independent sources for this incident.

Next comes the version in Mark 11:15–19, which is not at all a purification but rather a symbolic destruction. There is here, unlike the preceding case, first a physical *action* and then an interpretative *saying*. First of all, and in general, there was absolutely nothing wrong with any of the buying, selling, or money-changing operations conducted in the outer courts of the Temple. Nobody was stealing or defrauding or contaminating the sacred precincts. Those activities were the absolutely necessary concomitants of the fiscal basis and sacrificial purpose of the Temple. Second, Mark himself knows that Jesus was not just purifying but symbolically destroying the Temple, because he carefully framed his action within the fruitless fig tree's cursing in 11:12–14 and its withering in 11:20. As the useless fig tree was destroyed, so, symbolically, was the useless Temple.

> And they came to Jerusalem. And he entered the temple and began to drive out those who sold and those who bought in the temple, and he overturned the tables of the money-changers and the seats of those who sold pigeons; and he would not allow any one to carry anything through the temple.
>
> And he taught, and said to them, "Is it not written, 'My *house* shall be called a *house* of prayer for all the nations' [= Isaiah 56:7]? But you have made it a den of robbers [= Jeremiah 7:11]."

Notice, first of all, the balance of deed and word, action and comment. That action is not, of course, a physical destruction of the Temple, but it is a deliberate symbolical attack. It *destroys* the Temple by *stopping* its fiscal, sacrificial, and liturgical operations.

Finally, there is the account in John 2:14–17. Again, I show the balance of deed and word. But notice that, despite the use of a different Old Testament text, the word *house* is still there.

> In the temple he found those who were selling oxen and sheep and pigeons, and the money-changers at their business. And making a whip of cords, he drove them all, with

the sheep and oxen, out of the temple; and he poured out the coins of the money-changers and overturned their tables. And he told those who sold the pigeons,

"Take these things away; you shall not make my Father's *house* a *house* of trade." His disciples remembered that it was written, "Zeal for thy *house* will consume me [= Psalm 69:9]."

The Jews then said to him, "What sign have you to show us for doing this?" Jesus answered them, "Destroy this temple, and in three days I will raise it up." The Jews then said, "It has taken forty-six years to build this temple, and will you raise it up in three days?" But he spoke of the temple of his body. When therefore he was raised from the dead, his disciples remembered that he had said this; and they believed the scripture and the word which Jesus had spoken.

John has clearly developed the incident quite differently from Mark, just as he placed it at the start rather than the end of his description of Jesus' life. In John it is the authorities who are challenged to destroy Jesus' body as the symbolic Temple rather than Jesus himself who is symbolically destroying their Temple. But, in any case, destruction and not purification is the point of the debate.

I conclude, therefore, that an *action* and *saying* involving the Temple's symbolic destruction goes back to the historical Jesus. The *action* was as described in Mark and John; the *saying* was something like that in the *Gospel of Thomas*. That *saying* was developed and interpreted, in Mark and John, through appended but different biblical references, but those applications are later explanations of an action considered enigmatic to begin with and rendered even more so by the Temple's actual destruction in 70 C.E.. But even if that incident is historical, did it lead directly to Jesus' arrest and execution? There is clearly no such connection in the *Gospel of Thomas* 71. There is, however, equally clearly, a connection in Mark 11:18:

And the chief priests and the scribes heard it and sought a way to destroy him; for they feared him, because all the multitude was astonished at his teaching.

What about John? On the one hand, he locates the incident at the very start of Jesus' life, long before the arrest and crucifixion. But, on the other, it is immediately connected to that death, in a somewhat tortuous manner. Read it again in the text above. Notice the sudden shift from Jesus destroying the Temple to his hearers destroying his body. I think the reason for that shift is that John knows that the incident provoked Jesus' arrest but placed it programmatically at the start of Jesus' public life so that its long shadow would arch forward over everything else.

Here then is my historical reconstruction of what happened. I am not sure that poor Galilean peasants went up and down regularly to the Temple feasts. I think it quite possible that Jesus went to Jerusalem only once and that the spiritual and economic egalitarianism he preached in Galilee exploded in indignation at the Temple as the seat and symbol of all that was nonegalitarian, patronal, and even oppressive on both the religious and the political level. Jesus' symbolic destruction simply actualized what he had already said in his teachings, effected in his healings, and realized in his mission of open commensality. But the confined and tinderbox atmosphere of the Temple at Passover, especially under Pilate, was not the same as the atmosphere in the rural reaches of Galilee, even under Antipas, and the soldiers moved in immediately to arrest him.

∞ James the Just

If you think Jesus went regularly to Jerusalem, you must explain why something happened in the Temple only that one time. If you think, like I do, that he went there only once, you must explain why he went there that one time.

There are two connections between Jesus and Jerusalem apart from any pilgrimage relations with the Temple. One is his relationship with Mary, Martha, and Lazarus at Bethany, on Jerusalem's outskirts. Please do not think I am imagining Jesus going there to raise Lazarus from the dead; you have already seen how I interpret that narrative. But that family is very special. *It is a family of siblings; we never hear of a father or mother.*

How did Jesus know this family? Where did he meet them? Does that relationship have anything to do with his presence in Jerusalem that one time?

There is another and more significant possibility that takes us back to James the brother of Jesus. Josephus tells us about the execution of James, in *Antiquities* 20.197–203 (my italics):

> Upon learning of the death of Festus, Caesar sent Albinus to Judaea as procurator. The king removed Joseph from the high priesthood, and bestowed the succession to this office upon the son of Ananus, who was likewise called Ananus. . . . The younger Ananus . . . was rash in his temper and unusually daring. He followed the school of the Sadducees, who are indeed more heartless than any of the other Jews . . . when they sit in judgement. Possessed of such a character, Ananus thought that he had a favourable opportunity because Festus was dead and Albinus was still on the way. And so he convened the judges of the Sanhedrin and brought before them a man named James, the brother of Jesus who was called the Christ, and certain others. He accused them of having *transgressed the law* and delivered them up to be stoned. Those of the inhabitants of the city who were considered the most fair-minded and who were *strict in observance of the law* were offended at this. They therefore secretly sent to King Agrippa urging him, for Ananus had not even been correct in his first step, to order him to desist from any further such actions. Certain of them even went to meet Albinus, who was on his way from Alexandria, and informed him that Ananus had no authority to convene the Sanhedrin without his consent. Convinced by these words, Albinus angrily wrote to Ananus threatening to take vengeance upon him. King Agrippa, because of Ananus' action, deposed him from the high priesthood which he had held for three months and replaced him with Jesus the son of Damascus.

Because he had used the interlude between the departure of Festus and the arrival of his replacement, Albinus, to have James and some others put to death in 62 C.E., the High Priest Ananus the Younger brought down on himself the wrath of the Herodian ruler Agrippa II and the Roman governor Albinus. Josephus tells us that Ananus was a Sadducee, but he was much more than that. His father, Ananus the Elder, was High Priest from 6 to 15 C.E., and is known to us from the gospels as Annas. The elder Ananus was father-in-law of Joseph Caiaphas, High Priest from 18 to 36 C.E., a figure also known to us from the gospels. He was furthermore the father of five other High Priests—Eleazar, Jonathan, Theophilus, Matthias, and Ananus the Younger, of present concern. Finally, he was the grandfather of Matthias, High Priest in 65 C.E.. The immediate family of Ananus the Elder had dominated the high priesthood for most of the preceding decades, with eight High Priests in sixty years, yet the execution of James resulted in the deposition of Ananus the Younger after only three months in office. An abstract illegality could hardly have obtained such a reaction, so James must have had powerful, important, and even politically organized friends in Jerusalem. Who were they? Josephus's phrase "inhabitants . . . who were strict in observance of the law" probably means Pharisees. Was James a Pharisee? And, more important, how long had he been in Jerusalem? We know for sure, as seen earlier, that he was there by about 38 C.E., when Paul first met him. Did he come there only after the execution of Jesus, *or had he been there long before it?* I realize how tentative all this is, but much more explanation for James's presence and standing in Jerusalem needs be given than is usually offered. Did he leave Nazareth long before and become both literate and involved within scribal circles in Jerusalem? Could his earlier presence there and Jesus' (single?) visit to Jerusalem be somehow connected with this unit in John 7:3–5?

> His brothers said to him, "Leave here and go to Judea, that your disciples may see the works you are doing. For no man works in secret if he seeks to be known openly. If you do these things, show yourself to the world." For even his brothers did not believe in him.

All of that is terribly hypothetical, and I am quite well aware that it is. But we need to think much more about James and how he reached such status among Jewish circles that, on the one hand, he had to be executed by a Sadducee and that, on the other, his death could cause a High Priest to be deposed after only three months in office. Above all, was he in Jerusalem long before Jesus' death, and did his presence there invite, provoke, challenge Jesus' only journey to Jerusalem?

∞ That Charming Pontius Pilate

What do we know about Pontius Pilate apart, for the moment, from the New Testament gospels? After the division of Herod the Great's kingdom between his three sons in 4 B.C.E., Archelaus ruled for only a decade over its southern and central parts—Idumea, Judea, and Samaria. After Augustus deposed him in 6 C.E., his territories came under the direct control of a Roman governor while Galilee remained under indirect Roman control through Antipas, an indigenous client ruler. From that date until 44 C.E., when all of the Jewish homeland came under direct Roman control, seven second-rank governors or prefects governed those central and southern areas from Caesarea, on the coast. They had only auxiliary forces, but legal and military intervention was always possible from the first-rank governor or legate of Syria backed by his four legions. A legion, by the way, consisted of six thousand men at full strength, primarily heavy infantry but with some scouting cavalry and about sixty pieces of artillery for hurling arrows or stones. As fighting engineers, they were at their absolute best moving straight across any terrain toward a set and fixed goal, building roads, bridges, and forts and besieging or defending objectives.

The Roman administration of Judea depended, of course, on the cooperation of the native Jewish aristocracy and especially on the collaboration of the Temple's High Priest, whom the Romans deposed and replaced with a regularity calculated to keep such collaboration if not fervent at least secure. Pontius Pilate governed for ten years, from 26 to 36 C.E., and Joseph Caiaphas remained as High Priest from 18 to 36 C.E. No other High Priest lasted anywhere near as long as he did, and only Valerius Gratus, his predecessor as governor, outlasted Pilate. And that, in the circumstances, is probably not a compliment for either Pilate or Caiaphas. Both of them, in any case, were removed from office at the same time, and that probably reflects pejoratively on their preceding cooperation and administration, even from the Roman point of view. We now have, by the way, archaeological as well as literary evidence for both those worthies. In 1961, in the amphitheater at Caesarea, a dedicatory stone to the emperor Tiberius was found bearing the inscription "Pontius Pilate, prefect of Judea." That is surely and certainly our Pilate. And in 1990, just south of Jerusalem, a tomb was discovered containing an elaborately decorated ossuary with the name, in Hebrew, "Joseph son of Caiaphas," inscribed twice upon it. That is possibly and plausibly our Caiaphas.

Earlier, discussing overt peasant Jewish resistance to Roman imperialism before the First Roman-Jewish War broke out in 66 C.E., we looked at *apocalyptic prophets* and *messianic claimants*. There were also several instances of *massed protesters* in that same period, large groups of ordinary people who gathered at Jerusalem or Caesarea to complain about some action or demand relief of some grievance. Josephus recounts two such incidents during Pilate's governorship and Philo narrates one, in his *Embassy to Gaius* 199–305, but it is most likely a simple variant of Josephus's first story.

The first episode is that of the *Military Standards,* as told in the twin versions of *War* 2.169 and *Antiquities* 18.56. I quote the latter account:

> Now Pilate, the procurator of Judaea, when he brought his army from Caesarea and removed it to winter quarters in Jerusalem, took a bold step in subversion of the Jewish practices, by introducing into the city the busts [embossed medallions] of the emperor that were attached to the military standards, for our law forbids the making of images. It was for this reason that the previous procurators, when they entered the city, used standards that had no such ornaments. Pilate was the first to bring the images into Jerusalem and set them up, doing it without the knowledge of the people, for he entered at night.

The ordinary people of Jerusalem went to Caesarea, gathering country reinforcements as they went, and implored Pilate to remove the offending emblems. He refused, and "they fell prostrate around his house and for five whole days and nights remained motionless in that position" (*War* 2.171). To break this sit-down strike, Pilate hid his soldiers in the stadium, had the demonstrators come there for an audience, and then threatened them with immediate death unless they submitted. When all immediately and simultaneously offered to accept martyrdom, Pilate was himself forced to submit rather than massacre so many.

The second incident is that of the *Temple Funds*, again with twin versions in *War* 2.175-176 and *Antiquities* 18.60-62. Here is the former narrative.

> He provoked a fresh uproar by expending upon the construction of an aqueduct the sacred treasure known as Corbonas; the water was brought from a distance of 400 furlongs. . . . He, foreseeing the tumult, had interspersed among the crowd a troop of his soldiers, armed but disguised in civilian dress with orders not to use their swords, but to beat any rioters with cudgels.

The logic of that tactic derives from Pilate's previous experience. In the *Military Standards* incident he had suddenly opposed a Jewish crowd with armed soldiers and, confronted with their readiness for mass unresisting martyrdom, had been forced to back down. In the *Temple Funds* case he infiltrated the crowd with disguised soldiers, planning to stampede the crowd into violent action or headlong flight. Both events probably happened in relatively close proximity to one another, soon after Pilate first became governor. It is clear in any case that Pilate had simple methods of crowd control.

There is also a third incident concerning Pilate, but this one concerns *apocalyptic prophets* rather than *massed protesters*. Those former resisters were Jews, and they reenacted the archetypal Mosaic deliverance by moving from the desert, across the Jordan, and into the Promised Land. This present case concerns not Jews but Samaritans, descendants of Jewish peasants and Assyrian colonists from the eighth century B.C.E. They had their own Temple on Mount Gerizim, in opposition to the Jewish one on Mount Zion in Jerusalem, and *their* Mosaic reenactment involved finding the original sacred vessels that would vindicate their Temple over its rival. The incident of the *Samaritan Prophet* is told only in *Antiquities* 18.85-87.

> A man who made light of mendacity and in all his designs catered to the mob, rallied them [the Samaritans], bidding

them go in a body with him to Mount Gerizim, which in their belief is the most sacred of mountains. He assured them that on their arrival he would show them the sacred vessels which were buried there, where Moses had deposited them. His hearers, viewing this tale as plausible, appeared *in arms*. They posted themselves in a certain village named Tirathana, and, as they planned to climb the mountain in a great multitude, they welcomed to their ranks the new arrivals who kept coming. But before they could ascend, Pilate blocked their projected route up the mountain with a detachment of cavalry and heavy-armed infantry, who in the encounter with the firstcomers in the village slew some in a pitched battle and put the others to flight. Many prisoners were taken, of whom Pilate put to death the principal leaders and those who were most influential among the fugitives.

Once again, as with earlier cases of apocalyptic or millennial prophets, Josephus's rhetoric turns particularly nasty. This incident, however, ended Pilate's governorship. Afterward, according to *Antiquities* 18.88–89, the Samaritan authorities appealed against Pilate to his superior, the Syrian legate Vitellius, "for, they said, it was not as rebels against the Romans but as refugees from the persecution of Pilate that they had met at Tirathana." Vitellius found in their favor and sent Pilate to explain his conduct before Tiberius in Rome, where the emperor's timely death saved his life if not his career. Vitellius also, according to 18.95, "removed from his sacred office the high priest Joseph surnamed Caiaphas."

There is, however, something wrong with or at least missing from that story. If the crowd was really "in arms," it is hard to see what Pilate did wrong, from a Roman point of view, and it is equally hard to see how the Samaritan authorities were able to persuade Vitellius to dismiss him. However, if they were not armed and had only apocalyptic rather than military intentions, the crowd at Tirathana could plausibly be described as "refugees" and the action of Pilate as excessive cruelty. I am inclined, therefore, to doubt quite strongly the veracity of Josephus's "in arms," and for three reasons. One, as just seen, is the Samaritan and Roman reaction. Another is the general expectation that apocalyptic prophets and their followers will be unarmed since they expect divine power to solve a sociocultural situation already far beyond human redress. It is not so much that they are pacifists as that all necessary violence will be of transcendental rather than human derivation. Their part is to reenact the ritual act that invokes the eschatological scenario— to jump-start, as it were, the apocalypse. Finally, there is the much more pejorative view of the Samaritans in the later *Antiquities* as compared with that in the earlier *War*. Pilate, in other words, was dismissed from office for excessive cruelty or unnecessary brutality, even by Roman imperial standards. And we may well suspect the same reason for Caiaphas's simultaneous dismissal.

My point is not that Pilate was a monster. He was an ordinary second-rank Roman governor with no regard for Jewish religious sensitivities and with brute force as his normal solution to even unarmed protesting or resisting crowds. Like any Roman governor he was also careful to distinguish between the rich and the poor, the powerful and the powerless, the important and the unimportant, the aristocrat and the peasant.

∞ Barabbas Was *Not* a Robber

In the New Testament gospel accounts Pilate is completely just and fair. He wished to acquit Jesus but was forced, reluctantly and against his will, to crucify him because of the insistence of Jewish authority and Jerusalem crowd. And he held lengthy discussions with Jesus during which he repeatedly proclaimed his innocence of any crime worthy of death. Here, for example, is Mark 15:6–15:

> Now at the festival he used to release a prisoner for them, anyone for whom they asked. Now a man called Barabbas was in prison with the rebels who had committed murder during the insurrection. So the crowd came and began to ask Pilate to do for them according to his custom. Then he answered them, "Do you want me to release for you the King of the Jews?" For he realized that it was out of jealousy that the chief priests had handed him over. But the chief priests stirred up the crowd to have him release Barabbas for them instead. Pilate spoke to them again,

"Then what do you wish me to do with the man you call the King of the Jews?" They shouted back, "Crucify him!" Pilate asked them, "Why, what evil has he done?" But they shouted all the more, "Crucify him!" So Pilate, wishing to satisfy the crowd, released Barabbas for them; and after flogging Jesus, he handed him over to be crucified.

I judge that narrative to be absolutely unhistorical, a creation most likely of Mark himself, and for two reasons. One is that its picture of Pilate, meekly acquiescent to a shouting crowd, is exactly the opposite of what we know about him from Josephus. Brutal crowd control was his specialty. Another is that a custom such as *open* amnesty, the release of *any* requested prisoner at the time of the Passover festival, is against any administrative wisdom. Philo, for example, writing about a decade later, described what decent governors did for crucified criminals on festival occasions. They could postpone the execution until after the festival, or they could allow burial of the crucified by his family. He says nothing whatsoever about abrogation on demand. In *Against Flaccus* 81–84, an indictment of Flaccus, Roman governor of Egypt, because of the anti-Jewish pogroms during the emperor Caligula's birthday on 31 August 38 C.E., he writes:

Rulers who conduct their government as they should and do not pretend to honour but do really honour their benefactors make a practice of not punishing any condemned person until those notable celebrations in honour of the birthdays of the illustrious Augustan house are over. . . . I have known cases when on the eve of a holiday of this kind, people who have been crucified have been taken down and their bodies delivered to their kinsfolk, because it was thought well to give them burial and allow them the ordinary rites. For it was meet that the dead also should have the advantage of some kind treatment upon the birthday of the emperor and also that the sanctity of the festival should be maintained. But Flaccus gave no orders to take down those who had died on the cross. Instead he ordered the crucifixion of the living, to whom the season offered a short-lived though not permanent reprieve in order to postpone the punishment though not to remit it altogether.

But if the Barabbas incident did not actually happen, why did Mark create such a story? It does not seem, like the Triumphal Entrance incident, to have been created to show prophetic fulfillment. What then was its purpose?

Apart from massed protesters, apocalyptic prophets, and messianic claimants, there was one final group of peasant resisters in the first-century Jewish homeland. Josephus repeatedly mentions *rebel bandits*—for example, peasants forced off their farms who took to the hills and banditry rather than to the roads and beggary. In his classic study of that subject, Eric J. Hobsbawm calls them *social bandits* to distinguish them from plain robbers.

> They are peasant outlaws whom the lord and state regard as criminals, but who remain within peasant society, and are considered by their people as heroes, as champions, avengers, fighters for justice, perhaps even leaders of liberation, and in any case as men to be admired, helped and supported. . . . [Social banditry] is found in one or other of its three main forms . . . the noble robber or Robin Hood, the primitive resistance fighter or guerilla unit . . . and possibly the terror-bringing avenger.*

The rebel bandits or outlaws that Josephus speaks of were probably not all as nice as the sainted Robin Hood (who was Prince not of *Thieves* but of *Outlaws,* by the way). It is necessary neither to romanticize nor canonize them but to understand that their increasing presence always indicates that the oppressed lower classes are being pushed below even subsistence level and are being forced into armed resistance, however sporadic, ineffective, or desperate. In Greek the technical term for such a rebel bandit is *lēstes,* and that is exactly what Barabbas is called. He was a bandit, a rebel, an insurgent, a freedom fighter—depending always, of course, on your point of view. But Mark was written soon after the terrible consummation of the First Roman-Jewish War in 70 C.E., when Jerusalem and its Temple were totally destroyed. We already saw how the Zealots, a loose coalition of bandit groups and peasant rebels forced into

---

* Eric J. Hobsbawm, *Bandits,* 2d ed. (Middlesex: Penguin Books, 1985; first published 1969), pages 17 and 20.

Jerusalem by the tightening Roman encirclement, fought within the city for overall control of the rebellion in 68 C.E. There, says Mark, was Jerusalem's choice: it chose Barabbas over Jesus, an armed rebel over an unarmed savior. His narrative about Barabbas was, in other words, a symbolic dramatization of Jerusalem's fate, *as he saw it*. Finally, whenever such stories are judged to be authorial creations, their author's purpose is seldom just literary embellishment. It is usually either *symbolic dramatization,* as here (process become event in my earlier terms); or *prophetic fulfillment,* as with the Triumphal Entrance; or both, as with the infancy stories seen in Chapter 1.

That conclusion about the Barabbas incident raises, however, a far wider question. How did Jesus' first followers know so much about his death and burial? How did they know those almost hour-by-hour details given in fairly close and remarkable agreement by all four New Testament gospels and by the *Gospel of Peter* outside the New Testament?

∞ Searching the Scriptures Once Again

Recall, first, how "searching the Scriptures" created Jesus' infancy narratives in Matthew, Luke, and even before them. My heading's "once again" directs you back to that opening section of this book. Recall, second, that I said at the start of this chapter that it was the most difficult one for two reasons. One was the difficulty in looking unswervingly at the horror of torturous crucifixion and possible nonburial. The other is the need to explain where those detailed passion accounts came from and how they were constructed. But first, one brief word of background. The Jewish sect of the Essenes, whose home at Qumran was destroyed during the First Roman-Jewish War and whose hidden library has given us the Dead Sea Scrolls, applied prophetic writings from the Hebrew Scriptures to their own past history and present situation. They were a priest-led group who withdrew from Jerusalem's Temple to a settlement on the Dead Sea's northwest coast. They judged that the Temple was polluted after the usurpation of the high priesthood by Jewish rulers of the Hasmonean dynasty, Jonathan and Simon, between 152 and 134 B.C.E. Their biblical applications evince a dense intertextual weave between old and new, past and present—the work of skilled exegetes and learned scribes where intense concentration is often needed to distinguish Bible from Commentary. Their applications come in two main types. One is *sequential exegesis,* where a certain biblical text from one single book is given verse by verse, with commentary or interpretation after each verse. The other is *anthological exegesis,* where an anthology or collection of biblical verses from different books is interspersed with commentary or interpretation after each verse. Let me give you an example of this second type—just to make your head spin a little. It was found in Cave 4 at Qumran, where tens or even hundreds of thousands of fragments from about six hundred manuscripts were discovered in 1952. It has been called a "Midrash (or Commentary) on the Last Days," or, more prosaically, 4Q Florilegium or 4Q174. I give the biblical texts in italics and enclose their locations in square brackets. But imagine, as you are reading, how this would have read or sounded originally, without any such distinctions.

> Explanation of *How blessed is the man who does not walk in the counsel of the wicked* [Psalm 1:1]. Interpreted, this saying [concerns] those who turn aside from the way [of the people]; as it is written in the book of Isaiah the Prophet concerning the last days, *It came to pass that [the Lord turned me aside, as with a mighty hand, from walking in the way of] this people* [Isaiah 8:11]. They are those of whom it is written in the book of Ezekiel the Prophet, *The Levites [strayed far from me, following] their idols* [Ezekiel 44:10]. They are the sons of Zadok who [seek their own] counsel and follow [their own inclination] apart from the Council of the Community.

Those interwoven biblical texts are applied to the strife between the Temple priesthood, "the sons of Zadok" or Sadducees, and the Qumran Essenes or "Council of the Community." But as text merges with text and as event merges with citation, it could easily get extremely difficult to know where anything starts and something else finishes. Prophecy and history could begin to interweave, mutually influencing and even creating each other.

Obviously, of course, all such activity demands a most sophisticated scribal and exegetical capability. This is not at all the work of illiterate peasants, no matter how orally skilled or performatively brilliant. It is exclusively the domain of text and book, literacy and exegesis, reading, interpretation, and commentary. But all the evidence is that there were such people among Jesus' followers, probably at Jerusalem and probably at a very early stage.

My proposal is that Jesus' first followers knew almost nothing whatsoever about the details of his crucifixion, death, or burial. What we have now in those detailed passion accounts is not *history remembered* but *prophecy historicized*. And it is necessary to be very clear on what I mean here by *prophecy*. I do not mean texts, events, or persons that predicted or foreshadowed the future, that projected themselves *forward* toward a distant fulfillment. I mean such units sought out *backward*, as it were, sought out *after* the events of Jesus' life were already known and his followers declared that texts from the Hebrew Scriptures had been written with him in mind. Prophecy, in this sense, is known after rather than before the fact.

I distinguish three stages in the development of the passion stories. One is the *historical passion*—what actually happened to Jesus, what anyone present would have seen. That he was crucified is as sure as anything historical can ever be, since both Josephus and Tacitus, in texts to be seen in the final chapter, agree with the Christian accounts on at least that basic fact. Next comes the *prophetic passion*—the search by scribally learned followers from, in Lenski's stratification, the Retainer rather than the Peasant class to find basis or justification in the Hebrew Scriptures for such a shocking eventuality. How could God's Chosen One have been so treated, and if he had been so treated, could he still be God's Chosen One? Finally came the *narrative passion*—the placing of such prophetic fulfillments into a sequential narrative with its origins well hidden within a plausible historical framework. I want you to understand at least the plausibility of that claim, so rather than looking at the entire story in general, I look at one incident in particular. If this does not persuade you, more of the same will probably not do so either.

In testing this hypothesis, forget all you know about Easter Sunday from accounts written in our gospels between forty and sixty years after the event. Imagine, instead, learned followers of Jesus beginning to search their scriptures *immediately* after the crucifixion. Imagine what preceded any writings of twenty, forty, sixty years later and without which they might never have existed. Imagine, in other words, the thirties in certain circles of the Kingdom movement.

Locate yourself on the first Holy Saturday, *a day that is going to last about, say, five or ten years.* You are among certain followers of Jesus who are not at all peasants, are not at all interested in miracles, are not at all interested in collecting, preserving, or creating Jesus sayings, but are very, very interested in studying the scriptures to understand your past, reclaim your present, and envisage your future. What do you find? What do you produce? You know, first of all, exactly what you are looking for. You search for texts that show death not as end but as beginning, not as divine judgment but as divine plan, not as ultimate defeat but as postponed victory for Jesus. You are, therefore, especially looking for texts with a certain duality, a certain hint of two stages, two moments, two phases, or two levels.

One such text is the ritual of the Jewish Day of Atonement, which has *two* goats, one driven out into the desert carrying the sins of the people and the other presented for sacrifice in the Temple. The basic text is in Leviticus 16:7–10 and 21–22, describing the ritual as mandated by God to Aaron, the first High Priest.

> He [Aaron] shall take the two goats and set them before the Lord at the entrance of the tent of meeting; and Aaron shall cast lots on the two goats, one lot for the Lord and the other lot for Azazel. Aaron shall present the goat on which the lot fell for the Lord, and offer it as a sin offering; but the goat on which the lot fell for Azazel shall be presented alive before the Lord to make atonement over it, that it may be sent away into the wilderness to Azazel. . . . Then Aaron shall lay both his hands on the head of the live goat, and confess over it all the iniquities of the people of Israel, and all their transgressions, all their sins, putting them on the head of the goat, and sending it away into the wilderness by means of someone designated for the task.

The goat shall bear on itself all their iniquities to a barren region; and the goat shall be set free in the wilderness.

You, as a Jerusalem Jew, have probably seen that actual ritual and are not just imagining it from the biblical text alone. We, however, also know four precise details about that ritual's actual process from the *Mishnah*, the rabbinical code of law organized around 200 C.E. by Judah the Patriarch. The two goats had to be alike and equal; scarlet wool was placed on the scapegoat's head; it was abused by the people as it was hurried toward the desert; and before it was killed there, the scarlet wool was attached between a rock and its horns. You would have known that the scarlet wool recalled Isaiah 1:18 and God's promise: "Though your sins are like scarlet, they shall be like snow; though they are red like crimson, they shall become like wool." And, as long as you were thinking about Isaiah, that abuse in which the people symbolically and emphatically transferred their sins to the poor doomed animal reminded you of Isaiah 50:6: "I gave my back to those who struck me, and my cheeks to those who pulled out the beard; I did not hide my face from insult and spitting." You knew that the people spat their sins onto the scapegoat and that they used reeds to poke and hurry the poor animal toward its desert fate. Such spitting and poking or piercing were not, of course, just cruelty but a physical participation in the ritual itself.

Your choice of the Day of Atonement and its twin goats was not, to be quite frank, a very happy one. Jesus could easily be interpreted as the scapegoat, the goat driven and killed outside the city as an atonement for the sins of the people. But that second goat is also sacrificed, albeit in the Temple itself, and that sounds just like another but different version of the passion. Something more was clearly needed, and it was there, as far as we can see, from the beginning.

As you read Leviticus 16 or recalled the ritual you must have noted that Aaron is told in 16:23–24 to change his garments:

> Then Aaron shall enter the tent of meeting, and shall take off the linen vestments that he put on when he went into the holy place, and shall leave them there. He shall bathe his body in water in a holy place, and put on his vestments; then he shall come out and offer his burnt offering

and the burnt offering of the people, making atonement
for himself and for the people.

And that change of garments by the High Priest Aaron easily
reminded you of Zechariah 3:3–5, where, in the late sixth century B.C.E. just after the Jewish leadership had returned from the
Babylonian Exile, the High Priest Joshua is imagined having his
garments changed by an angel:

> Now Joshua was dressed with filthy clothes as he stood
> before the angel. The angel said to those who were stand-
> ing before him, "Take off his filthy clothes." And to him he
> said, "See, I have taken your guilt away from you, and I
> will clothe you with festal apparel [in Greek: a long robe]."
> And I said, "Let them put a clean turban on his head." So
> they put a clean turban on his head and clothed him with
> the apparel; and the angel of the Lord was standing by.

Now your search is starting to get somewhere. Of the twin
goats, the first or scapegoat's death worked best as a prophetic
model for Jesus' execution; the second was a little redundant.
But those twin garments, one filthy and one clean, worked
much better as a prophetic *type* (the technical term for such a
model) of Jesus, first dishonored at the cross, and then triumphant at his second coming. And, as long as you were in
Zechariah, and thinking along those lines, it was easy enough to
go from 3:3–5 on to 12:10:

> And I will pour out a spirit of compassion and suppli-
> cation on the house of David and the inhabitants of
> Jerusalem, so that, when they look on the one whom they
> have pierced, they shall mourn for him, as one mourns for
> an only child, and weep bitterly over him, as one weeps
> over a firstborn.

You have now arched beautifully and completely from past to
future, from passion to parousia, from Jesus crucified to Jesus
triumphant, from the day of piercing to the day, at the end of the
world, when those who pierced Jesus would mourn both for
him and for what they had done.

I now give you a Christian document that shows the entire
exegetical procedure. It combines all four strata: the *two goats*
of Leviticus 16 from the Bible and *Mishnah* (which I indicate
with underlined type); the *crowning and robing* of Zechariah 3

(in boldface type); the *seeing and piercing* of Zechariah 12 (in boldface italic type); and the *spitting* of Isaiah 50 (in ordinary italic type). These stata are all laminated into one demonstration that Jesus' past crucifixion pointed inevitably toward his future victory. The text is to be found in the *Epistle of Barnabas,* a book written toward the end of the first century C.E. but showing no knowledge of the New Testament gospels. The section at 7:6–12 is developed through four questions based on the actual ritual of the Day of Atonement:

> Note what was commanded: "Take two goats, goodly and alike, and offer them, and let the priest take the one as a burnt offering for sins."

(1) But what are they to do with the other?

> "The other," he says, "is accursed." Notice how the type of Jesus is manifested: "*And do ye all spit on it, and goad [pierce] it,* and bind the scarlet wool about its head, and so let it be cast into the desert." And when it is so done, he who takes the goat into the wilderness drives it forth, and takes away the wool, and puts it upon a shrub [instead of the rock]. . . .

(2) What does this mean?

> Listen: "The first goat is for the altar, but the other is accursed," and note that the one that is accursed is **crowned** because then "*they will see him on that day*" with the long scarlet robe "**down to the feet**" on his body, and they will say, "Is not this he whom we once crucified and rejected *and pierced and spat upon?* Of a truth it was he who then said that he was the Son of God."

(3) But how is he like the goat?

> For this reason: "The goats shall be alike, beautiful, and a pair," in order that when they see him come at that time they may be astonished at the likeness of the goat. See then the type of Jesus destined to suffer.

(4) But why is it that they put the wool in the middle of the thorns?

> It is a type of Jesus placed in the Church, because whoever wishes to take away the scarlet wool must suffer much because the thorns are terrible and he can gain it only

through pain. Thus he says, "Those who will see me, and attain to my kingdom must lay hold of me through pain and suffering."

If, by the way, our eyes or heads are now spinning, that is part of the process. We are persuaded of the validity of the argument by the sheer difficulty in taking it apart. It is almost easier just to listen and nod or read and agree than to analyze, explore, and disentangle.

Exegetical laminations such as the above were what certain learned followers of Jesus were creating in the years immediately after his death, and notice that it was passion and parousia rather than passion and resurrection on which they were concentrating. They were interested in linking the departure of Jesus on the cross to his return at the end of the world. That Day of Atonement symbolism, and other similar examples, are what the *prophetic passion* looked like for years and continued to look like for skilled exegetes long after the next stage, the *narrative passion*, developed and separated from it.

How did that next stage develop? The intertextual dexterity of the *Epistle of Barnabas* 7 is quite brilliant, and it is also supportive or probative, from the Hebrew Scriptures, for the passion-parousia destiny of Jesus. But it can hardly be called a good story or even a narrative sequence, let alone a historical memoir. Something more is absolutely necessary to change exegesis into story; some model is required to change argument into narrative. Compare, for example and in contrast, the following historical anecdote. Philo of Alexandria, in *Against Flaccus* 32–39, recounts how the Alexandrian mob mocked the Jewish Agrippa I when, having been made king of the Jewish homeland by the emperor Caligula, he sailed home via Alexandria in August of 38 C.E.

> There was a certain lunatic Carabas, whose madness was not of the fierce and savage kind, which is dangerous both to the madmen themselves and those who approach them, but of the easy-going, gentler style. He spent day and night in the streets naked, shunning neither heat nor cold, made game of by the children and the lads who were idling about. The rioters drove the poor fellow into the gymnasium and set him up on high to be seen by all and put on

his head a sheet of byblos spread out wide for a diadem, clothed the rest of his body with a rug for a royal robe, while someone who had noticed a piece of the native papyrus thrown away in the road gave it to him for his sceptre. And when in some theatrical farce he had received the insignia of kingship and had been tricked out as a king, young men carrying rods on their shoulders as spearmen stood on either side of him in imitation of a bodyguard. Then others approached him, some pretending to salute him, others to sue for justice, others to consult him on state affairs. Then from the multitude standing round him there rang out a tremendous shout hailing him as Marin, which is said to be the name for "lord" in Syria. For they knew that Agrippa was both a Syrian by birth and had a great piece of Syria over which he was king.

Carabas's mockery as pseudo-king involves not physical abuse or torture but rather a theatrical mime with throne, crown, robe, scepter, bodyguard, salutation, consultation, and especially his proclamation as Lord.

Supposing, now, that one took a prophetic exegesis such as that of *Barnabas* 7 and a historical story such as that of poor Carabas and fused them together. One would get, I propose, a story like that in Mark 15:16–20:

Then the soldiers led him into the courtyard of the palace (that is, the governor's headquarters); and they called together the whole cohort. And they clothed him in a purple cloak; and after twisting some thorns into a crown, they put it on him. And they began saluting him, "Hail, King of the Jews!" They struck his head with a reed, spat upon him, and knelt down in homage to him. After mocking him, they stripped him of the purple cloak and put his own clothes on him. Then they led him out to crucify him.

Let me focus the argument a little. Compare the *crown (of wool) among thorns* at the end of the *Epistle of Barnabas* 7 text given earlier with the *crown of thorns* on Jesus' head here. I can easily imagine a development from former to latter but not the reverse. In fact, I cannot conceive of a human imagination reading Mark 15:16–20 and developing *Epistle of Barnabas* 7 out of it, but the reverse process, with a little help from the Carabas farce, is quite comprehensible. Or again, that spitting or striking with a reed comes not from what actually happened to Jesus, but from the popular ritual of spitting one's sins out upon the scapegoat and hurrying it toward the desert by poking or striking it with sharp reeds. To prove my hypothesis would demand a similar argument for every incident in our present passion narratives. I have done that in previous scholarly books; here I wanted to look in fine focus at just one paradigmatic example.

My best historical reconstruction of what actually happened is that Jesus was arrested during the Passover festival and those closest to him fled for their own safety. I do not presume at all any high-level consultations between Caiaphas or Pilate about or with Jesus. They would no doubt have agreed before such a festival that fast and immediate action was to be taken against any disturbance and that some examples by crucifixion might be especially useful at the start. I doubt very much if Jewish police and Roman soldiery needed to go too far up the chain of command in handling a Galilean peasant like Jesus. It is hard for us, I repeat, to bring our imagination down low enough to see the casual brutality with which he was probably taken and executed. The details in our gospels are, in any case, *prophecy historicized* and not *history memorized.*

∞ A Respected Member of the Council

We know, from both literary and archaeological evidence, that a crucified body could be given back to its family for burial. Philo mentioned that as a possibility on certain festal occasions, and Yehochanan's corpse was honorably buried in the family tomb. There were also found, by the way, in Ossuary 1 of Tomb 4 at Giv'at ha-Mivtar, the bones of a sixteen- to seventeen-year-old male who had been burned to death on the rack and his bones left there long enough to bear the marks forever. In a patronal society, of course, even such burial concessions would have taken at least some influence—at least the ability to approach, indirectly if not directly, the powers involved. During the destruction of Jerusalem in 70 C.E., for instance, Josephus, who was present as an aide, interpreter, and client to the Roman commanding general Titus, tells us this story in the autobiographical appendix to his *Jewish Antiquities* known as the *Life*. In this document, defending his operations as Jewish general and Roman prisoner during the First Roman-Jewish War of 66–73 C.E., he writes in *Life* 75:

> When I . . . saw many prisoners who had been crucified, and recognized three of my acquaintances among them, I was cut to the heart and came and told Titus with tears what I had seen. He gave orders immediately that they should be taken down and receive the most careful treatment. Two of them died in the physicians' hands; the third survived.

In general, however, if one had influence, one was not crucified, and if one was crucified, one would not have influence enough to obtain burial. It would have been impossible, without influence or bribery, to obtain a crucified's corpse. And it might also be very dangerous to request it, lest even familial association with a condemned criminal be judged as part of the problem and handled accordingly.

In normal circumstances the soldiers guarded the body until death and thereafter it was left for carrion crow, scavenger dog, or other wild beasts to finish the brutal job. That nonburial consummated authority's dreadful warning to any observer and every passerby. Deuteronomy 21:22–23, however, as noted in this chapter's epigraph from Martin Hengel, gave this command:

> When someone is convicted of a crime punishable by death and is executed, and you hang him on a tree, his corpse must not remain all night upon the tree; you shall bury him that same day, for anyone hung on a tree is under God's curse. You must not defile the land that the Lord your God is giving you for possession.

Notice, by the way, that *prior* execution followed by being hung (dead) on a tree is in question there. The hanging is not to kill the condemned person but for ultimate dishonor and public warning. In such a situation removal by nightfall makes sense. In the case of actual crucifixion it makes much less sense since it could be late in the day when execution took place.

In early June of 1967 the Jewish archaeologist Yigael Yadin obtained possession of the largest of all the Dead Sea Scrolls. It had been discovered in Cave 11 at Qumran and had been copied around 50 C.E., although the original may have been composed as early as 150–125 B.C.E., after the Essenes had broken with the Sadducees, departed from Jeruslaem for Qumran, and left the Sadducees in control of the Temple. It is twenty-seven feet long, contains sixty-six columns of text, and is called the *Temple Scroll* because most of it concerns detailed plans for Jerusalem's purified Temple. It also, however, contains a catalog of certain crimes for which crucifixion is decreed, and in that context Deuteronomy 21:23 is again invoked in column 64, lines 11–13. Biblical injunction and Essene commentary tell us clearly what pious Jews deemed right *if or when* they themselves had control over the Jewish homeland and especially over Jerusalem and its Temple. We cannot, however, immediately conclude that Pilate respected Jewish piety in this regard, although it is possible that he did. Indeed, to the contrary, by telling us what the Qumran Essenes hoped to legislate when and if they regained control of Jerusalem and the Temple, the *Temple Scroll* tells us what was *not being done* when it was composed.

What actually and historically happened to the body of Jesus can best be judged from watching how later Christian accounts slowly but steadily increased the reverential dignity of their burial accounts. But what was there at the beginning that necessitated such an intensive volume of apologetic insistence? If the Romans did not observe the Deuteronomic decree, Jesus' dead body would have been left on the cross for the wild beasts. And his followers, who had fled, would know that. If the Romans did observe the decree, the soldiers would have made certain Jesus was dead and then buried him themselves as part of their job. In either case, his body left on the cross or in a shallow grave barely covered with dirt and stones, the dogs were waiting. And his followers, who had fled, would know that, too. Watch, then, how the horror of that brutal truth is sublimated through hope and imagination into its opposite.

A first example is in the *Gospel of Peter,* a fragmentary text not in the New Testament but discovered about a hundred years ago in Egypt. Here is 5:15–6:21, a section I judge independent of the New Testament gospels. It explicitly refers to the Deuteronomic decree and presumes that those who crucified Jesus took him down from the cross and buried him in compliance with that biblical law.

> Now it was midday and a darkness covered all Judaea. And they became anxious and uneasy lest the sun had already set, since he was still alive. [For] it stands written for them: the sun should not set on one that has been put to death. And one of them said, "Give him to drink gall with vinegar." And they mixed it and gave him to drink [to hurry death by poisoning him]. And they fulfilled all things and completed the measure of their sins on their head. And many went about with lamps, [and] as they supposed that it was night, they went to bed [or: they stumbled]. And the Lord called out and cried, "My power, O power, thou hast forsaken me!" And having said this he was taken up. And at the same hour the veil of the temple in Jerusalem was rent in two. And then the Jews drew the nails from the hands of the Lord and laid him on the earth. And the whole earth shook and there came a great fear.

That text bespeaks a very early Christian hope against hope that those who crucified Jesus would also, in deference to Deuteronomy 21:22–23, have buried him themselves. That is also the beginning of the process not of knowledge but of hope: he was buried, surely, by his enemies? And the answer to the fear that his enemies would not have bothered to do so is: they would have done so, surely, in obedience to biblical law? But once we move from burial by enemies to burial by friends, we no longer hear anything about Deuteronomy 21:22–23. Then it is simply a matter of burial before the Sabbath starts. You need Deuteronomy only to explain why his *enemies* might have buried him.

The dilemma is painfully clear. Political authority had crucified Jesus and was thus against him. But, his followers knew, it also took authority or at least authority's permission to bury him. How could one have it both ways? How could authority be both against and for Jesus at the same time? The trajectory of the burial tradition sought, after that rather negative beginning, to move from burial by enemies to burial by friends, from inadequate and hurried burial to full, complete, and even regal embalming. The first problem was how to create a story in which Jesus was buried by his friends. If they had power, they were not his friends; if they were his friends, they had no power. Mark 15:42–46 solves that dilemma by creating one Joseph of Arimathea:

> When evening had come, and since it was the day of Preparation, that is, the day before the sabbath, Joseph of Arimathea, a respected member of the council, who was also himself waiting expectantly for the kingdom of God, went boldly to Pilate and asked for the body of Jesus. Then Pilate wondered if he were already dead; and summoning the centurion, he asked him whether he had been dead for some time. When he learned from the centurion that he was dead, he granted the body to Joseph. Then Joseph bought a linen cloth, and taking down the body, wrapped it in the linen cloth, and laid it in a tomb that had been hewn out of the rock. He then rolled a stone against the door of the tomb.

The naming of Joseph, as with Barabbas earlier, does not necessarily guarantee historicity. If you are creating a person, it is easy to give him a name as well. But notice what Mark has done. Joseph is both "a respected member of the council"—that is, on the side of those who crucified Jesus—and also "waiting expectantly for the kingdom of God"—that is, on the side of Jesus' followers. Joseph is exactly what is needed to turn the vague hope that *they* would have buried him into a specific and definite event. Moreover, far from a hurried, indifferent, and shallow grave barely covered with stones from which the scavenging dogs would easily and swiftly unbury the body, there is now a rock tomb and a heavy rolling stone for closure and defense.

Matthew and Luke, each using Mark as a source, try to improve on that creation. Its weakest element is how Joseph could be on both sides at the same time. Matthew 27:57–60 solves the ambiguity one way by stressing Joseph's Christian rather than his Jewish credentials:

> When it was evening, there came a rich man from Arimathea, named Joseph, who was also a disciple of Jesus. He went to Pilate and asked for the body of Jesus; then Pilate ordered it to be given to him. So Joseph took

the body and wrapped it in a clean linen cloth and laid it in his own new tomb, which he had hewn in the rock. He then rolled a great stone to the door of the tomb and went away.

That is much simpler. Joseph is now a "disciple of Jesus," but he is also "rich" and that explains why he has access to Pilate. There is nothing at all about him being, as in Mark, "a respected member of the council" that had just condemned Jesus to death. And, furthermore, the tomb is now a "new tomb" so that Jesus is the only body in it.

Luke 23:50–54 focuses on the other half of the Joseph dilemma and explains his Jewish rather than his Christian credentials.

Now there was a good and righteous man named Joseph, who, though a member of the council, had not agreed to their plan and action. He came from the Jewish town of Arimathea, and he was waiting expectantly for the kingdom of God. This man went to Pilate and asked for the body of Jesus. Then he took it down, wrapped it in a linen cloth, and laid it in a rock-hewn tomb where no one had ever been laid. It was the day of Preparation, and the sabbath was beginning.

Luke follows Mark more closely, but he is just as aware as Matthew of the problem created by having Joseph in both camps at the same time. Hence he adds in the explanatory comment that although Joseph was "a member of the council" that had just condemned Jesus, he "had not agreed to their plan and action." He also explicitly emphasizes that "no one had ever yet been laid" in the tomb before Jesus.

This deliberate, almost desperate, but terribly understandable defensiveness about the nonburial of Jesus comes to a magnificent climax in John 19:38–42, which is, in my opinion, dependent on those other gospel accounts just seen. He combines their Joseph of Arimathea with Nicodemus, whom we had met twice earlier in his own gospel:

After these things, Joseph of Arimathea, who was a disciple of Jesus, though a secret one because of his fear of the Jews, asked Pilate to let him take away the body of Jesus. Pilate gave him permission; so he came and removed his

> body. Nicodemus, who had at first come to Jesus by night, also came, bringing a mixture of myrrh and aloes, weighing about a hundred pounds. They took the body of Jesus and wrapped it with the spices in linen cloths, according to the burial custom of the Jews. Now there was a garden in the place where he was crucified, and in the garden there was a new tomb in which no one had ever been laid. And so, because it was the Jewish day of Preparation, and the tomb was nearby, they laid Jesus there.

Joseph is now a secret disciple, and he is accompanied by Nicodemus. Jesus is now fully and even regally buried. This is not a hurried enshrouding but, finally, a complete and appropriate burial according to custom. Finally, that brand-new tomb is now located in a garden, which of course increases its magnificence.

At the start, as history's real terror, were his enemies and the dogs. At the end, as faith's unreal apologetics, were his friends and the spices. But no amount of apologetics can conceal what their intensity only confirms. With regard to the body of Jesus, by Easter Sunday morning, those who cared did not know where it was, and those who knew did not care. Why should even the soldiers themselves remember the death and disposal of a nobody? Still, Matthew 27:19 records that Pilate's wife had troubled dreams the previous night. That never happened, of course, but it was true nonetheless. It was a most propitious time for the Roman Empire to start having nightmares.

SEVEN

How Many Years Was Easter Sunday?

Wʜᴇɴ Narcissus died, the flowers of the field were desolate and asked the river for some drops of water to weep for him. "Oh!" answered the river, "if all my drops of water were tears, I should not have enough to weep for Narcissus myself. I love him." "Oh!" replied the flowers of the field, "how could you not have loved Narcissus? He was beautiful." "Was he beautiful?" said the river. "And who should know better than you? Each day, leaning over your bank, he beheld his beauty in your waters." "If I loved him," replied the river, "it was because, when he leaned over my waters, I saw the reflection of my waters in his eyes."

Oscar Wilde, "The Disciple" (quoted in Richard Ellmann, *Oscar Wilde* [New York: Knopf, 1988])

Charisma as a term expresses less a quality of person than of relationship; it contains the acceptability of a leader by a following, the endorsement of his personality, and the social endowment of power.... *Charisma* is a sociological, and not a psychological concept.... [It] expresses the balance of claim and acceptance—it is not a dynamic, causally explanatory, concept; it relates to an established state of affairs, when the leader is already accepted, not to the power of one man to cause events to move in a particular direction.

> Bryan R. Wilson, *Magic and the Millennium:*
> *A Sociological Study of Religious Movements of*
> *Protest Among Tribal and Third-World Peoples*
> (New York: Harper & Row, 1973)

∞ The Living Jesus

What happened after the death and burial of Jesus is told in the last chapters of the four New Testament gospels. On Easter Sunday morning his tomb was found empty, and by Easter Sunday evening Jesus himself had appeared to his closest followers and all was well once again. Friday was hard, Saturday was long, but by Sunday all was resolved. Is this fact or fiction, history or mythology? Do fiction and mythology crowd closely around the end of the story just as they did around its beginning? And if there is fiction or mythology, on what is it based? I have already argued, for instance, that Jesus' burial by his friends was totally fictional and unhistorical. He was buried, if buried at all, by his enemies, and the necessarily shallow grave would have been easy prey for scavenging animals. We can still glimpse what happened before, behind, and despite those fictional overlays precisely by imagining what they were created to hide. What happened on Easter Sunday? Is that the story of one day? Or of several years? Is that the story of *all* Christians gathered together as a single group in Jerusalem? Or is that the story of but one group among several, maybe of one group who claimed to be the whole?

First of all, *resurrection* is but one way, not the only way, of expressing Christian faith. Second, *apparition*—which involves trance, that altered state of consciousness already looked at in Chapter 4—is but one way, not the only way, of expressing Christian experience. Third, Christian faith experiences the *continuation* of divine empowerment through Jesus, but that continuation began only after his death and burial. Christian faith itself was there beforehand among Jesus' first followers in Lower Galilee, and it continued, developed, and widened across time and space after his execution. It is precisely that *continued* experience of the Kingdom of God as strengthened rather than weakened by Jesus' death that is Christian or Easter faith. And that was not the work of one afternoon. Or one year.

Since the Easter story at the end is, like the Nativity story at the beginning, so engraved on our imagination as factual history rather than fictional mythology, I begin with the two earliest non-Christian accounts of what happened *both before and after* Jesus's execution: a Jewish one from 93–94 C.E., and a Roman one from the 110s or 120s C.E.

The Jewish witness is Flavius Josephus, whom we have met often throughout this book. The problem is that Josephus's account is too good to be true, too confessional to be impartial, too Christian to be Jewish. There are sentences in it that could hardly have been written by a Jewish writer, sentences that assert Christian beliefs, sentences that could have been written only by a Christian believer. Remember that Josephus's works were preserved and copied by Christian rather than Jewish editors; such additions would have been easy to insert. I italicize those later Christian inserts within Josephus's text in *Antiquities* 18:63:

> About this time there lived Jesus, a wise man, *if indeed one ought to call him a man.* For he was one who wrought surprising feats and was a teacher of such people as accept the truth gladly. He won over many Jews and many of the Greeks. *He was the Messiah.* When Pilate, upon hearing him accused by men of the highest standing amongst us, had condemned him to be crucified, those who had in the first place come to love him did not give up their affection for him. *On the third day he appeared to them restored to life, for the prophets of God had prophesied these and countless other marvellous things about him.* And the tribe of the Christians, so called after him, has still to this day not disappeared.

Omit, therefore, those italicized sentences. Without them Josephus's account is carefully and deliberately neutral. He does not want, apparently, to be embroiled in any controversy about this Jesus, and such debate may have been quite possible within circles important to him at the time. So he was cautiously impartial and some later Christian editor delicately Christianized his account, but only to the extent that it was at least plausible and credible for the Jewish Josephus to have written it.

Those Christian insertions, however, should not diminish the importance of Josephus's commentary. That is how Jesus and early Christianity looked to a very prudent, diplomatic, and cosmopolitan Roman Jew in the early last decade of the first century: miracles and teachings, Jews and Greeks, our "men of highest standing" and Pilate, crucifixion and continuation. He did not, of course, mention resurrection, but he did admit that "the tribe of the Christians, so called after him, has still to this day not disappeared."

The pagan Roman witness is Cornelius Tacitus, whom we have also met before. He was writing, in the early decades of the second century, about the decline and fall of Augustus's Julio-Claudian dynasty. He tells, in *Annals* 15.44, how a rumor blamed that dynasty's last emperor, Nero, for the disastrous fire that swept Rome in 64 C.E.:

> Therefore to scotch the rumour, Nero substituted as culprits, and punished with the utmost refinements of cruelty, a class of men, loathed for their vices, whom the crowd styled Christians. Christus, the founder of the name, had undergone the death penalty in the reign of Tiberius, by sentence of the procurator Pontius Pilatus, and the pernicious superstition was checked for the moment, only to break out once more, not merely in Judaea, the home of the disease, but in the capital itself, where all things horrible or shameful in the world collect and find a vogue.

Instead of Josephus's neutral language, we now have Tacitus's intensely pejorative language. But, apart from that difference, the two outlines are in close agreement. There was a movement in Judea. Its founder was executed under Pontius

Pilate. But the movement, instead of stopping, has now reached Rome itself. Neither author needs to mention Christian faith in Jesus' resurrection to agree, one with prudent impartiality and the other with sneering contempt, that the "Christian" movement, far from being stopped by his execution, had now reached all the way to Rome itself.

Think now of two different groups or emphases or even classes among Jesus' earliest followers; one we have seen before his death and the other after it. We have, from before his execution, those missionaries who went out in imitation of Jesus' own life-style, practicing free healing and open commensality. Did they all stop their activities on the day of his death? Did they all immediately lose their faith? Or, if they found themselves just as empowered as before, was he not somehow still with them, and how could that absent presence best be expressed? The *Gospel of Thomas*, for example, uses only one title for Jesus. He is "the Living Jesus," who acts yesterday, today, and tomorrow as the Wisdom of God here on earth, and his missionaries participate in that divine Wisdom by how they live, not just by how they talk. They do not speak of resurrection but of unbroken and abiding presence. We have also, but from after his execution, those scribal exegetes who searched the scriptures to understand what had happened. You do not, by the way, search the scriptures when you have lost your faith. In the example from the *Epistle of Barnabas* 7 discussed in the previous chapter, they were concerned with departure and return, passion and parousia, not death and resurrection. They could imagine Jesus being with God and returning in triumph but never have to mention resurrection at all. Where, then, did all the emphasis on resurrection come from? In a word, from Paul.

∞ First Fruits of Them That Sleep

During the winter of 53 or 54 C.E.—that is, from twenty to forty years before the New Testament gospels gave us their last chapters—Paul was writing to the church he had founded at Corinth and defending the possibility and actuality of bodily resurrection. As you read 1 Corinthians 15:12–20 watch very carefully the logic of his argument, and pay special attention to the verses I have italicized:

> Now if Christ is proclaimed as raised from the dead, how can some of you say there is no resurrection of the dead? *If there is no resurrection of the dead, then Christ has not been raised;* and if Christ has not been raised, then our proclamation has been in vain and your faith has been in vain. We are even found to be misrepresenting God, because we testified of God that he raised Christ—whom he did not raise if it is true that the dead are not raised. For *if the dead are not raised, then Christ has not been raised.* If Christ has not been raised, your faith is futile and you are still in your sins. Then those also who have died in Christ have perished. If for this life only we have hoped in Christ, we are of all people most to be pitied. But in fact Christ has been raised from the dead, the first fruits of those who have died.

Paul never argues that Jesus' resurrection was a special privilege afforded only to him. That would have been a perfectly possible proposal, since Judaism believed that Elijah, for example, had been taken up to heaven but never widened that privilege to all others as well. Why was Jesus not just another special case, another individual prerogative with no wider application than himself? Why, as my italics emphasize, is Jesus' resurrection actually dependent on the general resurrection?

It has often been said that Paul believed the end of the world was at hand. It is more accurate to say that he believed it *had already begun,* for that is his logic in the preceding passage. As a Pharisee he believed in the general resurrection at the end of time. But Jesus, he claims, has already risen as the start of the general resurrection. Notice his metaphor. Jesus is the "first fruits"—that is to say, the beginning of the harvest, the start of the general resurrection. That is why he can argue in either direction: no Jesus resurrection, no general resurrection; or, no general resurrection, no Jesus resurrection. They stand or fall together, and Paul presumes that only the mercy of God delays the final consummation, the ending of what has already started. The *Titanic* has, as it were, already hit the iceberg, and Paul's mission is to waken the cabins as far and as wide as possible— while God gives time. In such a theological vision, resurrection is the only possible way to articulate the presence of Jesus for Paul, but it is also inextricably linked to the *imminent* general resurrection at the end of the world. But if the end is not imminent, is resurrection still the best way to put it? Is *first fruits* a credible metaphor if the harvest is long delayed? For Paul, in any case, bodily resurrection is the only way that Jesus' continued presence can be expressed. But I repeat my question: Was that the only way other individuals and groups in earliest Christianity expressed their continuing and unbroken faith in Jesus? The question is not what it is that Paul means, because that is surely clear enough. The question is whether he speaks for all Christians then and thereafter. Is resurrection, so understood, the only way or just one of the ways to express faith in the continuing power and presence of Jesus in the world?

∞   Last of All to Me

My point is not that Paul was wrong but that his emphasis on *resurrection* was but one way of expressing early Christian faith and should not be taken as normative for all others. Consider another section in 1 Corinthians 15:1–11, and focus especially on *apparition* to see, once again, how Paul's own experience and expression have been taken as normative for all others rather than as one among many.

> Now I would remind you, brothers and sisters, of the good news that I proclaimed to you, which you in turn received, in which also you stand, through which also you are being saved, if you hold firmly to the message that I proclaimed to you—unless you have come to believe in vain. For I handed on to you as of first importance what I in turn had received: that Christ died for our sins in accordance with the scriptures, and that he was buried, and that he was raised on the third day in accordance with the scriptures, and that he *appeared* to Cephas [Simon Peter], then to the twelve. Then he *appeared* to more than five hundred brothers and sisters at one time, most of whom are still alive, though some have died. Then he *appeared* to James, then to all the apostles. Last of all, as to one untimely born,

he *appeared* also to me. For I am the least of the apostles, unfit to be called an apostle, because I persecuted the church of God. But by the grace of God I am what I am, and his grace toward me has not been in vain. On the contrary, I worked harder than any of them—though it was not I, but the grace of God that is with me. Whether then it was I or they, so we proclaim and so you have come to believe.

What I emphasize from that text, and throughout the rest of this chapter, is its profoundly political implications. It is not primarily interested in trance, ecstasy, apparition, or revelation, but in authority, power, leadership, and priority.

The thrust of that description is not just its emphasis on the risen apparitions of Jesus but its insistence that Paul himself is an *apostle*—that is, one specifically called and designated by God and Jesus to take a leadership role in the early church. Notice three elements. There is, first of all, the balance of Cephas and the Twelve against James and the apostles. Normally one thinks of the Twelve Apostles with Peter mentioned always in first place. For certain Christian groups, as we saw earlier, the Twelve Apostles represented in microcosm the New Testament just as the Twelve Patriarchs represented the Old Testament. But here the Twelve seem distinct from the apostles. But of course they have to be, or else Paul himself cannot be an apostle. That is why he mentions "to all the apostles" just before mentioning himself as "the least of the apostles." He cannot claim to be one of the Twelve but can and does claim to be an *apostle*, one *sent* (that is what the Greek term *apostolos* means) by God and Jesus. And despite the admission of belatedness at the end, as well as the insistence on divine grace, that final sentence puts it bluntly: there is *I* and there is *they*, but we are all apostles; *I* am *their* equal.

Before continuing, and lest this seem to place an unfair emphasis on apostolic legitimacy and authority over divine apparition and revelation, recall a text mentioned earlier, but only in passing, from Acts 1:15–17 and 20–26:

In those days Peter stood up among the believers [literally: brothers] (together the crowd numbered about one hundred twenty persons) and said, "Friends [literally: men, brothers], the scripture had to be fulfilled, which the Holy Spirit through David foretold concerning Judas, who became a guide for those who arrested Jesus—for he was numbered among us and was allotted his share in this ministry. . . . For it is written in the book of Psalms, 'Let his homestead become desolate, and let there be no one to live in it' [Psalm 69:25]; and 'Let another take his position of overseer [Psalm 109:8].' So *one of the men* who have accompanied us during all the time that the Lord Jesus went in and out among us, beginning from the baptism of John until the day when he was taken up from us—one of these must become a witness with us to his resurrection." So they proposed two, Joseph called Barsabbas, who was also known as Justus, and Matthias. Then they prayed and said, "Lord, you know everyone's heart. Show us which one of these two you have chosen to take the place in this ministry and apostleship from which Judas turned aside to go to his own place." And they cast lots for them, and the lot fell on Matthias; and he was added to the eleven apostles.

As far as Luke who wrote the Acts of the Apostles is concerned, Paul was not one of the Twelve Apostles and could never have been one since he had not been with Jesus from the beginning. For Luke, there are only Twelve Apostles and, even with Judas gone, it is not Paul who replaces him. Paul is, for Luke, the great missionary to the pagans but not an Apostle. Hence Paul, who insists on his apostolic authority at the start of so many letters, must, in 1 Corinthians 15:1–11, distinguish between "the twelve" and "all the apostles," for if there are but Twelve Apostles, he is outside that charmed inner circle forever.

There is a second element dependent on that first one. Paul is very interested in equating his own experience of the risen Jesus with that of all others before him. Hence he always uses that same expression, *appeared to* or *was revealed to* (the latter is a literal and better translation of the Greek expression *ōphthē*), in all instances. There can be no doubt that Paul's own experience involved trance—that altered state of consciousness discussed in Chapter 4. Luke gives three accounts of Paul's initial revelatory experience, in Acts 9:3–4, 22:6–7, and 26:13–14. They all agree on its dissociative character.

(1) Now as he was going along and approaching Damascus, suddenly a light from heaven flashed around him. He fell to the ground and heard a voice saying to him, "Saul, Saul, why do you persecute me?"

(2) "While I was on my way and approaching Damascus, about noon a great light from heaven suddenly shone about me. I fell to the ground and heard a voice saying to me, 'Saul, Saul, why are you persecuting me?'"

(3) "At midday along the road ... I saw a light from heaven, brighter than the sun, shining around me and my companions. When we had all fallen to the ground, I heard a voice saying to me in the Hebrew language, 'Saul, Saul, why are you persecuting me? It hurts you to kick against the goads.'"

When Paul himself describes that same experience in Galatians 1:16 he simply calls it a "revelation." But it is possible that he is also referring to it in 2 Corinthians 12:2–3:

I know a person in Christ [that is, Paul himself] who fourteen years ago was caught up to the third [or highest] heaven—whether in the body or out of the body I do not know; God knows. And I know that such a person—whether in the body or out of the body I do not know; God knows—was caught up into Paradise and heard things that are not to be told, that no mortal is permitted to repeat.

Paul's experience of the risen Jesus certainly occurred in a trance. But recall from Chapter 4 that trance neither furnishes any new information nor creates the raw materials of faith, but only confirms, strengthens, or enforces what was already there. Paul, for example, tells us repeatedly that he was a persecutor of Christianity before he was called to become the apostle to the pagans. He knew enough about this new Jewish sect to oppose it deeply, and the result of his dissociative experience was not just to stop persecution, not just to become a Christian, not just to become a missionary, but to become the apostle of the pagans. I suspect that it was the Christians' opening of Judaism to paganism and their willingness to abandon any ritual tradition standing in their way that had caused his initial persecution of Christianity, and that it was precisely what he had persecuted them for that he now accepted as his destiny.

I take very cautiously, therefore, the presumption that Paul's entranced experience of the risen Jesus was the only or even dominant experience of earliest Christianity after the crucifixion. Paul needs, in 1 Corinthians 15:1–11, to equate his own experience with that of the preceding apostles. To equate, that is, its validity and legitimacy but not necessarily its mode or manner. Jesus *was revealed* to all of them, but Paul's own entranced revelation should not be presumed to be the model for all others. What, once again, about those peasant followers in Galilee who were living the Jesus life-style and who knew full well the opposition and even derision about which he had warned them? Did they experience his continued presence in trance or in life? And what about those learned exegetes, presumably in Jerusalem, who were searching their scriptures to see if a crucified leader could be the Elect of God? Does one do exegesis in a trance? Maybe we should keep *trance, life-style,* and *exegesis* a little separate from one another—as different options and combinations for different followers and different groups within earliest Christianity.

Finally, notice in Paul's account of those apparitions or revelations that there are three types of recipients. There are three *specific leaders,* such as Peter, James, and Paul himself; there are two *leadership groups,* such as the Twelve and the apostles; and there is one single *general community,* the five hundred brethren. For the rest of this chapter, I explore those three categories with two main proposals. First, that what are often taken, in the last chapters of the New Testament gospels, as entranced revelations, simply because of the analogy with Paul, are not such at all. They bear no marks of such phenomena (no blinding light, nobody knocked to the ground, no heavenly voices) but are rather quite deliberate political dramatizations of the priority of one *specific leader* over another, of this *leadership group* over that *general community.* Those stories, then, are primarily interested not in trance and apparition but in power and authority. They presume rather than create the Christian community; they are about how it will continue, not how it began.

They detail the origins of Christian leadership, not the origins of Christian faith. Second, I propose that other stories in the gospels, ones from before the execution of Jesus—the so-called *nature miracles*—serve the same function. They are not about Jesus' physical power over the world but about the apostles' spiritual power over the community.

∞ A Meal of Bread and Fish

Recall, from the preceding section, Paul's mention of a revelation from Jesus to five hundred members of the community at once. We never hear of that five hundred again, but are there any indications of similar revelations to a *general community* elsewhere in the New Testament gospels? There are, in fact, certain very interesting examples where revelations to *specific leaders* and/or *leadership groups* come to overpower and suppress revelations to the *general community*. Such narratives, once again, are not about trance or ecstatic experiences but are ways of expressing who is in charge. *Apparition is the conferral of authority.* That is why Jesus spends no time in revealing heavenly mysteries or divine secrets. What is important is to whom he appears, not what he says. When the village atheist and the pious pastor argue about whether we are dealing here with valid trance or weird hallucination, they are both totally off the point. The point is that here, unlike with Paul, we are dealing with quite a different phenomenon. These are dramatizations of power and visualizations of authority.

Emmaus and Jerusalem

A first example is in Luke 24:13–46. Note especially its integrated and rounded structure, as emphasized in the headings:

(A) SCRIPTURES (24:13–27)
Now on that same day two of them were going to a village called Emmaus, about seven miles from Jerusalem, and talking with each other about all these things that had happened. While they were talking and discussing, Jesus

himself came near and went with them, but their eyes were kept from recognizing him. . . . Then he said to them, "Oh, how foolish you are, and how slow of heart to believe all that the prophets have declared! Was it not necessary that the Messiah should suffer these things and then enter into his glory?" Then beginning with Moses and all the prophets, he interpreted to them the things about himself in all the scriptures.

(B) BREAD (24:28–33a)

As they came near the village to which they were going, he walked ahead as if he were going on. But they urged him strongly, saying, "Stay with us, because it is almost evening and the day is now nearly over." So he went in to stay with them. When he was at the table with them, he took bread, blessed and broke it, and gave it to them. Then their eyes were opened, and they recognized him; and he vanished from their sight. They said to each other, "Were not our hearts burning within us while he was talking to us on the road, while he was opening the scriptures to us?" That same hour they got up and returned to Jerusalem.

(C) SIMON PETER (24:33b–35)

And they found the eleven and their companions gathered together. They were saying, "The Lord has risen indeed, and he has appeared to Simon!" Then they told what had happened on the road, and how he had been made known to them in the breaking of the bread.

(B') FISH (24:36–43)

While they were talking about this, Jesus himself stood among them and said to them, "Peace be with you." They were startled and terrified, and thought that they were seeing a ghost. He said to them, "Why are you frightened, and why do doubts arise in your hearts? Look at my hands and my feet; see that it is I myself. Touch me and see; for a ghost does not have flesh and bones as you see that I have." And when he had said this, he showed them his hands and his feet. While in their joy they were disbelieving and still wondering, he said to them, "Have you anything here to eat?" They gave him a piece of broiled fish, and he took it and ate in their presence.

(A') SCRIPTURES (24:44–46)

Then he said to them, "These are my words that I spoke to you while I was still with you—that everything written about me in the law of Moses, the prophets, and the psalms must be fulfilled." Then he opened their minds to understand the scriptures, and he said to them, "Thus it is written, that the Messiah is to suffer and to rise from the dead on the third day."

The two most striking aspects of that complex are, first, its overall linked and balanced structure and, second, the awkward syntax of the central section, unit C.

The structure emphasizes that we are dealing with a *general community*. Out from Jerusalem go two missionaries, leaving behind them "the eleven gathered together and those who were with them," and it is back to those that they return. Nowhere in the framing units of A/B and B'/A' does Jesus deal exclusively with a *specific leader* or even a *leadership group*. What we have here is not an event from Easter Sunday but a process that happened over many years. The presence and empowerment of Jesus remain in the community as it studies the scriptures "about" him and shares a meal of bread and fish together. This is not trance but exegesis, not ecstasy but eucharist. Luke, however, has broken up that eucharist of bread and fish so that now only the bread is a eucharist while the fish is a remarkably crude proof that Jesus is not a ghost. Meal as presence becomes meal as proof. But you can still see what was there before Luke started work on it: two missionaries leave Jerusalem, experience the full presence of Jesus through Scripture and especially Meal, most probably of bread and fish, and return to Jerusalem to report.

The awkward syntax of 24:33–35 has been smoothed over in the English translation used above. Here is that section in a more literal translation.

And they found gathered together the eleven and those with them saying that "The Lord has risen indeed, and he has appeared [*ōphthē*] to Simon!" Then they told what had happened on the road, and how he had been made known to them in the breaking of the bread.

But that awkward syntax is quite deliberate. We have just seen those two followers encounter Jesus, but *before* they can tell the others, the others tell them about Simon Peter. Only then do they get to recount their story. Peter's witness preempts theirs: *specific leader* over *general community.*

There is still, however, one major problem with the account in Luke 24, even after Peter has been established in primacy. Who exactly is mandated to be Jesus' witnesses to the world? Read 24:33b together with 24:47–53, and note the italicized words:

> [Jesus commands] the eleven *and their companions gathered together* . . . "that repentance and forgiveness of sins is to be proclaimed in his [Christ's] name to all nations, beginning from Jerusalem. You are witnesses of these things. And see, I am sending upon you what my Father promised; so stay here in the city until you have been clothed with power from on high." Then he led them out as far as Bethany, and, lifting up his hands, he blessed them. While he was blessing them, he withdrew from them and was carried up into heaven. And they worshiped him, and returned to Jerusalem with great joy; and they were continually in the temple blessing God.

That apostolic mandate is given to the community at large, and they all observe Jesus' Ascension into heaven. Even though the Eleven are specifically mentioned, they are not exclusively singled out as the only ones to receive authority or to see that Ascension. But, horror of horrors, then as now, there might have been—must have been—women among "those who were with them." Are women, too, apostles? That was all taken care of when Luke rewrote the ending of his gospel in starting his Acts of the Apostles. Watch how he rephrases the ending of his former volume as he begins the latter one, in Acts 1:1–4, 8, and 12–14:

> In the first book [Luke's gospel] . . . I wrote about all that Jesus did and taught from the beginning until the day when he was taken up to heaven, after giving instructions through the Holy Spirit *to the apostles whom he had chosen.* After his suffering he presented himself alive to them by many convincing proofs, appearing to *them* during forty days and speaking about the kingdom of God. While staying with *them,* he ordered *them* not to leave Jerusalem, but to wait there for the promise of the Father. . . . "You will receive power when the Holy Spirit has come upon

you; and you will be my witnesses in Jerusalem, in all Judea and Samaria, and to the ends of the earth." Then *they* returned to Jerusalem from the mount called Olivet, which is near Jerusalem, a sabbath day's journey away. When *they* had entered the city, they went to the room upstairs where they were staying, Peter, and John, and James, and Andrew, Philip and Thomas, Bartholomew and Matthew, James son of Alphaeus, and Simon the Zealot, and Judas son of James. *All these* were constantly devoting themselves to prayer, *together with* certain women, including Mary the mother of Jesus, as well as his brothers.

All is now clear. Jesus was talking *only* to the Apostles. They and they alone receive apostolic authority and observe the Ascension. The Eleven are clearly distinguished from all others, including the women. Finally, as we saw already, the Eleven are restored to Twelve Apostles by a choice among "the men" who had been with Jesus from the beginning in Acts 1:21. Luke has finally got it right. There is a *specific leader*, Peter; there is an exclusively male *leadership group*, the Twelve Apostles; and there is everyone else, including the women.

Community and Leadership

A second example is the miracle of the loaves and fishes as told independently in Mark 6:35–44 and John 6:5–13. There is another account of this miracle in Mark 8:1–9, but that is best seen not as separate tradition but as a deliberate doubling of the story by Mark himself. He thereby obtains a miracle on the lake's western shore in a Jewish context and on its eastern shore in a Gentile context. And that prepares him for this scene in the middle of the lake, in Mark 8:14–21.

Now the disciples had forgotten to bring any bread; and they had only one loaf with them in the boat. And he cautioned them, saying, "Watch out—beware of the yeast of the Pharisees and the yeast of Herod." They said to one another, "It is because we have no bread." And becoming aware of it, Jesus said to them, "Why are you talking about having no bread? Do you still not perceive or understand? Are your hearts hardened? Do you have eyes, and fail to see? Do you have ears, and fail to hear? And do you not remember? When I broke the five loaves for the five thousand, how many baskets full of broken pieces did you collect?" They said to him, "Twelve." "And the seven for the four thousand, how many baskets full of broken pieces did you collect?" And they said to him, "Seven." Then he said to them, "Do you not yet understand?"

Mark satirizes the disciples' failure to understand that there is one loaf for Jews and Gentiles alike and that it is more than enough for all. They are more interested, Mark notes ironically, in their own lack of bread than in the profusion Jesus has created for both sides of the lake. That second Markan multiplication in 8:1–9 was created by Mark himself to double the original one in 6:35–44 and thus render doubly culpable the disciples' failure to understand in 8:14–21. That second multiplication in 8:1–9 must be left aside, therefore, in considering his first account in 6:35–44 and its independent parallel in John 6:5–13.

From here on the nature miracles from Jesus' earthly life will be included with apparitional scenes from after his death. Note, in the present case, that all apparitional scenes concern bread and fish; that all have four key verbs—*took, blessed, broke, and gave*—for Jesus' action; and, most especially, that Jesus' presence to the *general community* is mediated only through the actions of a *leadership group*. My final justification for treating *all* nature miracles together, whether from before or after Jesus' death, will be given only in the next section, concerning the miraculous catch of fishes in Luke 5 and John 21.

For now I will concentrate on the story in Mark and John of how Jesus multiplied loaves and fishes to feed a multitude. That story, however, is only the surface narrative. Even though both versions are independent of one another, each, in its own way, emphasizes that all is done *only* through the disciples. It is clearly not a miracle for the disciples themselves, but it is just as clearly a miracle for the people only through the mediation and authority of the disciples. The *general community* is fed by Jesus not directly and immediately but through, and only through, a *leadership group*. The twin accounts from Mark 6:35–44 and John 6:5–13 are given in tandem and in that order to show how each underlines, in different ways, the mediating role of the disciples.

There are five basic elements in the story. The first is the problem itself, the question about what to do for a multitude without food in a desert place:

(1) When it grew late, his disciples came to him and said, "This is a deserted place, and the hour is now very late; send them away so that they may go into the surrounding country and villages and buy something for themselves to eat." But he answered them, "You give them something to eat." They said to him, "Are we to go and buy two hundred denarii worth of bread, and give it to them to eat?" And he said to them, "How many loaves have you? Go and see." When they had found out, they said, "Five, and two fish."

(2) When he looked up and saw a large crowd coming toward him, Jesus said to Philip, "Where are we to buy bread for these people to eat?" He said this to test him, for he himself knew what he was going to do. Philip answered him, "Six months' wages would not buy enough bread for each of them to get a little." One of his disciples, Andrew, Simon Peter's brother, said to him, "There is a boy here who has five barley loaves and two fish. But what are they among so many people?"

In John it is Jesus himself who raises the issue, but in Mark it is the disciples who do so. Yet in both cases Jesus and the disciples plan together to solve a problem for the crowds, not for themselves.

The second element concerns the preparation, the seating arrangements for the crowds. Note once again who commands it.

(1) Then he ordered them to get all the people to sit down in groups on the green grass. So they sat down in groups of hundreds and of fifties.

(2) Jesus said, "Make the people sit down." Now there was a great deal of grass in the place; so they sat down, about five thousand in all.

In both cases Jesus commands the crowds only through the disciples. In John this is quite clear. In Mark the translation depends on how one understands the Greek.

The third element is the multiplication and distribution of the food. Does Jesus do it himself or only through the disciples?

(1) Taking the five loaves and the two fish, he looked up to heaven, and blessed and broke the loaves, and gave them to his disciples to set before the people; and he divided the two fish among them all.

(2) Then Jesus took the loaves, and when he had given thanks, he distributed them to those who were seated; so also the fish, as much as they wanted.

Once again it seems a small point, but what Jesus does himself in John he does through the disciples in Mark, explicitly for the bread and presumably for the fish as well.

Finally, there is the collection of food left over. In Mark it is done by a vague and unspecified "they," but in John it is the disciples who are commanded to do so:

(1) And all ate and were filled; and they took up twelve baskets full of broken pieces and of the fish. Those who had eaten the loaves numbered five thousand men.

(2) When they were satisfied, he told his disciples, "Gather up the fragments left over, so that nothing may be lost." So they gathered them up, and from the fragments of the five barley loaves, left by those who had eaten, they filled twelve baskets.

All of the points I raised are so small that they can easily be overlooked. Throughout his life Jesus performed healings and exorcisms for ordinary people. *He performs what are usually called nature miracles only for his disciples.* Except here: this is the single case where a nature miracle is performed for ordinary people. Yet the disciples keep appearing as mediators and are commanded by Jesus to act in that capacity. Is that just coincidence?

The open commensality of Jesus' life was ritualized separately after his death either as a eucharist of bread and fish meal or a eucharist of bread and wine. The two accounts just given are examples of that former ritual retrojected into the earthly life of Jesus. But in both cases, even if in different ways, hierarchy and authority have been reintroduced into the meal. Open commensality has been both ritualized, which was probably inevitable, and ruined, which was not.

Lambs and Sheep

In the two preceding sections it was the supremacy of a *specific leader* or a *leadership group* over the *general community* that was emphasized against the background of a eucharistic meal of bread and fish. Jesus' eucharistic presence is primarily concerned, in other words, with authority and priority. In this third example, the competition is rather between specific leaders, but once again the context is that of a bread-and-fish eucharist. To appreciate its functions we must begin with an earlier scene.

In John 18:17–18 and 25–27, at the High Priest's house, Peter denied Jesus three times in association with a charcoal fire just before dawn:

> (1) The woman said to Peter, "You are not also one of this man's disciples, are you?" He said, "I am not." Now the slaves and the police had made a *charcoal fire* because it was cold, and they were standing around it and warming themselves. Peter also was standing with them and warming himself. . . .
>
> (2) Now Simon Peter was standing and warming himself. They asked him, "You are not also one of his disciples, are you?" He denied it and said, "I am not."
>
> (3) One of the slaves of the high priest, a relative of the man whose ear Peter had cut off, asked, "Did I not see you in the garden with him?" Again Peter denied it, and at that moment the cock crowed.

This early triad of denial in John 18:17–18 and 25–27 must be negated by the later triad of confession as Peter is placed in charge in John 21:9–17. And the artificial nature of the confessional triad is emphasized by the fact that there are only two categories for it to handle: lambs and sheep.

The scene takes place after the execution of Jesus, when seven of his disciples are fishing on the Sea of Galilee. I will look at John 21:1–8 in the next section; here I concentrate on 21:9–17.

> When they had gone ashore, they saw a *charcoal fire* there, with fish on it, and bread. Jesus said to them, "Bring some

of the fish that you have just caught." So Simon Peter went aboard and hauled the net ashore, full of large fish, a hundred fifty-three of them; and though there were so many, the net was not torn. Jesus said to them, "Come and have breakfast." Now none of the disciples dared to ask him, "Who are you?" because they knew it was the Lord. Jesus came and took the bread and gave it to them, and did the same with the fish.

This was now the third time that Jesus appeared to the disciples after he was raised from the dead.

When they had finished breakfast,

(1) Jesus said to Simon Peter, "Simon son of John, do you love me more than these?" He said to him, "Yes, Lord; you know that I love you." Jesus said to him, "Feed my lambs."

(2) A second time he said to him, "Simon son of John, do you love me?" He said to him, "Yes, Lord; you know that I love you." Jesus said to him, "Tend my sheep."

(3) He said to him the third time, "Simon son of John, do you love me?" Peter felt hurt because he said to him the third time, "Do you love me?" And he said to him, "Lord, you know everything; you know that I love you." Jesus said to him, "Feed my sheep."

There is a charcoal fire just after dawn, and there is a triple statement of love from Peter to Jesus and a triple statement of mandate from Jesus to Peter. The text's apologetical overtones are quite heavy, and they are not exactly subtle.

Apart from the restoration of Peter's standing, it is clear that he is being put in charge of the entire flock—lambs and sheep—by Jesus. He loves Jesus "more than these" and is put in charge of all. Peter is a *specific leader* given authority over both a *leadership group* and the *general community*.

Commensality and Eucharist

If Jesus himself had ritualized a meal in which bread and wine were identified with his own body and blood, it would be very difficult to explain the complete absence of any such symbolization in eucharistic texts such as those of *Didache* 9–10. It was, therefore, open commensality during his life rather than the

Last Supper before his death that was the root of any later ritualization. And open commensality could be ritualized into eucharists of bread and fish just as well as eucharists of bread and wine. Hence the bread-and-fish eucharists in the early tradition. For how could those have ever been created if a bread-and-wine symbolization had already officially antedated them? But, despite the eventual ascendancy of the bread-and-wine eucharist, it is impossible to emphasize too greatly the early importance of the bread-and-fish alternative.

The continuity between open commensality during Jesus' life and both forms of eucharist, that of bread and fish and that of bread and wine, after his death is preserved in the four key verbs describing Jesus' action: *took, blessed* (or *gave thanks), broke,* and *gave.* That foursome appears, for example, with the bread both at the Last Supper in Luke 22:19 and at the Emmaus meal just seen in Luke 24:30. What is their importance, and why should they have become ritualized expressions for those eucharists, whether of bread and wine or of bread and fish?

Return once more for comparison to those Qumran Essenes who left us their library as the Dead Sea Scrolls. Hierarchical rank rather than egalitarian commensality was emphasized symbolically in their ritual meals. Here are two examples found in Cave 1, where the group hid their precious library during the First Roman-Jewish War of 66–73 C.E. The first one is taken from the *Rule of the Community* or *Manual of Discipline* and the second one from its badly fragmented appendix, *The Rule of the Congregation* or *Messianic Rule;* both are from manuscripts dated to about 100 B.C.E.:

(1) And when the table has been prepared for eating, and the new wine for drinking, the Priest shall be the first to stretch out his hand to bless the first-fruits of the bread and new wine.

(2) And [when] they shall gather for the common [tab]le, to eat and [to drink] new wine, when the common table shall be set for eating and the new wine [poured] for drinking, let no man extend his hand over the first-fruits of bread and wine before the Priest; for [it is he] who shall bless the first fruits of bread and wine, and shall be the first

[to extend] his hand over the bread. Thereafter, the Messiah of Israel shall extend his hand over the bread, [and] all the Congregation of the Community [shall utter a] blessing, [each man in the order] of his dignity.

There the emphasis is on hierarchy, precedence, and the order of dignity. A very different emphasis appears in Jesus' commensality. Even as early communities ritualized the contents of Jesus' open commensality, they also continued one major feature implicit in those few verbs. *Took, blessed, broke,* and *gave* have profound symbolic connotations and may well stem from that inaugural open commensality itself. They indicate, first of all, a process of *equal sharing,* whereby whatever food is there is distributed alike to all. But they also indicate something even more important. The first two verbs, *took* and *blessed,* and especially the second, are the actions of the master; the last two, *broke* and *gave,* and especially the second, are the actions of the servant. Jesus, as master and host, performs the role of servant, and all share the same food as equals. There is, however, one further step to be taken. Most of Jesus' first followers would have known about but seldom experienced being served at table by slaves. The male followers would think more experientially of females as preparers and servers of the family food. Jesus took on himself the role not only of servant but of female. Not only *servile* but *female hosting* is symbolized by the *juxtaposition* of those four verbs. Far from reclining and being served, Jesus himself serves, like any housewife, the same meal to all, including himself.

∞ Nothing and Nowhere All Night

All Jesus' *nature miracles* before his death and all his *risen apparitions* afterward should be grouped together and analyzed in terms of the authority of this or that *specific leader* over this or that *leadership group* and/or over this or that *general community.* The first example I present here shows that conjunction of nature miracle and risen apparition most clearly and is the primary justification for their combination.

Fishing Without Jesus

There are two separate and independent versions of this narrative. One, a nature miracle, is in Luke and takes place before the death of Jesus; the other, a risen apparition, is in John 21 and takes place after Jesus' death. It is this story above all that confirms for me the original unity of *nature miracle* and *risen apparition*.

The Lukan version of the story is given as Luke narrates the very start of Jesus' public life; its conclusion, in Luke 5:10–11, has been combined with the call of the first disciples from Mark 1:16–20. I leave aside that conjunction to focus on the miraculous catch of fishes in Luke 5:2–9:

> [Jesus] saw two boats there at the shore of the lake; the fishermen had gone out of them and were washing their nets. He got into one of the boats, the one belonging to Simon, and asked him to put out a little way from the shore. Then he sat down and taught the crowds from the boat. When he had finished speaking, he said to Simon, "Put out into the deep water and let down your nets for a catch." Simon answered, "Master, we have worked all night long but have caught nothing. Yet if you say so, I will let down the nets." When they had done this, they caught so many fish that their nets were beginning to break. So they signaled their partners in the other boat to come and help them. And they came and filled both boats, so that they began to sink. But when Simon Peter saw it, he fell down at Jesus' knees, saying, "Go away from me, Lord, for I am a sinful man!" For he and all who were with him were amazed at the catch of fish that they had taken.

The symbolic message is, once again, quite clear. Jesus chooses Peter's boat above the other one, and it is from there that he teaches and catches fish. The disciples have toiled all night, but without Jesus in command they have caught nothing. Now, with Jesus in command of the boat, they catch almost more than they can handle. Without Jesus nothing; with Jesus everything. Notice, however, that in its present context, Peter's confession of sinfulness is difficult to understand. Were this miracle instead a risen apparition coming after his triple denial, however, Peter's confession would be both comprehensible and necessary. And it is as a *risen apparition* that this *nature miracle* is told in John 21:2–8:

> Gathered there together were Simon Peter, Thomas called the Twin, Nathanael of Cana in Galilee, the sons of Zebedee, and two others of his disciples. Simon Peter said to them, "I am going fishing." They said to him, "We will go with you." They went out and got into the boat, but that night they caught nothing. Just after daybreak, Jesus stood on the beach; but the disciples did not know that it was Jesus. Jesus said to them, "Children, you have no fish, have you?" They answered him, "No." He said to them, "Cast the net to the right side of the boat, and you will find some." So they cast it, and now they were not able to haul it in because there were so many fish. That disciple whom Jesus loved said to Peter, "It is the Lord!" When Simon Peter heard that it was the Lord, he put on some clothes, for he was naked, and jumped into the sea. But the other disciples came in the boat, dragging the net full of fish, for they were not far from the land, only about a hundred yards off.

That is the same symbolic message: without Jesus nothing; with Jesus everything. But notice, for later reference, a slight tension in this version between "the disciple whom Jesus loved" and Peter. The former recognizes Jesus first, but the latter jumps overboard to get to him first. As the story continues in John 21, of course, as we have just seen, Simon Peter is put clearly and unequivocally in charge of disciples and community.

Sailing Without Jesus

I find exactly the same symbolic meaning in Jesus' walking on the waters as in the miraculous catch of fishes: without Jesus the disciples are endangered and get nowhere, but with Jesus they get where they are going swiftly and safely. There are two accounts of the calming of the waters in Mark 4:35–41 and 6:45–51 just as there were two accounts of the multiplication of loaves and fishes in 6:35–44 and 8:1–9. In both cases Mark doubled his given tradition for exactly the same reason: to increase the incomprehension and thus the culpability of the disciples, against whom he is waging an increasingly forceful polemic throughout his gospel. Here are his twin versions, in Mark 4:35–41 and 6:45–51, respectively.

(1) On that day, when evening had come, he said to them, "Let us go across to the other side." And leaving the crowd behind, they took him with them in the boat, just as he was. Other boats were with him. A great windstorm arose, and the waves beat into the boat, so that the boat was already being swamped. But he was in the stern, asleep on the cushion; and they woke him up and said to him, "Teacher, do you not care that we are perishing?" He woke up and rebuked the wind, and said to the sea, "Peace! Be still!" Then the wind ceased, and there was a dead calm. He said to them, "Why are you afraid? Have you still no faith?" And they were filled with great awe and said to one another, "Who then is this, that even the wind and the sea obey him?"

(2) Immediately he made his disciples get into the boat and go on ahead to the other side, to Bethsaida, while he dismissed the crowd. After saying farewell to them, he went up on the mountain to pray. When evening came, the boat was out on the sea, and he was alone on the land. When he saw that they were straining at the oars against an adverse wind, he came towards them early in the morning, walking on the sea. He intended to pass them by. But when they saw him walking on the sea, they thought it was a ghost and cried out; for they all saw him and were terrified. But immediately he spoke to them and said, "Take heart, it is I; do not be afraid." Then he got into the boat with them and the wind ceased. And they were utterly astounded.

That first version is simply a Markan duplication of the traditional one given in second place. That is why, independent of Mark, the early tradition knows only *one* meal miracle and *one* sea miracle, those in Mark 6:35–44 and 45–51, respectively. In what follows, therefore, only Mark 6:45–51 will be considered and 4:35–41 will be ignored.

Here is the second and independent version of that sea story, in John 6:15b–21:

When Jesus realized that they were about to come and take him by force to make him king, he withdrew again to the mountain by himself. When evening came, his disciples went down to the sea, got into a boat, and started across the sea to Capernaum. It was now dark, and Jesus had not yet come to them. The sea became rough because a strong wind was blowing. When they had rowed about three or four miles, they saw Jesus walking on the sea and coming near the boat, and they were terrified. But he said to them, "It is I; do not be afraid." Then they wanted to take him into the boat, and immediately the boat reached the land toward which they were going.

The point is surely clear: without Jesus the disciples get nowhere all night, but when Jesus arrives all is immediately well. But there are also three motifs in Mark 6:45–51, a nature miracle from before the death of Jesus, that are remarkably similar to ones in Luke 24, apparitional accounts from after the death of Jesus. Those common elements help emphasize the common matrix from which both nature miracles and risen apparitions were originally derived. First, the time. Jesus walks to them on the waters "early in the morning," or, literally, "about the fourth watch of the night," between 3:00 and 6:00 A.M., in Mark 6:48. So also, in Luke 24:1 and 24:22 the tomb of Jesus is found empty "at early dawn" or "early in the morning."

Next, the reaction. There are four close verbal similarities between Mark 6:49–50 and Luke 24:37–38 (I keep translations consistent with the Greek words):

(1) But when they saw him walking on the sea, they thought it was a *ghost* [*phantasma*] and cried out; for they all saw him and were *frightened*. But immediately he spoke to them and said, "Take heart, *it is I*; do not be *terrified*."

(2) They were startled and *terrified*, and thought that they were seeing a *ghost* [*pneuma*]. He said to them, "Why are you *frightened*, and why do doubts arise in your hearts? Look at my hands and my feet; see that *it is I* myself."

Finally, the necessary invitation. There is a rather strange comment in Mark 6:48 when Jesus approaches the boat walking on the waters: "he intended to pass them by." Similarly, at Emmaus in Luke 24:28, "as they came near the village to which they were going, he walked ahead as if he were going on." In both cases, they must react to get Jesus to join them.

The messages are surely most clear. Fishing all night without Jesus, the disciples catch nothing. Sailing all night without Jesus, the disciples get nowhere. Jesus returns and immediately there is a great catch or a safe harbor. The symbolism is devastatingly obvious, but it is a symbolism for a *specific leader,* namely Peter, in the former case, and for a *leadership group* in the second one. Here, then, is a question: How does one get a specific leader, namely Peter, dominant in that second case—over, that is, the *leadership group?* Hint: Who is it that gets to walk (or sink) on the water with Jesus, but only in Matthew 14:28–33?

∞ The Race to the Empty Tomb

We have seen the exaltation of *specific leader* over *leadership group* and of each over the *general community* throughout the preceding conjunction of *nature miracle* and *risen apparition.* Those stories were not concerned with control over nature before Jesus' death or with entranced apparitions after it; rather, they were quite dramatic and symbolic narratives about power and authority in the earliest Christian communities. That is what they were intended to be, and that is how we should read them. All of this process reaches something of a climax in John 20, where "the disciple whom Jesus loved" is exalted over three other individuals—first Peter, then Mary Magdalene, and finally Thomas.

We already saw a competitive tension between the Beloved Disciple and Peter in John 21, but in that chapter, which scholars judge to be a later addition to John's gospel, it is resolved in Peter's favor. Here in John 20, in the original last chapter of that gospel, Peter loses badly. Look first, however, at Luke 24:12, a verse omitted from some manuscripts but most likely originally present in that chapter:

> But Peter got up and ran to the tomb; stooping and looking in, he saw the linen cloths by themselves; then he went home, amazed at what had happened.

Suppose, now, that you knew that piece of tradition and could not ignore it, but that you also wanted to exalt the Beloved

Disciple over Peter. How could you both admit that tradition and then negate it at the same time. This is how, in John 20:3–10; note the four steps:

> Then Peter and the other disciple [the one whom Jesus loved] set out and went toward the tomb.
>
> (1) The two were running together, but the other disciple *outran* Peter and reached the tomb first.
>
> (2) He bent down to look in and *saw* the linen wrappings lying there, but he did not go in.
>
> (3) Then Simon Peter came, following him, and *went into* the tomb. He saw the linen wrappings lying there, and the cloth that had been on Jesus' head, not lying with the linen wrappings but rolled up in a place by itself.
>
> (4) Then the other disciple, who reached the tomb first, also went in, *and he saw and believed;* for as yet they did not understand the scripture, that he must rise from the dead. Then the disciples returned to their homes.

The Beloved Disciple reaches the tomb first and looks into the tomb first. Peter is allowed, however, in deference to tradition, to enter the tomb first. But *only* the beloved Disciple is said to believe. That takes care of Peter.

Mary Magdalene is next; indeed, her denigration frames that of Peter. But read first this narrative in Matthew 28:8–10, just after the women leave the empty tomb on Easter Sunday:

> So they [Mary Magdalene and the other Mary] left the tomb quickly with fear and great joy, and ran to tell his disciples. Suddenly Jesus met them and said, "Greetings!" And they came to him, took hold of his feet, and worshiped him. Then Jesus said to them, "Do not be afraid; go and tell my brothers to go to Galilee; there they will see me."

Suppose, once again, that you knew this piece of tradition. And suppose that you wanted both to admit it and to suppress it at the same time. Understand, of course, that I am not imagining these as historical but as fictional units, as competing visualizations about priority and primacy. Here is what John 20:1–2 and 11–18 does with Mary:

> (1) Early on the first day of the week, while it was still dark, Mary Magdalene came to the tomb and saw that the stone

had been removed from the tomb. So she ran and went to Simon Peter and the other disciple, the one whom Jesus loved, and said to them, *"They have taken the Lord out of the tomb, and we do not know where they have laid him."*. . .

(2) But Mary stood weeping outside the tomb. As she wept, she bent over to look into the tomb; and she saw two angels in white, sitting where the body of Jesus had been lying, one at the head and the other at the feet. They said to her, "Woman, why are you weeping?" She said to them, *"They have taken away my Lord, and I do not know where they have laid him."*

(3) When she had said this, she turned around and saw Jesus standing there, but she did not know that it was Jesus. Jesus said to her, "Woman, why are you weeping? Whom are you looking for?" Supposing him to be the gardener, she said to him, "Sir, *if you have carried him away,* tell me where you have laid him, and I will take him away." Jesus said to her, "Mary!" She turned and said to him in Hebrew, "Rabbouni!" (which means Teacher). Jesus said to her, "Do not hold on to me, because I have not yet ascended to the Father. But go to my brothers and say to them, 'I am ascending to my Father and your Father, to my God and your God.'" Mary Magdalene went and announced to the disciples, "I have seen the Lord"; and she told them that he had said these things to her.

Mary gets to give the wrong interpretation of the empty tomb three times: to the disciples, to the angels, and finally to Jesus himself. She does not even recognize Jesus when he appears to her, at least until he addresses her. She is told to announce not the resurrection but the ascension. And if you object that at least she gets to see Jesus, read on to see what John 20 has to say about *seeing* the risen Jesus rather than, like the Beloved Disciple, believing after *seeing* only an empty tomb and empty grave cloths.

The final exaltation of the Beloved Disciple is over Thomas. Recall that Simon was nicknamed Rocky or "the Rock"—*Petros* in Greek and *Cephas* in Aramaic. Another follower of Jesus called Jude or Judas (not Iscariot, of course) also had a bilingual nickname, "the Twin"—*Didymos* in Greek and *Thomas* in Aramaic or Syriac. This is the figure here immortalized as Doubting Thomas. We know about his leadership and authority, and his competition with alternative figures such as Peter and Matthew, from the *Gospel of Thomas* 13:

> Jesus said to his followers, "Compare me to something and tell me what I am like."
>
> Simon Peter said to him, "You are like a just messenger [or: angel]."
>
> Matthew said to him, "You are like a wise philosopher."
>
> Thomas said to him, "Teacher, my mouth is utterly unable to say what you are like." Jesus said, "I am not your teacher. Because you have drunk, you have become intoxicated from the bubbling spring that I have tended." And he took him, and withdrew, and spoke three sayings to him.
>
> When Thomas came back to his friends, they asked him, "What did Jesus say to you?"
>
> Thomas said to them, "If l tell you one of the sayings he spoke to me, you will pick up rocks and stone me, and fire will come from the rocks and consume you."

But the story in John 20 exalts the Beloved Disciple over Thomas just as the preceding dialogue exalts Thomas himself over Peter and Matthew. In John 20:19–23 Jesus appears to the disciples but Thomas is not present. When they tell him about their experience in 20:24–25 he refuses to believe until and unless he can see and touch the wounds from the crucifixion. The story concludes in 20:26–29:

> A week later his disciples were again in the house, and Thomas was with them. Although the doors were shut, Jesus came and stood among them and said, "Peace be with you." Then he said to Thomas, "Put your finger here and see my hands. Reach out your hand and put it in my side. Do not doubt but believe." Thomas answered him, "My Lord and my God!" Jesus said to him, "Have you believed because you have seen me? Blessed are those who have not seen and yet have come to believe."

That takes care of Thomas. The Beloved Disciple *saw* only empty cloths and empty grave but believed; Thomas needed to *see* and even wanted to touch the risen Jesus himself. That also takes care, by the way, of those disciples who needed to see Jesus, touch him, and watch him eat before they believed, in Luke 24.

∞   In Remembrance of Her

The stories from the preceding sections tell us nothing whatsoever about the origins of Christian *faith* but quite a lot about the origins of Christian *authority*. They tell us about power and leadership in the earliest Christian communities. They tell us about the establishment of *leadership groups* over *general communities* and they tell us very clearly about competing *specific leaders* within and among those groups. The last story, for instance, tells us that, at least for the community of the Beloved Disciple, Mary Magdalene's authority needed to be opposed just as much as did that of Peter or Thomas. And we cannot tell whether the Beloved Disciple represents an individual person or a different mode of leadership. Maybe, for example, the title is left unspecified in order to designate a charismatic rather than an institutional primacy. But all of that presumes a community or communities that have been around for a long time—in fact, for one or two generations. Those stories were not, in other words, about events that first Easter Sunday. Or, if you prefer, Easter Sunday lasted quite a few years.

What happened historically is that those who believed in Jesus before his execution *continued* to do so afterward. Easter is not about the start of a new faith but about the continuation of an old one. That is the only miracle and the only mystery, and it is more than enough of both. Of course there may have been trances and visions. There always are such events in every religion, and there is no reason to think Paul was alone in his. But that is not all that happened. There were those, first of all, whose unshod feet hurt and continued to hurt from Galilean roads. And there were also those who searched the scriptures to see what this all meant. It is a terrible trivialization to imagine that all Jesus' followers lost their faith on Good Friday and had it restored by apparitions on Easter Sunday. It is another trivialization to presume that even those who lost their nerve, fled, and hid also lost their faith, hope, and love. It is a final trivialization to mistake stories about competing Christian authority for stories about inaugural Christian experience.

I leave aside, therefore, all the stories about named individuals, whether female or male, and all the stories about what happened after the death of Jesus to look, in conclusion, at one unnamed individual who believed before it, despite it, or even because of it. The story is in Mark 14:3–9:

> While he was at Bethany in the house of Simon the leper, as he sat at the table, a woman came with an alabaster jar of very costly ointment of nard, and she broke open the jar and poured the ointment on his head. But some were there who said to one another in anger, "Why was the ointment wasted in this way? For this ointment could have been sold for more than three hundred denarii, and the money given to the poor." And they scolded her. But Jesus said, "Let her alone; why do you trouble her? She has performed a good service for me. For you always have the poor with you, and you can show kindness to them whenever you wish; but you will not always have me. She has done what she could; she has anointed my body beforehand for its burial. Truly I tell you, wherever the good news is proclaimed in the whole world, what she has done will be told in remembrance of her."

Why is this unnamed woman so important? Why does she get that absolutely stunning accolade from Jesus at the end? Why is this precise action and none other in any other gospel singled out for such an extraordinary comment?

As Jesus and his male disciples journeyed to Jerusalem and his death, he told them three times that he would die and rise again. Those three prophecies, in Mark 8:31–33, 9:30–32, and 10:32–37, were created by Mark himself, as were the reactions of the disciples after each one. They ignore, deny, dismiss, or avoid discussing those fatal predictions, and this is another part of their programmatic denigration throughout Mark's gospel.

> (1) Then he began to teach them that the Son of Man must undergo great suffering, and be rejected by the elders, the chief priests, and the scribes, and be killed, and after three days rise again. He said all this quite openly.
>
> And Peter took him aside and began to rebuke him. But turning and looking at his disciples, he rebuked Peter and

said, "Get behind me, Satan! For you are setting your mind not on divine things but on human things."

(2) They went on from there and passed through Galilee. He did not want anyone to know it; for he was teaching his disciples, saying to them, "The Son of Man is to be betrayed into human hands, and they will kill him, and three days after being killed, he will rise again."
But they did not understand what he was saying and were afraid to ask him.

(3) He took the twelve aside again and began to tell them what was to happen to him, saying, "See, we are going up to Jerusalem, and the Son of Man will be handed over to the chief priests and the scribes, and they will condemn him to death; then they will hand him over to the Gentiles; they will mock him, and spit upon him, and flog him, and kill him; and after three days he will rise again."
James and John, the sons of Zebedee, came forward to him and said to him, "Teacher . . . grant us to sit, one at your right hand and one at your left, in your glory."

The disciples have never, as Mark sees it, understood or accepted Jesus' impending crucifixion. But now, in the home of Simon the Leper, for the first time somebody believes that Jesus is going to die and that unless his body is anointed now, it never will be.

Earlier commentators often discussed whether the unnamed young man fleeing naked into the night from the garden of Gethsemane in Mark 14:51–52 might be Mark himself obliquely and indirectly signing his narrative. It is just as possible, even more credible, but unfortunately quite as unprovable, to suggest that the unnamed woman in Mark 14:3–9 is "Mark" herself obliquely and indirectly signing her narrative. That, however, is not the point. We cannot ever be sure whether Mark was a woman or a man. We can, however, be absolutely sure that the author of this gospel chose an unnamed woman for the supreme model of Christian faith—for the faith that was there before, despite, or even because of Jesus' death. Easter, for her, came early that year.

EPILOGUE

From Jesus to Christ

THE voices that speak to us from antiquity are overwhelmingly those of the cultured few, the elites. The modern voices that carry on their tale are overwhelmingly those of white, middle-class, European and North American males. These men can, and do, laud imperialistic, authoritarian slave societies. The scholarship of antiquity is often removed from the real world, hygienically free of value judgements. Of the value judgements, that is, of the voiceless masses, the 95% who knew how "the other half" lived in antiquity. . . .

The peasants form no part of the literate world on which most reconstructions of ancient history focus. Indeed, the peasants—the pagani—did not even form part of the lowly Christian (town dweller's) world. They are almost lost to historical view, because of their illiteracy and localism.

Thomas F. Carney, *The Shape of the Past: Models and Antiquity* (Lawrence, KS: Coronado Press, 1975)

Class, then, essentially a relationship, *is* above all the collective social expression of the *fact of exploitation* (and of course of resistance to it): the division of society into economic classes is in its very nature the way in which exploitation is effected, with the propertied classes living off the non-propertied. I admit that in my use of it the word "exploitation" often tends to take on a pejorative colouring; but essentially it is a "value-free" expression, signifying merely that a propertied class is freed from the labour of production through its ability to maintain itself out of a surplus extracted from the primary producers, whether by compulsion or by persuasion or (as in most cases) by a mixture of the two.

G. E. M. de Ste. Croix, "Karl Marx and the
History of Classical Antiquity"
Arethusa 8 (1975)

This epilogue is both summary and challenge. The summary looks backward and condenses the preceding chapters into a historical synthesis. The challenge looks forward and asks about the relationship between any and every historically reconstructed Jesus and any and every theologically accepted Christ. The twin sections that follow are, respectively, historical summary and theological challenge.

∞   The One as Yet Unknown

He comes as yet unknown into a hamlet of Lower Galilee. He is watched by the cold, hard eyes of peasants living long enough at subsistence level to know exactly where the line is drawn between poverty and destitution. He looks like a beggar, yet his eyes lack the proper cringe, his voice the proper whine, his walk the proper shuffle. He speaks about the rule of God and they listen as much from curiosity as anything else. They know all about rule and power, about kingdom and empire, but they know it in terms of tax and debt, malnutrition and sickness, agrarian oppression and demonic possession. What, they really want to know, can this Kingdom of God do for a lame child, a blind parent, a demented soul screaming its tortured isolation among the graves that mark the village fringes? Jesus walks with them to the tombs, and in the silence after he has exorcised the woman they brought him to see, the villagers listen once more, but now with curiosity giving way to cupidity, fear, and embarrassment. He is invited, as honor demands, to the home of the village leader. He goes, instead, to stay in the home of the dispossessed woman. Not quite proper, to be sure, but it would be unwise to censure an exorcist, to criticize a magician. The village could yet broker this power to its surroundings, could give this Kingdom of God a localization, a place to which others would come for healing, a center with honor and patronage enough for all—even, maybe, for that dispossessed woman herself. But the next day he leaves them, and now they wonder aloud about a divine kingdom with no respect for proper protocols—a kingdom, as he had said, not just for the poor, like themselves, but for the destitute. Others say that the worst and most powerful demons are found not in small villages but in certain cities. Maybe, they say, that was where the exorcised demon went—to Sepphoris or Tiberias, or even Jerusalem, or maybe to Rome itself, where its arrival would hardly be noticed amid so many others already in residence. But some say nothing at all and ponder the possibility of catching up with Jesus before he gets too far.

Even Jesus himself had not always seen things that way. Earlier he had received John's baptism and accepted his message of God as the imminent apocalyptic judge. But the Jordan was not just water, and to be baptized in it was to recapitulate the ancient and archetypal passage from imperial bondage to national freedom. Herod Antipas moved swiftly to execute John, there was no apocalyptic consummation, and Jesus, finding his own voice, began to speak of God not as imminent apocalypse but as present healing. To those first followers from the peasant villages of Lower Galilee who asked how to repay his exorcisms and cures, he gave a simple answer—simple, that is, to understand, but hard as death itself to undertake. You are healed healers, he said, so take the Kingdom to others, for I am not its patron and you are not its brokers. It is, was, and always will be available to any who want it. Dress as I do, like a beggar, but do not beg. Bring a miracle and request a table. Those you heal must accept you into their homes.

That ecstatic vision and social program sought to rebuild a society upward from its grass roots, but on principles of religious and economic egalitarianism, with free healing brought directly to the peasant homes and free sharing of whatever they had in return. The deliberate conjunction of magic and meal, miracle and table, free compassion and open commensality, was a challenge launched not just on the level of Judaism's strictest purity regulations, or even on that of the Mediterranean's patriarchal combination of honor and shame, patronage and clientage, but at the most basic level of civilization's eternal inclination to draw lines, invoke boundaries, establish hierarchies, and maintain discriminations. It did not invite a political revolution but envisaged a social one at the imagination's most dangerous depths. No importance was given to distinctions of Gentile and Jew, female and male, slave and free, poor and rich. Those distinctions were hardly even attacked in theory; in practice, they were simply ignored.

What would happen to Jesus was probably as predictable as what had happened already to John. Some form of religiopolitical execution could surely have been expected. What he was saying and doing was as unacceptable in the first century as it would be in the twentieth—there, here, or anywhere. Still, the exact sequence of the events at the end of his life lacks multiple independent accounts, and the death is surer in its connection to the life than it is in its connection to the preceding few days. It seems clear that Jesus, confronted, possibly for the first and only time, with the Temple's rich magnificence, symbolically destroyed its perfectly legitimate brokerage function in the name of the unbrokered Kingdom of God. Such an act, if performed in the volatile atmosphere of Passover, a feast that celebrated Jewish liberation from inaugural imperial oppression, would have been quite enough to entail crucifixion by religiopolitical agreement. And it is now impossible for us to imagine the offhanded brutality, anonymity, and indifference with which a peasant nobody like Jesus would have been disposed of.

What could not have been predicted and might not have been expected was that the end was not the end. Those who had originally experienced divine power through his vision and his example continued to do so after his death. In fact, even more so, because now this power was no longer confined by time or place. A prudently neutral Jewish historian reported, at the end of the first century, that "when Pilate, upon hearing him accused by men of the highest standing amongst us, had condemned him to be crucified, those who had in the first place come to love him did not give up their affection for him. . . . And the tribe of the Christians, so called after him, has still to this day not disappeared." And an arrogant Roman historian reported, at the start of the second century, that "Christus, the founder of the name [of Christian], had undergone the death penalty in the reign of Tiberius, by sentence of the procurator Pontius Pilatus, and the pernicious superstition was checked for the moment, only to break out once more, not merely in Judaea, the home of the disease, but in the capital itself, where all things horrible or shameful in the world collect and find a vogue." Some of Jesus' own followers, who had initially fled from the danger and horror of the crucifixion, talked eventually not just of continued affection or spreading superstition but of resurrection. They tried to express what they meant by telling, for example, about the journey to Emmaus undertaken by two Jesus followers, one named and clearly male, one unnamed and probably female. The couple were leaving Jerusalem in disappointed and dejected sorrow. Jesus joined them on the road and, unknown and unrecognized, explained how the Hebrew Scriptures should have prepared them for his fate. Later that evening they invited him to join them for their evening meal, and finally they recognized him when once again he served the meal to them as of old beside the lake. And then, only then, they started back to Jerusalem in high spirits. The symbolism is obvious, as is the metaphoric condensation of the first years of Christian thought and practice into one parabolic afternoon. Emmaus never happened. Emmaus always happens.

Jesus has been interpreted in this book against an earlier moment in Judaism's encounter with Greco-Roman imperialism. It is not, however, the elite, literary, and sophisticated intellectual encounter of a Philo of Alexandria. It is, rather, the peasant, oral, and popular physical encounter of what might be termed, if adjective and noun are given equal weight, a Jewish Cynicism. Pagan Cynicism involved practice and not just theory, life-style and not just mind-set, in opposition to the cultural heart of Mediterranean civilization—a way of looking and dressing, of eating, living, and relating that announced its contempt for honor and shame, for patronage and clientage. Jesus and his first followers fit very well against *that* background; they were hippies in a world of Augustan yuppies. Greco-Roman Cynics, however, concentrated primarily on the marketplace rather than the farm, on the city dweller rather than the peasant. And they showed little sense, on the one hand, of collective discipline or, on the other, of communal action. Jesus and his followers do not fit well against *that* background. And both similarity and difference must be given equal respect.

The historical Jesus was a *peasant Jewish Cynic*. His peasant village was close enough to a Greco-Roman city like Sepphoris that sight and knowledge of Cynicism are neither inexplicable nor unlikely. But his work was among the houses and hamlets of Lower Galilee. His strategy, implicitly for himself and explicitly for his followers, was the combination of *free healing and common eating*, a religious and economic egalitarianism that negated alike and at once the hierarchical and patronal normalcies of Jewish religion and Roman power. And, lest he himself be interpreted as simply the new broker of a new God, he moved on constantly, settling down neither at Nazareth nor at Capernaum. He was neither broker nor mediator but, somewhat paradoxically, the announcer that neither should exist between humanity and divinity or between humanity and itself. Miracle and parable, healing and eating were calculated to force individuals into unmediated physical and spiritual contact with God and unmediated physical and spiritual contact with one another. He announced, in other words, the unmediated or brokerless Kingdom of God.

That reconstructed historical Jesus must be understood within his contemporary Hellenistic Judaism, a Judaism responding with all its antiquity and tradition to Greco-Roman culture undergirded by both armed power and imperial ambition. But that contemporary Judaism was, as modern scholarship insists ever more forcibly, a richly creative, diverse, and variegated one. By the end of the second century of the common era, two hundred years after Jesus, *rabbinic* Judaism, like *catholic* Christianity, was deeply involved in retrojecting its ascendancy onto earlier history; it would later be as difficult to discern any earlier plurality in one as in the other. By that time those two great religions had emerged as distinct products of a common matrix, as twin daughters of a common mother. Each claimed to be the only legitimate heir, and each had texts and traditions to argue that claim. Each, in fact, represented an equally legitimate, equally valid, equally surprising, and equally magnificent leap out of the past and into the future. It would, in truth, be difficult to say, had Moses woken from slumber around 200 C.E., which of the two would have surprised him the more. All that was, however, two hundred years *after* Jesus.

∞ The One Who Did Not Go Away

Is an understanding of the historical Jesus of any permanent relevance to Christianity itself? Is it all simply interesting historical background but quite irrelevant to faith itself? Is *any* historical reconstruction, and not just the preceding one, of *any* importance *ever*?

By *historical study* I mean an analysis whose theories and methods, evidence and arguments, results and conclusions are open, in principle and practice, to any human observer, any disciplined investigator, any self-conscious and self-critical student. Abstracting, then, from my own or anyone else's analysis, is such work mere background scenery, mere optional detail, or is it part and parcel of the whole? Granted, of course, that the historical Jesus is always an interpretive construct of its own time and place but open to all of that time and place, is such a construct always in dialectical tension with faith itself? Bluntly: Is Christian faith always (1) an act of faith (2) in the historical Jesus (3) as the manifestation of God? Imagine, for example, these responses from different observers, all of whom have heard and seen exactly the same phenomena in the life of Jesus:

> *He's dumb, let's ignore him.*
> *He's lost, let's leave him.*

He's dangerous, let's fight him.
He's criminal, let's execute him.
He's divine, let's worship him.

The last response represents Christian faith, which was there as soon as the phrase was uttered or carried out—*before* any death or resurrection just as well as *after* it. Christian belief is (1) an act of faith (2) in the historical Jesus (3) as the manifestation of God.

The New Testament itself contains a spectrum of divergent theological interpretations, each of which focuses on different aspects or clusters of aspects concerning the historical Jesus—or, better, different historical Jesuses. It may be, for example, only the sayings, or only the miracles, or only the death that is of primary concern for a given tradition, but any of those emphases presumes divergent historical Jesuses who said something, did something, and died in a certain way. Different visions of the historical Jesus appear in dialectic with different theological interpretations so that the New Testament itself is an obvious expression of that plurality's inevitability. But any analysis of a historical Jesus must be open to the disciplined historical methods of its *contemporary* world and must be able to stand up to its judgments without special pleading. It may also help, of course, to overturn those methods and judgments because, if scientific history cannot handle somebody that important, it may well be thereby indicating its own vacuity. Need I say, at this point, that the way in which the nineteenth century dreamed of uncommitted, objective, dispassionate historical study should be clearly seen for what it was—a methodological screen to cover various forms of social power and imperialistic control? I presume that there will always be divergent historical Jesuses, that there will always be divergent Christs built upon them, but I argue, above all, that the structure of a Christianity will always be: *this is how we see Jesus-then as Christ-now.* Christianity must repeatedly, generation after generation, make its best historical judgment about who *Jesus* was *then* and, on that basis, decide what that reconstruction means as *Christ now.* I am proposing that the dialectic between Jesuses and Christs (or Sons, or Lords, or Wisdoms) is at the heart of both tradition and canon, that it is perfectly valid, and that it has always been with us and probably always will be.

Finally, about three hundred years after the crucifixion of Jesus, on 28 October 312 C.E., the Roman emperor Constantine, believing that victory over his imperial rival Maxentius near Rome's Milvian Bridge had been obtained by Christ's power, converted to Christianity. It is interesting, by the way, that we know that event to the day but we know the date of Jesus' death only as sometime within a decade of years, from 26 to 36 C.E. In any case, Constantine, wanting a unified Christianity as the empire's new religion, ordered the Christian bishops to meet, under imperial subsidy, in lakeside Nicea, southeast of Constantinople, and there erase any major theological disagreements between them. Even if one is not already somewhat disquieted at imperial convocation, presence, and participation, it is hard not to become very nervous in reading this description of the imperial banquet celebrating the Council of Nicea's conclusion, from Eusebius's *Life of Constantine* 3.15:

> Detachments of the bodyguard and troops surrounded the entrance of the palace with drawn swords, and through the midst of them the men of God proceeded without fear into the innermost of the Imperial apartments, in which some were the Emperor's companions at table, while others reclined on couches arranged on either side. One might have thought that a picture of Christ's kingdom was thus shadowed forth, and a dream rather than reality.

A Christian leader now writes a life not of Jesus but of Constantine. The meal and the Kingdom still come together, but now the participants are the male bishops alone, and they recline, with the emperor himself, to be served by others. Dream or reality? Dream or nightmare?

It is, of course, an example of the dialectic just proposed between historical Jesus and confessional Christ, of peasant Jesus grasped now by imperial faith. Still, as one ponders that progress from open commensality with Jesus to episcopal banquet with Constantine, is it unfair to regret a progress that happened so fast and moved so swiftly, that was accepted so readily and criticized so lightly? Is it time now, or is it already too late, to conduct, religiously and theologically, ethically and morally, some basic cost accounting with Constantine?

INDEX

141, 142, 153, 161–62. *See also*
Jewish Antiquities; Jewish War
Joshua, 41, 42, 56. *See also* John the
Baptist
Judaism, 31–33, 36–37, 38, 40–41,
43–44, 54, 56–57, 77, 79–80, 89–90,
103–5, 119, 124, 135–36, 137–38,
140–41, 147–50, 154, 196–99. *See
also* Apocalypticism; Dead Sea
Scrolls; Jesus; *Mishnah;* Passover;
Purity code
Juvenal, 97–98

Kingdom of God, 47, 54–74, 83–84,
93, 121–22, 156, 194–95; apocalyp-
tic, 55–56; continued experience
of, 161; sapiential, 56–58. *See also*
Children; Family; Jesus; John,
gospel of; Luke, gospel of; Mark,
gospel of; Matthew, gospel of;
Poverty; *Q Gospel; Thomas,
Gospel of*
Kleinman, Arthur, 81–82
Kloppenborg, John S., 111–12
Klosinski, Lee Edward, 69

Last Supper, 129–30
Lazarus, 93–95, 133–34
Lenski, Gerhard, 24–25, 40, 55–58,
103, 145
Leper, healing of, 77–78, 82
Lepra, 78–84
Leprosy, 78–84
Leviticus, 79–80
Leviticus, 146–48, 149
Lewis, Ioan M., 88–89
Livy, 36
Luke, gospel of, x–xi, xiii, 1–2, 4,
5–10, 23, 26, 100–101; appearance
of Jesus after death in, 170–73,
180; baptism of Jesus in, 44–45;
birth of Jesus in, 18–21; burial of
Jesus in, 156–57; egalitarianism in,
106–7; exorcism in, 91–92; food
in, 112, 170–72; infancy story of

Jesus in, 4–10, 21; John the Baptist
in, 5–10, 21, 37–38, 46, 47, 48; healing of leper in, 84; Kingdom of
God in, 58–59, 60–61, 66, 67; Last
Supper in, 180; miraculous catch
of fishes in, 182–83; mission in,
108, 111–12, 114, 118; Peter at the
tomb of Jesus in, 186; Son of Man
expression in, 51; virginal conception of Jesus in, 16–18

Mack, Burton, 116
MacMullen, Ramsay, 24
Magic and the Millennium
(Wilson), 104, 159–60
Malherbe, Abraham, 117–18
Mark, gospel of, x–xi, xiii, 4, 23, 24,
35–37, 44, 48, 127; anointing of
Jesus by the unnamed woman in,
191–92; burial of Jesus in, 156–57;
calming of the waters by Jesus in,
183–86; cleansing of Temple in,
131–32; denial of impending crucifixion of, 191–92; dispute over
Barabbas incident in, 140–44;
entrance of Jesus into Jerusalem
in, 128–39; expulsion of demon
in, 89–90, 91–92, 100; healing of
leper by Jesus in, 77, 83; itinerancy
of Jesus in, 99–101; Jesus and
Pilate in, 140–41; Kingdom of
God in, 58–59, 63, 64–65; Last
Supper described in, 129; mission
in, 108–9, 114, 118; multiplication
of loaves and fishes in, 174–77;
passion narrative in, 151–52; walking on water by Jesus in, 183–86
Mary Magdalene, 186–88, 190
Mary, 1–2, 16–18, 19, 23–24, 26
Matthew, gospel of, x–xi, xiii, 4, 5,
23, 24, 100, 186; baptism of Jesus
in, 44–45; birth of Jesus in, 18–21;
burial of Jesus in, 156–57; children
in, 64; egalitarianism in, 106–7;
entrance of Jesus into Jerusalem